Selling 101

Other titles in
THE ADAMS BUSINESS ADVISORS

Accounting for the New Business, by Christopher R. Malburg
The All-In-One Business Planning Guide, by Christopher R. Malburg
Buying Your Own Business, Russell Robb
Do-It-Yourself Advertising, Direct Mail, and Publicity,
by Sarah White and John Woods
Entrepreneurial Growth Strategies, by Lawrence W. Tuller
Exporting, Importing, and Beyond, by Lawrence W. Tuller
Managing People, by Darien McWhirter
Marketing Magic, by Don Debelak
The Personnel Policy Handbook for Growing Companies, by Darien McWhirter
Service, Service, Service: The Growing Business' Secret Weapon,
by Steven Albrecht
The Small Business Legal Kit, by J. W. Dicks
The Small Business Valuation Book, by Lawrence W. Tuller
Winning the Entrepreneur's Game, by David E. Rye

Selling 101

A COURSE FOR BUSINESS OWNERS AND NON-SALES PEOPLE

INCLUDES:

- FINDING LEADS
- COLD CALLING
- HANDLING OBJECTIONS
- CLOSING SALES
- GROWING SALES

MICHAEL T. MCGAULLEY

Adams Publishing
Holbrook, Massachusetts

Published by Adams Media Corporation
260 Center Street, Holbrook, MA 02343

ISBN: 1-55850-545-8

Printed in the United States of America.

J I H G F E D C B A

Library of Congress Cataloging-in-Publication Data
McGaulley, Michael T.
Selling 101 : a course for business owners and non-sales people : includes finding leads, cold calling, handling objections, closing sales, growing sales / Michael T. McGaulley.
p. cm. — (An Adams business advisor)
Includes index.
ISBN 1-55850-545-8 (pb)
1. Selling. 2. Sales management. I. Title. II. Series.
HF5438.25.M398 1995
658.85—dc20 95-41507
CIP

Cover design: Marshall Henrichs

Contents

Preface

The Entrepreneurial Option

> I'm too old to get a good job and too young to retire. The only option I have is to go into business for myself.
>
> Laid-off Pan Am pilot, in *Newsweek*

> The baby-boom generation is entering its peak entrepreneurial years. There hasn't been a decade in living memory when the population of potential entrepreneurs has been bigger.
>
> David L. Birch, President, Cognetics, Inc.
> (an economic research firm), in *Fortune*

> Some New Grads Turn Entrepreneur, Not Employee: Tight Job Market Pushes a Growing Number to Try Starting Their Own Firms.
>
> Headline in The *Wall Street Journal*

"Downsizing," "right-sizing," "restructuring," "reductions in force," "cutbacks"—these are the key words in the new vocabulary of the job market, not only in the United States, but around the world, as well.

That's why, like it or not, ready or not, you may be finding that you are now—or soon will be—an entrepreneur, either marketing a product you've developed or marketing your own services as a self-employed person.

The pilot quoted above is not alone; for many of the managers, technical specialists, military people, and professionals who are finding themselves displaced, entrepreneurship or self-employment is the only reasonable choice.

It's much the same at the other end of the career pipeline: Many of the more than 1 million American college graduates each year are electing to try going it on their own, partly because of the scarcity of good jobs, but partly also because they hope to take control of their own destinies.

Opportunity—Welcome or Unwelcome

The shove into entrepreneurship or self-employment may be the opportunity you've fantasized about for most of your working life—you needed only the final push. Or self-employment may be involuntary, unwanted yet inescapable—a frightening new world.

But, whether your move was voluntary or involuntary, success as an entrepreneur depends on more than just good ideas and hard work. They're essential, but alone they're not enough.

Success, even survival, as a self-employed person or as an entrepreneur depends on more than technical abilities, job skills, energy, enthusiasm, and creativity. These are important, but even more important is the ability to market those abilities.

According to the U.S. Small Business Administration, half of all new business ventures fail within the first year, and the single greatest reason is simple lack of sales.

The old truism just isn't true: In these competitive times, the world will **not** ***beat a path to your door, not even for that legendary "better mousetrap."***

To-the-Point Reading, Targeting Practical How-To Skills

Selling 101: A Course for Business Owners and Non-Sales People is for the person—typically a new entrepreneur or newly self-employed—who needs a fast, practical crash course in marketing and selling.

The book is a boiled-down, "netted-out" adaptation of the kind of sales training programs offered in *Fortune* 500 firms, but specifically targeted at the special needs of the new entrepreneur and the self-employed. *Selling 101* stems from my experience as a management consultant working with some of America's most successful marketing organizations—companies including Xerox, Kodak, BankAmerica, GTE/Sylvania, and others. In the course of that work, I developed numerous sales and sales management training programs, guidebooks, and training materials for both beginning and experienced people.

Part of that work involved tapping the expertise of some of the very best sales reps and sales managers in these firms, people from around the company whose skills were considered so outstanding that they set the standard against which others were measured.

But as a struggling new entrepreneur, you don't have access to that kind of sales training. Indeed, you're probably so busy with other aspects of getting your venture going that you barely have time to think about learning to sell.

As one individual put it, "new entrepreneurs work twenty-eight hours per day." When you're trying to get a new enterprise started—and when you're struggling to keep it afloat—there's not the spare time to read books that are any longer than they absolutely have to be.

That's why I wrote *Selling 101* in the same lean, "netted-out" style that I used in the sales training programs I developed for these corporate clients. That means you'll be able to spend more of your time actually out selling and generating income, instead of back home reading a stack of books.

Several years ago, I developed an earlier version of this book to be the core of a sales training program for the sales reps of Rank-Xerox in Europe. When it was presented at a conference in Italy, the manager of sales training from the Swedish operating company said, "There's more practical content here in this book than in twenty other books on selling put together."

Since then, I've added more material and refined what I already had, targeting it to the special needs of the person who is new to selling. Now, I hope, *Selling 101* provides even more content than those "twenty other books on selling," especially the kind of practical how-to steps and tips you need.

In *Selling 101,* the focus is on the practical how-to, so that you **know where and how to get started next Monday morning...and how to keep going efficiently from then on.** I know there are a lot of books on selling on the market. What's unique about *Selling 101* is the following:

1. It guides you *step by step,* addressing practical, useful tips that a lot of books overlook—things like how to determine who within the organization you should be talking to (that is, who can really say yes) and even how to subtly remind the prospect to write you on the calendar.
2. It focuses on the *practical how-to* and doesn't get bogged down in side issues like motivational you-can-do-it fluff, qualities of a good salesperson, "war stories" of how the author made the great sales of his life, abstract theories of marketing, and the like. I set out to write a practical guide with all meat.

There's another reason I think that, as a new entrepreneur and beginning marketer, you'll find *Selling 101* especially helpful: Before I began my work developing these corporate sales training programs, I was, like you perhaps are, a sole entrepreneur, marketing both products and services. I saw at first hand just how much sales really are the key to success or failure.

That experience of struggling to learn how to sell gave me a special awareness of the kind of practical skills and guidance that new entrepreneurs and consultants need, and I've distilled that essence from the many hours of workshops and the hundreds of pages of sales guidebooks and job aids I wrote.

I wrote *Selling 101* to contain the kind of *comprehensive, step-by-step guidance* in professional selling skills, including the practical techniques and how-to, that I wished I'd had when I was a beginning entrepreneur.

Selling 101 is for the person—perhaps like yourself—who thinks, "I know my field, but I can't sell." It was designed from the start to give you the kind of help you need to move from ground zero in selling capability to the point where you have the skills and confidence to search out and approach potential clients.

But *Selling 101* is not only for beginners. Although the fundamentals are covered thoroughly, the content is rich with advanced techniques that will carry the beginner through to "master" level, be useful as well for the experienced salesperson looking for a refresher course, or provide an update on some fresh approaches.

In short, *Selling 101* meets your key needs if you are among

1. *The 1.3 million new entrepreneurs* who set up each year, for whom sales are the lifeblood of business survival.
2. *The new consultants and contractors* supplying specialized services to business and government. Increasingly, professionals and executives are becoming part of this contingent workforce. Demand is high for experts who are willing to work short-term as consultants and "contract managers" on turnaround projects. Some executives who took early retirement find consulting a way to retire without retiring—and to keep cash flowing in.

(A UCLA study predicts that by the end of the decade, a full 40 percent of all American workers will be consultants and contract employees.)

3. *The continuing influx—whether voluntary or involuntary—of new self-employeds* who have become contract or contingent workers marketing themselves for part-time or short-term projects.
4. *The year's 1.1 million-plus American college graduates beginning the job search.* When less than half of the graduates of some prestigious law and MBA programs are able to find work in their fields within the first six months, the pressures are especially heavy on those leaving with only bachelor's degrees. Many are finding that their only recourse is starting their own firm. But even those with business degrees have had no training in the practical skills covered in *Selling 101.*
5. **The 13,000,000 Americans who make their living selling**, and want to gain the benefit of the kind of professional sales training program offered by the *Fortune* 500 firms, or who have had training and want a quick, practical refresher and update.

Acknowledgments

This book could not have been written without the ideas and support provided by consulting clients, master salespeople, and friends, particularly Mary Casteel Bauer, Barry Blum, Ray Croft, Frank Dombroski, John Fairs, Paul Foster, Nick Iuppa, Stephanie Jackson, William F. Jordan, Paul Landauer, Claude Lineberry, John H. McGaulley, C.P.A., Larry Martin, William A. Mulligan, Neil Rackham, Phil Scatterday, Paul Tremlett, Bob Tuomey, and other salespeople who shared ideas and suffered having a silent partner watching them work.

Joe Harless introduced me to the three questions for diagnosing the core of "people problems" in Part 11.

Ray Croft, then with Xerox Office Systems Division, helped me realize that the quesitons I asked as a consultant in helping my clients diagnose the problem were virtually the same questions that I should be asking earlier, as I marketed to prospective clients, to help them reconize the need for my services. That insight formed the core of the Selling Wedge introduced in this book.

Special thanks to Susan McGaulley, whose contributions extended from technical input to the reading of endless drafts; to my agent, Michael Snell, who showed me how to sell a book on selling; and to my editor, Dick Staron, who guided me in expanding the original idea into a book with broader market appeal.

Xerox Corporation, Xerox of Canada, Rank-Xerox, Kodak, GTE/Sylvania, Motorola, and BankAmerica sponsored some of the consulting work that provided the background for the approaches in this book. The illustrations in Chapter 29 are from a training guide I developed for the Xerox Corporation, and are used with permission.

Introduction

Starting Questions

Marketing, someone has said, is like what generals do: Think "big picture" and develop broad strategies. Selling is like what the foot soldiers do: Get into the thick of it and bring those strategies into reality.

As a new entrepreneur, consultant, or self-employed person, you'll necessarily be both marketing strategist and front-line salesperson. The thrust of this book is toward the practical how-to, toward the details of actually selling, going out and working face-to-face with prospective customers and clients.

However, there are some broad, strategic questions that you do need to begin thinking about before you get too far down the pathway. Very likely, you won't know all the answers at the start, but that's normal in new enterprises. These questions are here to help you begin an evolving process of discovering and refining your marketing and sales approach. These are questions to consider now, but also to come back to and reconsider as your direction and methods evolve.

There are never any "final" answers to these questions. Effective marketers are constantly open to learning and adapting, both to adjust to changes in the market and to reflect new ideas and experience.

Economists make the distinction between "products" and "services." In this book, we'll use the terms interchangeably. Thus, if I write of "your product," read it to mean "your product or service."

There will be some differences between marketing a tangible product and marketing a less tangible service, such as consulting. I'll point those differences out as they become relevant.

In a nutshell, precisely what *is* the product or service that I am offering?

It may be clear enough to you, but just how are you going to explain—quickly—to the prospects you encounter just what it is that you do or sell? This is especially important if you're marketing intangibles, such as your services or expertise.

If you say, "I'm a consultant," the next question will inevitably be, "In what areas do you consult?" Unless you have a clear, succinct answer ready, you lose credibility.

It's true that, especially in the beginning, you don't want to lock yourself into a niche too soon, as you want to be open to what the marketplace tells you. You want to keep your options open so that you can move with the need. Yet you also have to be able to speak of one or a few areas in which your experience is relevant as a way of setting the context for what you are capable of. For instance, you could say, "My experience has been in the general field of _____, and I'm offering that expertise as a problem solver in related fields." Or you could respond, "I'm basically a problem solver, working in the general area of _____."

If possible, immediately back up these general statements with a capsule summary of one or two relevant accomplishments: "For example, for a large manufacturing company, I did _____. I anticipate offering those kinds of services to smaller firms in this area."

Who needs my product or service?

It's obvious to you just what kinds of things your product (or service) will accomplish. But will it be so immediately obvious to the prospects you approach?

Perhaps not. Even if the uses are clear, the need may not be so apparent. One of the themes in this book is that *people (and organizations) tend to buy if and only if they recognize that they do in fact face a need, and that the need is significant enough to be worth filling*. Therefore, in preparing to sell, think backward from your product or service to develop a clear perception of precisely how a prospect will be able to recognize a need for it.

Suppose, for example, you're selling software to make office paperwork flow more efficiently. What kind of concrete factors would signal you (and your prospect) that there really is a need for your product? How could you make this need clear to the prospect? The evidence might include the clutter of unfiled papers in the prospect's office, a recurring need to get back to clients who phone or write to find why their files have been lost, or a lot of staff time wasted looking for information and papers.

- When my product is in place here, or my work has been completed, how will the client recognize that it has been successful?
- What needs will it have filled?
- For what kinds of situations would a satisfied customer recommend my product or service to someone else?

Once you have those need indicators in mind, use them as checkpoints to work toward in structuring your selling strategy. If they show that a need exists, then you want to find ways of helping the key decision maker become vividly aware of them and their significance.

Instead of asking about needs, you could ask prospects about the problems they face. But there's a strange difference in buyers' psychology operating between the two words.

If you ask about problems, the Decision Maker will probably deny that any problems exist. After all, the existence of unsolved problems implies that he or she has been subpar in some way in performing his or her duties as a manager or person. Good managers don't let "problems" continue.

But if you probe for what *needs* exist—well, that's not so threatening, and you'll usually get a more open response that is helpful both to you and to the prospect you're there to assist.

What will my product (or service) *do* for those who buy it? That is, what specific needs will it fill? What service does it render?

Why is it worthwhile to fill those needs? What direct costs and indirect consequences result from the unfilled needs?

Will my product not only fill the needs, but also help pay for itself in savings, or by opening other opportunities?

People (and organizations) don't buy *things;* instead, they buy the *results* that flow from those things or services. For example, one doesn't buy a television set just to have a box with a screen on it, but rather to have a way of getting access to the programs: those programs are the results flowing from investing in the television box.

When you look from the buyer's perspective, you'll see that the buyer's interest is not in the innovations and features of your product (or service), but rather in *how those features translate into practical ways to make the buyer's life and things that matter to him or her operate better, more efficiently, more profitably,* and so forth.

Putting that differently, if you are to sell effectively, there are two assumptions that you should *not* make:

1. **Don't assume that the prospect is already aware of a need for your product or service.**

   Probably the single most important part of your job as a salesperson is to help the prospect become aware of that need, or become *more* aware of it. The stronger the prospect's sense of need is, the greater are your chances of making the sale.

2. **Don't assume that the prospect automatically sees the link between his or her need and how your product or service can fill it.**

   Once the customer becomes aware of a need, the next part of your job is to help that prospect see the link between the need and how your product or service can fill that need.

   You can't leave it to chance that prospects will make the link between the product or service that you present and precisely how it can help them and their work. Those practical benefits are perfectly clear to you, but they are almost certainly far less clear to a prospective customer who is seeing your product or service for the first time. Indeed, the prospect may even be seeing the whole technology on which your product or service is based for the first time.

We'll be talking a good deal in this book about helping prospective customers develop an awareness of the needs that your product can fill. By thinking through in advance just what kind of needs these might be, you'll be better prepared to convince the customers to buy.

Also, going even further back in the process, by thinking through what kinds of needs the customers will want to fill, you may be able to shape not only your selling message, but also the actual product and service as you develop it, so that it meets those needs more precisely, and so its advantages are easier to communicate.

In short, if your product or service is successful with your customers, precisely what will it do for them? How will they recognize and measure that success?

What, then, are my core selling messages?

If we could somehow replay all the sales calls that have been made since the beginning of time, I suspect we'd find that nearly as many prospects have been talked *out* of buying as have been talked *into* saying yes. Obviously, that was not what the salesperson intended, but it happened all the same. Why? Because the salesperson either talked too much or failed to have concise, to-the-point, positive reasons for buying.

Therefore, as you refine your sales approach, work toward boiling down the essence of your selling messages into neat, succinct, one- or two-sentence "core messages."

That takes discipline. You know an enormous amount about your product and what it can do. In fact, you're probably bursting with all of the good reasons to buy. But often less is more: To communicate, it's usually better to hit a few key points clearly than to overwhelm—and confuse—the prospective purchaser with a lot of not-necessarily-relevant detail.

Think of these core selling messages as like the "sound bites" you hear from the politicians who are quoted on the evening news. Those succinct little sayings don't just happen; savvy politicians know that the news organizations are looking for short, quotable nuggets, and so they take pains to boil down their comments into these memorable bits.

It's the same when you're selling. You need to learn how to boil down your key selling features and reasons to buy into short sound bites, each only a sentence or two long.

It's not that these sound bites are all that you say; you will amplify as needed. But it's good to lead with "netted-out," to-the-point, easily digestible core selling messages. Invest the time to prepare these messages in advance, and to rehearse them so that they flow easily.

It's a good idea, too, to develop similar short sound bites to respond to the most common questions and objections you encounter. The objective is to make sure you are able to get the core of your response across clearly and succinctly. If the other person then wants more detail, you can give it, but at least you can be certain that you have responded to the question without losing the point.

How can I most effectively bring my selling messages to prospects?

In *Selling 101*, we focus on one way of bringing your product to market: that is, *by making face-to-face sales calls directly on potential buyers.*

But face-to-face selling is not the only way of marketing your product or service. You can use direct mail. You can market by phone ("telemarketing"). You can buy space advertising in newspapers or magazines. You can hire students to put flyers on cars in shopping centers.

If your product is suitable, you can even market reasonably inexpensively via television. For a beginning entrepreneur with the right product, the cable marketing channels that will sell your product for a percentage of the proceeds may be practical and profitable.

Alternatively, you can sell through a network of dealers, wholesalers, and commission sales representatives. Or you can license the product for another organization to market, and even manufacture as well.

Which of these methods—or what combination of methods—will work best for you depends on a variety of factors, including the nature of your product or service, what it costs, who the appropriate users are, the money required to get it to market compared with the capital you have available, and your own inclinations and time availability.

In one of my entrepreneurial ventures, publishing educational kits and marketing them to schools, teachers, and parents, I worked through each of these approaches (except cable television, which was not feasible at the time). I began with mail order, using both space ads in magazines and direct mailings to schools. My space ads brought sales orders, and also queries from the networks of commission sales reps and wholesalers who market to schools. I made face-to-face sales calls on some of these dealers, and relied on telephone marketing to reach others in more distant parts of the country. Ultimately, the products were bought out by a division of a major publisher in a licensing arrangement, for which I got up-front cash plus continuing royalties.

The point is to be aware of the range of options open to you, so that you don't get locked into any of them too early. Realize, too, that what is the "best" choice may change as conditions evolve. In making your selection, the key consideration is, Which approach can most efficiently bring your message to those you have targeted as priority prospects? The answer may become apparent as you think about it, or as you tap into the thinking of friends and potential buyers. Or you may have to test each approach and see which works best for you.

Is there competition? If so, what is unique about my product or service?

Until you know who your main competitors are, and their costs, strengths, and weaknesses, you're not ready to sell. Further, until you can explain clearly and to the point the unique advantages of your product or service, you're not ready to sell. You can try to pretend that the competitors don't exist, but they'll be on your prospects' minds.

In looking for what is unique about your product or service, keep in mind that your special advantages may come from factors such as

- Lower cost. This can take various forms, such as lower purchase price, lower long-term operating costs, or lower personnel or training costs.
- Better service.
- Better financing terms.
- Your continuing personal involvement to ensure that your product does all that you claim it will.

Be sure to project yourself into the minds of several different hypothetical customers. Look at your product, along with the service, purchase terms, and the like, with the same kind of hard-nosed realism that you would use if you were actually the buyer instead of the seller. Exactly what questions would you be asking? What concerns would be in the back of your mind? It's better to know what these are and prepare to deal with them now rather than finding them when you are further down the line. If your product (or terms) has flaws, it's better to spot them yourself now rather than after you have committed more time and money.

Letting Your Competitors Educate You

There's another good reason for knowing your competition: They can be your best teachers.

- They can teach you by what they do or don't do, and they can teach you what you *should* do. You don't want to be a copycat, but if something works, you can learn from it, and maybe even tweak it into something better.
- They can teach you by the blunders they have made—there's no need to make your own mistakes if you can learn from those of others.
- They can point you to a specific niche in the market—that is, your own special place. By studying where your competitors are and are not, you can find where you can fit in and be unique—perhaps because you have a unique product, because of initial cost, because of overall cost savings, because of the quality of the service you provide, and so forth.

Key point: When you learn from your competition, make sure you model your firm on the *best* competitors. Don't just look at the nearby competitor who's barely managing to survive. Pay a lot more attention to the top firms in your field. Why have they survived—and prospered—when so many have failed? Why are customers willing to pay a premium to do business with them as industry leaders? Given your lower overhead as a small firm, what can you do to match or beat that level of product quality or service?

But What If There Is No Competition?

That could, obviously, be very good news: You've got the market to yourself—at least for a while. So you'd better be prepared to move fast.

But the lack of competition could also be a warning signal. You'd better do some checking. It could be that someone has already tested the market, only to find that it didn't pay off. Or perhaps what you're offering is *too* novel, and the market isn't—at least mentally—ready for it yet.

Summary

Before you get too far down the track, it's helpful to think through answers to eight key questions of strategy:

1. In a nutshell, precisely what *is* the product or service that I am offering?
2. Who needs my product or service?
3. What will my product (or service) *do* for those who buy it? That is, what specific needs will it fill? What service does it render?
4. Why is it worthwhile to fill those needs? What direct costs and indirect consequences result from the unfilled needs?
5. Will my product not only fill the needs, but also help pay for itself in savings, or by opening other opportunities?
6. What, then, are my core selling messages?
7. How can I most effectively bring my selling messages to prospects?
8. Is there competition? If so, what is unique about my product or service?
    - What can the competition teach me?
    - What does it mean if there is no competition?

Part One
Locating Priority Prospects

Regardless of how unique and innovative your product or service is, you can't effectively sell it to the whole world—at least, not at the start. Your time and energy, as well as your working capital, are limited. Don't spread them too thin.

Therefore, begin by narrowing in on the best groups of prospects, and target your efforts especially to them. It's a rule of thumb in marketing that 80 percent of your sales (and profits) will come from 20 percent of your customers. By finding and focusing on those high-payoff prospects early, you greatly increase your chances of surviving... and ultimately succeeding.

Those in this primary target market are individuals or organizations that have a particularly *strong need* for what you offer, have the *money*, and can be *reached efficiently.*

Others outside the target group may find their way to you and buy; that's fine. You won't turn them away, of course. But on the other hand, you can't afford to waste effort on the lost cause of trying to find these improbables.

Naturally, the composition of the target markets may change or expand over time as conditions change, or as your awareness of your best markets grows. But at the start, you need to have definite prospect groups in mind, since precisely who these high-probability buyers are is likely to influence the strategy and approach you evolve.

Continuous Learning

When you begin selling, you undertake a cycle of continuous learning. You start with good ideas, but the real world (mainly your prospects and your competition) gives you constant feedback on just how viable those ideas and products really are. You can ignore the feedback (not a good idea), or you can use it to prompt fresh thinking and better ideas and products.

While it is important to focus on the 20 percent of all prospects who will give you 80 percent of your profits, at the start you will not really know who makes up that productive 20 percent. Or you may think you know, only to be reeducated by the real world of the marketplace.

That's where feedback and flexibility and being open to continuous learning come in. Certainly, start out with ideas on how to sell and where to target your main efforts, but don't get locked into those starting points. For example, those that you hypothesize will be your prime prospects (the top 20 percent) may not be productive for you at all, for any of a variety of reasons.

- The ones you think will be heavy buyers in fact don't really need your product at all.
- They are not ready to recognize the need, and it's evident that it will not be cost-effective for you to try to educate them on that need.
- They were such obvious candidates that your competitors have been there long before you, and have skimmed off the profitability.
- These prospects are so lucrative that the big competitors focus all their efforts on them, and so you as a start-up don't stand a chance of breaking in.

But that feedback, though initially discouraging, actually may open up other, even better possibilities:

- The second-tier prospects (those that you ranked below the likely top 20 percent) may actually be more interested and more profitable for you, as they have not been picked over by competitors.
- By listening to what the top 20 percent bought, and what areas of dissatisfaction they have, you can adapt your product (or your service, purchase terms, and the like) to fill a niche in the main market. (Your competitors may have grown complacent and stopped listening to what their customers really want. By listening and adapting, you can squeeze into the holes they have left.)

The market is the great teacher. It's also the great spur to creativity and innovation for those who are open and flexible.

Chapter 1

Creating Your Prospect List

In finding who and where the prospects for the product or service you offer are, a lot will obviously depend on where you're located, what you're selling, and what kind of a marketplace you're working in.

Here's a checklist to trigger your thinking on other sources of leads:

1. Obvious or logical users of your product or service.

You probably already know a lot of prospective users of your product or service. You probably already know many of them by name. They may be people you worked with at your previous jobs, or they may be your counterparts in other organizations or people you know from professional or trade groups.

Others you may not know personally, but you know who they are by the organization within which they work and by their job titles. Or you may know that since they hold a particular kind of job, or live in a particular area, or have a particular kind of hobby, they are logical users of your product or service.

Write the names down as they come to you, regardless of how remote the chances of selling to them seem now. Develop your list of prospects first, and only later think about narrowing it down. The possibility you list may trigger other ideas, referrals, and leads.

The worksheet following may help you structure your thinking. List the prospects that occur to you in the left column. Then, in a word or two, sum up in the middle column why you think each is a good prospect. Finally, extend your thinking: given why this seems a good prospect, who else is similar?

For example, suppose you have developed an automatic telephone dialer to call patients and clients and remind them of upcoming appointments. You developed it with doctors in mind; they are good prospects because they don't want to have gaps in their schedules because patients forgot to come in, nor do they want to create unhappy patients by billing them for those appointments. Your system solves that problem.

But then you expand your opportunities: Doctors are not the only prospects. Open up your thinking, springboarding from the "why it's good" column to other possible prospects. What other businesses or professions don't want to have clients or customers forget appointments? You might come up with lawyers, hairdressers, airlines, hotels, auto repair shops, even salespeople like yourself, who don't want to waste time on calls only to find that the prospect has forgotten them.

This is just an example; adapt the worksheet to your own product or service to let the "obvious" prospects give you clues to those who may be less obvious.

Obvious/Logical Users	**Why My Product/Service Is Good for Them**	**Who Else Has Similar Needs?**

2. Your contacts.

If you're marketing the expertise you gained in your former job, then the people you met while working there—both within that organization and in other firms—may be potentials. Similarly, those you met through business and professional groups may be prospects for your services now, or at least may be able to suggest referrals for you to contact.

The people you know in a nonprofessional way may also be helpful contacts: people from your neighborhood, civic groups, church, or circle of friends and acquaintances.

You may ask them for help when you see them face to face, or you may decide to phone them for ideas. You could contact them to get their ideas on potential prospects. Even better, you might ask for their suggestions on your whole business plan. They will be flattered that you asked for their input, and they may well have some ideas that had not occurred to you.

3. Referrals.

We'll be discussing the use of referrals later. Ask for referrals from everyone who buys. Even ask for referrals from those who don't buy, but nonetheless seem interested in what you offer. (Although they may not have the money or need right now, they may still think you have a worthwhile idea, and want to pass it on to friends. Or they may want to help a beginning business.)

To ask for a referral, simply say something to the effect, "By the way, is there anyone else you could suggest I contact?"

If the person gives you a name, ask, "Do you mind if I mention your name when I call them?" (If you're lucky, the person may even offer to call up and make the introduction for you.)

If the person has trouble thinking of names, you can gently prompt him or her by suggesting, "For example, is there anyone else I should talk to in your company [or agency, if it is public sector]?" Pause and wait for an answer. Then prompt, "What about your counterparts in other organizations?"

4. Prospects you attract.

As we'll discuss in more detail in Chapters 32 and 33, additional leads may come to you from actions you take, including

- Appearances at trade shows and the like
- Talks before groups of potential users, such as civic and professional organizations
- Articles and interviews in trade journals and local media
- Contacts you make through volunteer work and similar activities
- Advertisements you run

5. "Smokestacking."

The name comes from the old days, when salespeople new to a town would begin by driving around looking for the factory smokestacks, as the smokestacks usually indicated where the business in that town was. Nowadays, when "smokestacking," you would be looking for office buildings, industrial parks, shopping centers, and other clusters of activity that may contain the offices and operations of likely prospects.

Generally, the most efficient way of smokestacking these days is to find your way to the Chamber of Commerce, as it will be pleased to supply you with maps, and directories of the businesses, nonprofits, and government agencies in the area. Most of the time, you'll be able to determine from these lists which organizations are viable prospects, or at least worth further exploration.

Also see if there are regional development agencies in the area, as they would have directories of manufacturers and other major industries. (The names of these agencies will vary with the state. It may be helpful to call your state's Department of Commerce, or even the governor's office, as these development or redevelopment agencies or authorities often either use public money or are funded by state bonds.)

But in some cases it will be helpful to go out and "eyeball" these business clusters, doing some on-site investigation. It may be that the directories are a year or so old, and there may have been turnover. Or some organizations' names may be too vague to tell you what you need to know.

In some cases, you can generate leads by quick "sweeps" through office buildings and commercial clusters, hardly more than poking your head into each office to see if it would be worthwhile to schedule an appointment later. We'll examine the how-to of sweeping in Chapter 5.

6. Paper research.

The easiest paper research can be done through telephone books and, if appropriate, by scanning ads and articles in local newspapers and magazines. The business sections in libraries are your other main source. (Actually, this is "paper" research only in name now, as much of this information is available on computer networks, microfilm, and other paperless modes.)

For guidance, see Chapter 33, "Prospecting Resources."

SUMMARY/ACTION PLAN

Before reading on, spend a few minutes making a first attempt at a concrete action plan to structure your search for prospects. Jot down at least three ideas in each category.

1. Who are the "obvious" or "logical" users of your product or service?
2. Your contacts:
   - From your previous work.
   - From business and professional groups.
   - From civic, church, and other nonbusiness groups.
3. Initial referrals. At the start, who might be able to help you generate lists of potential users, or make some introductions on your behalf?
4. Attracting prospects. Other than running ads, what inexpensive, feasible ways are there for you to spread the word about yourself and your product?
5. Smokestacking. Are there office buildings, industrial parks, and the like where users of your product or service may tend to cluster?
6. Paper research. What publications, directories, membership associations, and the like exist in your field that may help you find potential buyers? (See Chapter 33 for additional ideas.)

Chapter 2

Setting Priorities among Prospects

A sure way of failing in anything, especially marketing, is to spread yourself too thin. The whole world may be prospects for your product or service, but you can't call on everyone first. The taxi meter is running—especially in your first months—so it's crucial to focus on the prospects who have enough profit potential to make it worth your while.

If you are starting up a business, you probably have only limited capital—maybe only enough to keep going for a few months before the cash runs out. Even if you are more established, to the point of having some cash flowing in, it's helpful to view every prospect in the context of the value of your time.

Recent estimates indicate that the cost to the company of the average sales call ranges upward from $150. Even if your overhead is low and you don't have travel expenses, the cost of each face-to-face call will surprise you, particularly when you add in your commuting time to and from, as well as follow-up. To survive, you have to make your calls count.

Even at the start of your selling effort, you need to begin making conscious choices of which customers are worth calling on personally and which should best be approached by other, less costly methods or written off altogether. (Marketing by telephone, called "telemarketing," and direct mail are relatively low-cost ways of contacting low-priority prospects, or prospects who are spread over a wide geographic area.)

Even among those on whom it is important to make personal calls, some will be of higher priority than others. In setting priorities, use criteria such as the following, or add your own specific criteria appropriate to your product and your market.

1. The prospect's potential need for your product or service.

In assessing whether a prospect should be given high priority, ask yourself exactly how strong this prospect's need for your product or service is likely to be. Also, is the need for your product likely to be apparent to the prospect at the start, or will you have to develop the awareness of the need? Survival is precarious when your business is just getting started. That's not the time to be fighting lost causes.

Don't hesitate to go for the easy sales first. After all, you're in business to make a profit, not to build your character through unnecessary adversity. Some initial successes will ease the financial strain, and give you success stories to use in persuading others.

2. Dollar potential, both short and long term.

As you work, keep the 20/80 principle in mind: from 20 percent of your customers will come 80 percent of your sales and profits. It pays to find that productive 20 percent as quickly as possible, and focus most of your efforts on them.

But the rule also works in reverse: The other 80 percent of your customers will yield only 20 percent of your sales. That tells you that if you manage your time unwisely, that unproductive 80 percent can eat up your days so that you never get around to selling to the productive 20 percent.

3. Geographic desirability.

In selling, time is money, and travel is time. In the time that you spend going across town to see one prospect, you could perhaps see four or five other prospects that were more conveniently located.

On the other hand, the overall objective is to make a profit, not just to save travel time. It may be worth making an "inefficient" trip if that prospect offers the chance for a significant return on the investment of time.

4. "Wedge" potential.

What are the chances that a call on this prospect will result in not just a single sale, but will open the door for several other sales? For example, it may be worth investing extra effort to sell to one division of a company if that is reasonably likely to open the way to other divisions. Similarly, it may be worth investing extra effort to sell to the business leaders in your area, because success with them may open the doors to other prospects.

5. Chances of success/prospect's reputation for innovation and for working with new suppliers.

Especially in the early days, you're going to be short of capital, and hence operating against a tight deadline before you scrape against the bottom of your money barrel. Downgrade the companies that have a reputation for being slow to change, or for being the last to accept innovation. Experiment with them later, after you have built a reserve cushion.

6. Buying cycle.

Orders by government agencies and other large organizations often are substantial, but may be locked up a year in advance. In addition, there may be mandated buying procedures, such as a requirement to advertise for bids before making any purchases. If these organizations are prime prospects, talk to the contracting officer early, and do the necessary paperwork in time to get on the bidder's lists—at least for next year's cycle.

However, take what the contracting officers and others in the agency tell you with a grain of salt. More often than not, there are ways around the rigidities of the purchasing regulations. If you can generate enough interest among the people who will actually be using your product, they, as users, will probably be able to help you through the purchasing red tape. That's why it's so important to go past the purchasing department to find and talk directly to the person who has this power to say yes. (We discuss how to do this in the next chapter.)

SUMMARY

Particularly at the beginning, it's crucial to set priorities among prospects. You can't afford to work randomly, because you need to get cash flowing in with some early successes. In setting priorities, use criteria such as these; add others that are appropriate to your market and situation.

1. The prospect's potential need for your product or service
2. Dollar potential, both short and long term
3. Geographic desirability
4. "Wedge" potential
5. Chances of success/prospect's reputation for innovation and for working with new suppliers
6. Buying cycle

Part Two
Locating and Getting Through to the Appropriate Decision Maker

The core question addressed in this part is: Once I find an organization that might be interested, how do I get through to the right person there?

By this point, you have developed a working list of prospects, and you have targeted some priority prospects from that list. Now you need to find the name of the specific individual or group within each prospect organization to approach.

That person or team to approach is what we refer to as the *Decision Maker*—that is, the individual or team, working in the relevant area, who has the *Authority, Need, and Dollars* to enable them to say yes to what you are offering.

We address the how-to of finding this DM in Chapter 3, "Finding the Person or Team Who Can Say Yes."

In Chapter 4, "Getting Past the Decision Maker's Screen," we examine some useful methods of either quickly convincing the Screen to put you through to the Decision Maker or, alternatively, finding a way of getting around the screen to approach the DM directly.

Chapter 5, "Cold Calling—When You Must," focuses on the practical how-to for those times when cold calling is appropriate in selling.

Then, in Chapter 6, "Convincing the Decision Maker to Meet with You," we address the issue of how to quickly convince the DM to agree to invest time in hearing your message. ("Quickly" is the key; this is not the time for an extended conversation. Busy Decision Makers are reluctant to waste time, either on the phone or in meetings that threaten to be overly long.)

Finally, in Chapter 7, "Organizing and Learning from Your Phone Calls," we point out some ways of improving your telephone techniques.

Chapter 3

Finding the Person or Team Who Can Say Yes

Note: In this book, we'll put initial capitals at times on certain words such as Decision Maker, Decision Influencer, Screen, Authority, Need, Dollars, and others, in order to make clear that we are using them there with special meaning. For example, a Decision Maker (with initial capitals) is not just anybody who might make a decision, but specifically a person or team who appears to have the appropriate Authority, Need, and Dollars to say yes to what you are selling.

Basic rule: You can make a sale only if you deal with the person who can say yes to what you offer.

This sounds obvious enough, but it is often overlooked. Organizations are full of people who claim to have decision-making authority. But in reality, most of them have only *negative* decision-making authority. That is, they have the authority to say no to you. But, no matter what or how good a deal you offer, they're just not able to say yes.

People with only negative decision-making authority typically range from the guard at the plant gate to the purchasing manager to the Decision Maker's secretary or subordinate.

They tend to be easily accessible, and so it's tempting to meet with them and get a sense that you're making progress. But that progress is an illusion. If you do make your presentation to them, you'll generally find that nothing happens—at least, nothing positive. After all, they can't say, "Yes, we'll buy." They can only say either no or "I'll have to think about it"—which really means, "If I happen to think of it, I'll carry your message up to my boss, the real decision maker."

Consider the possibilities. First possibility: If this person who has only the authority to say no *does* say no, the sale is just as dead as if you had made the case to the right person. The opportunity is gone, even though you never had the chance to talk to the person who might have said yes.

Second possibility: Even if they say they'll pass the word on to the real decision maker, the sale is almost certainly equally dead. Sure, you might be lucky. But the fact is that it's very unlikely that they'll make the kind of strong case for your product or service that you could make if you met directly with the Decision Maker.

For one thing, they don't know your product as well as you, and won't be ready to explain why it is better than the competition. Besides, selling your product is not a priority to them; their other responsibilities have the first call on their time and energy. If the Decision Maker says no, they aren't likely to risk their job by pushing on as you would.

The AND Test

The "Decision Maker," as we use the term here, is the person (or team) who has the ability to say yes to what you're offering—whether that yes means to buy a product, to hire you or retain your services, or to take the next step, such as agreeing to a trial run.

In small organizations, the Decision Maker (DM) will typically be the person at the top—the owner of a small business, the managing partner of a law firm, the president of a company, the director of a public agency.

It may take more effort to spot the appropriate DM in larger organizations. Begin looking for the appropriate DM early, as soon as you start your preliminary research to develop your prospect list. As you research the company, and particularly as you talk to people both within and outside the organization, keep your antennae out for the person (or work team) who seems to be in charge in the area in which you would propose to work, and who meets the "AND" test.

The AND test is this: The Decision Maker is the person (or team) who possesses three key characteristics, *Authority, Need,* and *Dollars* (AND).

"A" Represents Authority

The person to whom you make your presentation must be at a level to have the authority, or "authorization," to make a buying commitment for the amount appropriate to your projected work.

Thus, if your cheapest model costs $5,000, and the person with whom you meet has a $3,000 purchasing limit, then you cannot expect a yes decision from that person. That individual, therefore, is not the Decision Maker, in our meaning of the term. He may be a part of a team that has full decision-making power. Or he may be a *Decision Influencer*—that is, someone whose advice is heeded by the actual Decision Maker.

Incidentally, it's usually not good to ask directly, "Do you have authority to buy?" The person may feel too embarrassed to admit if he or she does not, and may fib and say yes. A more professional way is to ask something to the effect, "I realize it's early to address this, but if later in the process you should want to buy, is there anyone else who we'll need to bring in?" (Still another approach: "Is there anyone else who'll need to sign off on this?")

"N" Represents Need

Find your way to the person (or department) with a problem that your product or service can solve. That is, *find your way to the person who has the need for your product.*

If your product is a janitorial cleaning tool, for instance, there is obviously no point in meeting with the head of data processing. Similarly, the purchasing manager is usually the wrong person, as the purchasing manager probably does not have a first-hand need. (We look at the role of the purchasing department later in this chapter.)

"D" Represents Dollars

A person can have the Authority to buy and a Need for the product, yet still not be a Decision Maker because she lacks Dollars (or budget).

It may not be easy to find out whether or not money is available to spend on your product or service. There is no tactful way of asking straight out if someone has the money. But you can sometimes ask indirectly, by questions such as, "Suppose we find that this product does meet your needs. Will it be possible for you to buy in this present budget cycle?"

However, don't necessarily believe a Decision Maker who claims poverty; usually that's just an excuse to get rid of salespeople.

Finding Your Way to the Decision Maker with AND

Your Knowledge of the Field

You may already know from contacts in your professional organizations, from scuttlebutt in the industry, and from your reading of news articles and business journals who's who in the hierarchies of potential client organizations.

But caution: The person who is apparently in charge of an area may *not* be the person with the necessary AND to make purchases for that area. For instance, the person in charge of the word-processing unit in a firm is probably not the person with the AND to sign off on the purchase of new software or equipment.

In most cases, you may be wiser to avoid talking to that user altogether, and instead begin further up the chain with the person who has overall responsibility for profitability and productivity in the area relevant to your product or service.

While you could ask the user (such as the head of word-processing) for guidance on who has the Authority, Need, and Dollars, there is a risk that, once you open contact with that person, you may be locked into making your case to her. You would then be drawn into working with her, rather than directly with the real Decision Maker, with the disadvantages we discussed earlier.

Your Research within the Prospect Organization

This can be the easiest way of all—if it works. Simply phone the company and ask the operator who is the person in charge of the area that your product relates to. Get the person's name first, then the job title. The title is important, as you need to be sure that this is the manager, not just a junior clerk.

While you are on the phone, take an extra few seconds to ask who that person reports to—just in case the decisions are made at the next-higher level.

As you probe for this information, it's usually best not to identify yourself as a salesperson, as the operator may try to refer you to the purchasing department. You will usually get further if the operator assumes that you are a customer.

If the operator asks why all these questions, you might say simply, "I need to talk to the person in charge of that area." Or, you could admit that you are hoping to sell to the organization, but you need to first explore whether there really is a need for your product there. If you are able to establish the right rapport with this receptionist, you may get all the help you need.

Alternatively, you might say, "I'm conducting an industry survey"—which is true, at least in the sense that you are surveying the industry for prospects.

But don't tell any fibs, because you will be back there later, and they could return to haunt you. Also, do not let the operator connect you to this person yet. At this point you are only determining who the person is; you are not yet ready to talk business.

Client Literature

A brochure or other company literature, such as an annual report to shareholders, can be a very helpful source of information, as it may give you a better idea of what the organization is about, what the key themes are, and perhaps even who's who in the management structure. You could ask the receptionist to send this literature, or you might drop by and pick it up in person.

Actually, dropping by for literature can be a good way of doing some on-site investigation of the organization as a prospect, as well as finding who the likely Decision Maker for your product would be.

When you go for the literature, don't go out of your way to say that you are there on a selling mission. A receptionist who assumes that you are a potential customer or shareholder will often be more generous with information. (And if the receptionist recognizes you when you come back later on a sales call? Well, plans change, and who can blame you for following up on a business opportunity you chanced upon!)

Your Network in the Organization or in the Industry

Those whom you meet during your early general "scouting" of the organization may be able to give you a sense of where to make contact.

Your present clients may give you guidance on who their counterparts with AND buying authority in other firms or agencies are. (They may even be willing to make telephone introductions for you, or at least allow you to use them as referrals.)

Leads from Other Salespeople

Trade leads with other salespeople who work in the same general field, but are not your direct competitors. (That is, if you sell brushes, trade leads with those who sell paint.)

Business Directories

Local directories, perhaps from the Chamber of Commerce, may give you the guidance you need. Or, if you're working in a specialized field, determine what trade or professional societies the manager with the responsibility for this area would probably belong to. Phone that society's local or national headquarters to get the directory.

If you will be doing significant selling to those in this field, you might even consider joining these societies, provided you are eligible. The time and membership fees you invest will probably pay off in access to a variety of decision makers in other organizations. It may also open the way for you to advertise in the group's newsletter. In time, you could be invited to give a talk or presentation to the group.

For a more extensive listing of directories and other research sources, see Chapter 33.

If You Can't Locate the Decision Maker with AND

Sometimes, no matter how much probing and research you do, you still can't determine who actually has the Authority, Need, and Dollars within the organization.

Rule of thumb: The person at the very top of the organization *will* have positive decision-making authority, *or at least* will be able to *make things happen* by shifting budgets. Even if the top person refers you down, you have at least opened a channel, so that you can later ask to move back upstairs for funding.

Therefore, if in doubt, start as high as possible. If necessary, go to the very top: Call the president's office. Chances are, you'll be referred downward. But then you can honestly say, "Mr. Roberts in the president's office suggested that I call you."

In a large organization, the person you are directed to may not be the right DM. Most often, the mistake will be to direct you to the person slightly *above* the level of the actual DM. But that is typically to your advantage, as you can again benefit from being referred downward, and being able to say that you are calling "at the suggestion of" that higher-level person.

It's better to start a level or so too high and be referred downward than to start too low and be locked into a position where you don't have direct contact with the real Decision Maker.

Decision Influencers

Even if the user, or the person in charge of an area, does not have the level of Authority, Need, and Dollars to be the actual Decision Maker, he or she may nonetheless be an important "Decision Influencer." That is, even though this person can't make the final call, his or her input and suggestions are listened to with respect. Such people may have the Need, but Authority and Dollars reside with their boss, or their boss's boss. You don't want to offend them by first seeing them, then appearing to skip over their heads.

Decision Influencers may include

- Those who will be the *actual users* of your product or service. (For instance, in midsized and larger companies, the person who uses the computer you sell will generally not be the Decision Maker [because he lacks Authority, Need, or Dollars], but will probably have a significant influence, as that person will be technically knowledgeable and will be living with whichever computer is selected.)
- *Financial advisers* such as the firm's accountant or chief financial officer. They may say whether or not the firm can afford what you offer, and may also have input on finance alternatives, such as leasing versus purchasing and the like.
- *The Decision Maker's Mentor.* That is, the person who has Decision-Making Authority, Need, and Dollars may still want to check with the "old hand" in the company who has helped him along the way. Chances are, you won't know who that mentor is, and you may never meet him or her; just be aware that there may be such a person feeding suggestions, questions, and other concerns to the DM.
- *The purchasing manager.* That influence may be more on the technical aspects of how to make the purchase happen, given the organization's policies on purchasing. But since the purchasing manager may have this influence, you don't want to antagonize him. Go around him to get to the real DM, but do it quietly and in a nice, unobtrusive way.

When to Begin with the Purchasing Manager, And When Not To

Contrary to what you might expect, it is usually *not* a good idea to begin your contact with the purchasing manager. More often than not, the purchasing manager will have clear authority only to say no—at least with respect to a new product, service, or idea.

In most organizations, the purchasing manager's role is to coordinate the buying of known commodities. If you're selling copy paper, or paint, or any other kind of standard item, the purchasing office probably *is* the place to begin.

But if you're selling something innovative (either because it's a new idea or new product, or because it accomplishes the job in a new way), then it's best to find your way to the actual potential user and create the sense of need at that level.

Unconvinced? Project yourself back a couple of decades, and imagine that you were selling one of the first personal computers. If you had started with the purchasing department, they might have said, "Well, we do have a mandate to buy a dozen Selectric typewriters and a dozen adding machines. But this strange-looking box you're offering clearly isn't a Selectric, and it doesn't fit the specifications we've set up for the adding machine, so we're not interested. Sorry."

But suppose, instead, you had found your way to the head of the engineering department, or to someone in the legal department who faced the need to grind out endless versions of the same form. Once you showed just what your little computer could accomplish, they probably would have found a way to open the necessary doors for you.

That's why I suggest you use the purchasing department only as a last resort. (The same goes for the personnel department if you're marketing your services.) Instead, find your way to the person or department with the actual need.

For anything innovative or novel, the purchasing manager probably lacks the Authority to buy. The purchasing manager certainly lacks Need, unless your product happens to be relevant to the purchasing area. And the purchasing manager has Dollars only within prescribed limits.

Nonetheless, there are *some* occasions when it *is* good strategy to contact the purchasing manager:

- Contact the purchasing department if you cannot otherwise find the person who has AND to make a positive decision in your field. You can generally do this best by telephone, as you are less likely to be drawn into making a full presentation of what you are offering. This phone contact should be as short as possible, generally not more than about 30 seconds. Here's a model to adapt:

> "My name is Greta Ross, and I'm with 21st Century Containers. We've developed radically new types of safety containers for shipping fragile or especially valuable items. I know that your firm manufactures computer drives, which are exactly the kind of product suitable for our containers. Who in your organization would you suggest I talk to?"

If necessary, further clarify as you "negotiate" your way to the proper decision maker:

> "From our experience, the shipping department is generally not appropriate, as the packaging choice is usually made earlier in the process."

- Contact purchasing if you know that the wheels are already in motion to buy what you are offering, so that the purchasing manager has the Authority and Dollars, and the Need has been communicated from another part of the organization.
- Contact purchasing to get on the organization's approved list of bidders. (But don't sit around waiting for the organization to solicit you; continue taking active steps to meet with the appropriate managers, regardless.)

Training Directors: When to Begin There, and When Not To

If you are selling packaged training products, such as audio or video tapes, or seminars on this year's hot topic, then it is probably productive to start with the organization's director of training, or personnel director, or human relations coordinator (or some similar title, depending on the organization). He may have Authority, Need, and Dollars for things like that, particularly if your product focuses on areas that have received a lot of publicity, such as employee safety practices.

But suppose instead that you are selling not packaged products but rather your consulting services as an expert on this topic (for illustration, employee safety practices). Or suppose you don't think much of the packaged (or "canned") safety training programs that are on the market, and propose to develop custom training specifically for this organization.

In that case, the training department might be a dead end. The training director probably does not have the Need to improve safety—at least in any novel way. Thus, your best approach would be to bypass the training and personnel departments and find your way to the manager who *does* have a real reason to be concerned with safety. This may be the company president, who has an incentive to lower insurance costs, or it may be the plant manager.

Summary

In finding your way to the appropriate Decision Maker for your product, look for the individual or working team with AND: *Authority* to make a buying commitment, *Need* for your product or service, and the *Dollars* to pay for it.

Your ingenuity is your best tool for finding your way to the right Decision Maker for what you're offering. But here are some starting points:

1. Your knowledge of who's who in the field.
2. Your research in the prospect organization. As you talk to people there, in person or on the phone, stay alert for clues that can direct you to the person or team with AND.
3. The client company's literature, such as brochures, annual reports, press clippings, and the like.

4. The network you develop, both in this prospect organization and in the industry.
5. Trading leads with the other salespeople you meet—those who cover the same ground as you, although with noncompeting products.
6. Business directories. You probably already know the key publications in your field; for a broader introduction, see Chapter 33.

Rule of thumb: If you can't spot the real Decision Maker, start at the top of the organization, and let yourself be guided downward. When you contact the suggested person, you can honestly say that it is "at the suggestion" of the president (or whomever you contacted).

The time you invest in locating the appropriate DM will be worth it. If you call the wrong individual (one too low in the hierarchy, or otherwise lacking Authority, Need, and Dollars), you will often be locked into dealing with that person. You can then move on only at the risk of offending that first contact, who may later turn out to be a significant influencer of the decision.

While the purchasing manager is usually the *wrong* person (or office) with which to begin your contact, there are some situations in which purchasing *is* the place to begin:

- When the purchasing office seems to be the only source that can tell you who really has Authority, Need, and Dollars
- When the purchasing apparatus is already in motion, so that Need is recognized, the Dollars have been allocated, and now the purchasing manager has been delegated the Authority to buy
- When your objective is to get on the organization's list of authorized bidders or suppliers

If You're Selling Yourself for a Consulting Role or Full-Time Job

What was said here about going to the purchasing department only as a last resort applies equally if you're job-hunting. Begin with the personnel department only as a last resort.

Instead, invest effort in finding your way to the department—or, even better, the individual—with the Authority, Need, and Dollars to take you on. Using approaches adapted from those covered in this chapter help that person see a need that you, uniquely, can fill. If you can convince her of that, she'll get you through the personnel hoops.

As someone put it, personnel departments tend to see their first step as discarding the square pegs that arrive in order to more easily spot the round pegs to fit round holes. If you're a perfectly round peg, then all is well for you. But if you're a little different—that is, if you bring something unique—then you're far better off bypassing the sorting-out process and going directly to the place where your unique potential can be recognized.

Chapter 4

Getting Past the Decision Maker's Screen

People with the kind of positive decision making authority you need—that is, who have Authority, Need, and Dollars—tend to be busy people with many responsibilities. To minimize interruptions, they often set up various types of "Screens" around themselves.

Screens may extend from the security guard at the gate, to the telephone receptionist, to the executive secretary who guards the door to the DM's office. The Screen's function is to minimize distractions so that the Decision Maker can focus on what is truly significant to the well-being of the organization.

That means that the Screen will open for you if, and only if, you communicate, through your words and professionalism, that you have the potential of bringing something of significant value to the organization—that is, if you present a sound business purpose for seeing the Decision Maker.

How can you get that sense of significance across before the Screen's mind clicks shut? We'll examine some techniques in this chapter. But first we need to address an important question.

Whether to "Cold Call" or Work by Appointment

It's easy enough to "cold call" (that is, drop in at Decision Maker's office in the hope of slipping in at a convenient time). But salespeople who rely on cold calling waste a lot of productive time waiting in reception rooms and driving to meetings that never take place because the DM couldn't fit them in.

You have only so many good hours in a business day. Is the best use of those hours waiting for other people's meetings to end so that you can have a few minutes to make your presentation?

Investing the time to phone ahead for your appointments pays off in several ways:

- It projects to the DM a businesslike respect for the value of time, both your own and that of the DM.
- By making a fixed appointment, you set up an environment that permits some control over the proceedings, free from phone calls and interruptions.
- It allows you to better prepare for the meeting; since you know for sure who you will be meeting, you can take the time to do a little more research in advance.

In some situations, you have no real choice other than to work by appointment, since executives with real decision-making power often can be seen only by appointment.

Getting Through (or Around) the Screen

Whether you choose to cold call or to phone ahead for an appointment, you still need to get past the Screen so that you can talk directly to the Decision Maker. Here are some methods to get you started, useful in both phoning and cold calling in person.

Whenever possible, make your contact through referrals or other "pre-introductions."

If you are calling this DM at the suggestion of another of your clients or of a mutual friend, make that clear at the very start, both to the Screen and later to the DM: "I'm calling at the suggestion of Peter Wenders of GMR Industries."

If you already know the Decision Maker from another context, mention this to the Screen, but be careful how you word it. You don't want the Decision Maker to come to the phone (or to avoid you) because he thinks you're setting up a golf tournament at the country club or asking for a donation to the alumni fund.

Flag that other context as a door-opener in the Screen's mind, but then quickly move on to your present business purpose. Here's a good model to follow:

> "At the Rotary luncheon the other day, I was talking with Ms. Tompkins. I later came upon an idea that I realized might be helpful to her work here. I'd like to set a time to drop by and explain it to her. I wonder if you can help me arrange a time, please?"

Or,

> "Mr. Parsons dropped by our booth at the NATL show, and asked me to get in touch with him to arrange a meeting to explore some possibilities he saw there. I have the information ready now. Do you think Wednesday morning or Thursday afternoon would be more convenient for him?"

Make the Screen your ally.

When you phone an organization, listen closely to the name of the person who answers. It may be someone you met earlier when you were on the premises researching the organization as a potential client. If the name is familiar, remind the person of your previous conversation:

> "Mrs. Johnson, this is Jack Thomas of Computers for Business. You may remember me from my visit to your office last week." (Pause a moment to give thinking time.) "We spoke at that time about how your organization handles inventory. Since then, I've had a chance to give some more thought to what we discussed. I have some ideas that I think Mr. Rabin will find of interest. Perhaps you could schedule an appointment for me with him. It should take about twenty minutes at most. I'm available both Tuesday morning and Wednesday afternoon. Would either of these times be convenient for him to meet?"

If the questions you asked during that earlier conversation were well focused, perhaps suggesting problem areas for which you might offer a solution, then you may have intrigued the Screen, raising the thought that perhaps you have the potential of solving a problem with which the Screen is familiar.

For example, if one of your questions was, "Do you have crunch periods during the month when you're very overloaded?" the DM's secretary may assume that you have a remedy available, and hence will be eager to put you through to the boss.

Presell the Screen. But speak only in broad concepts. *Do not* become drawn into the details.

In persuading the Screen to put you through to the DM, you'll obviously need to talk some about your business purpose for calling. But beware of saying too much.

Granted, this puts you on the horns of a dilemma. If you are too vague, you will not get the appointment. But, conversely, the more you talk of the specifics of what you are offering, the more reasons you'll give the Screen for keeping you out: "You work with computers, you say? Well, there's no point in your seeing Mr. Chase, as we already have our own in-house computer expert."

Keep in mind the basic principle: You can't make the sale over the phone, but you can *lose* it.

Therefore, when you're on the phone, speak in overall conceptual terms of what your product or service will *do* for the organization, not of what it *is*, or of its technical features.

Thus if your consulting focus is on introducing computer systems for increasing productivity, do *not* say "computers." Instead, speak of "methods for increasing productivity" or "techniques for developing more efficient work flows."

In explaining to the Screen, focus your communication beyond what your product or service *is* in order to speak of what it can *do* for the purchaser. For example, if your specialty is training in telephone marketing, you could say,

> "We've been able to help organizations extend their marketing reach to smaller customer accounts, and those in hard-to-reach places. As a result, we typically help our clients increase sales by 15 to 20 percent."

Notice that in this example there is no mention at all of "telephone," and no mention of "training." But since you're offering the prospect of increasing sales by 20 percent, how could a Screen reasonably turn you away?

Here are some models you can adapt:

> "I'd like to speak to Mr. Dobson about some methods that may be able to increase your organization's productivity by 10 percent or more, as we have with other firms."

Or,

> "I'm a design consultant, and I'd like to propose some suggested designs for Ms. White to consider for your next series of advertisements."

Or,

> "I represent a consulting firm that specializes in financial management. We've worked with a number of organizations like yours, and I believe that we may be able to help you. I do need to speak with Ms. Jensen to find out what your present needs are, and in what directions you'll be moving in the next couple of years."

Ask questions the Screen won't be able to answer.

The way to get through the Screen is to communicate that you have a *sound business reason* for talking to the DM—one that will help the DM or the organization work better.

Thus, if the Screen is putting you on the defensive with questions, switch from defense to attack by asking your own questions, as in this dialogue:

Screen: "And what is it you want to talk to Mr. Builder about?"

Salesperson: "Mr. Builder is the construction engineer on the PDM Center, isn't he?"

Screen: "Yes, of course. But why do you need to talk to him?"

Salesperson: "I'm calling to determine whether the PDM Center is being built in accord with the NEPA Standards on hydro-thallaxic transfaxions."

Screen: "I have no idea. For that you'll have to talk to Mr. Builder. Hold, please."

With a little ingenuity, you can come up with a repertoire of unanswerable questions like these. The questions should be relevant to the reason for your call to the DM, but a little more technical or detailed than a receptionist or secretary would be willing to address.

If necessary, call when the Screen is away.

If you find that you just can't break through the Screen, try phoning before or after normal business hours, or even over the lunch hour. Key Decision Makers are typically at their desks earlier or later, or both, to take advantage of the quiet time when the office is empty.

In off hours, Decision Makers often answer their own phones. If you do get the DM on the line, be particularly brief and to the point, respecting the fact that she is in the office at this time precisely in order to avoid interruptions.

The Screen's "Buying Signals"

Be alert for the subtle clues that indicate that the Screen is relaxing the barrier. When you sense this opening, don't hesitate. Use the momentum that you've built up, and move on to ask for what you want, which is, ultimately, to meet with the DM.

In some organizations, the Screen is authorized to set up the appointment, and can write you onto the calendar without your needing to speak to the DM at this point. That's ideal, as it means that you don't have to make your case again to the DM over the phone. If you sense that this may be the case, work on this assumption, and suggest to the Screen a pair of alternative times from which to choose:

> "I'm free to meet Mr. Bolger next Tuesday afternoon. Or would Thursday morning be better?"

Just what these buying signals consist of will depend a lot on the individual's own mannerisms. Here are some to watch for; in time you will develop a sixth sense for when the mood has changed.

- Change in phone manner. The Screen may be less formal and less curt, or may become more informal and relaxed.

- Questions may be buying signals. Watch for the switch from questions about the product (which are basically looking for reasons to say no) to questions that relate to practical things like where you are located or when you can come in.
- Some statements may be indirect buying signals. A Screen who says, "Mr. Watkins is out of town all this week" is, consciously or not, telling you that you've won, and it's now just a matter of settling on a mutually convenient time. When this happens, stop making your case, and say something to the effect, "Fine. I'll be in your area next Tuesday and Thursday. Which would be better?"
- Sometimes interest in what you are selling does convey a buying signal. Listen for subtle clues. If you're selling, for example, productivity improvement software for the office, the Screen might probe for reasons to say No. But the Screen might also want to know more because he is very eager to find a way of easing his own workload. Often, the difference will be perceptible in voice tone, energy, and enthusiasm—perhaps even in the kinds of questions. If the questions are somewhat technical, that may be a clue that the organization has already begun shopping for something like what you offer.

When You Encounter Voice Mail

It's increasingly likely that you will encounter voice mail or answering machines when you call the Decision Makers in both small and large organizations. Think through in advance just how you will respond.

- Will you leave a message, or will you keep trying to reach the DM directly? If you leave your name, then whether or not to respond is in the DM's hands, and you lose control. If the DM doesn't return your call, then it gets awkward: Does that mean no interest, or just too busy? But sometimes leaving your name and number is the only way. Besides, if the DM does call you back, that puts you in a good position, as it shows some level of interest.
- As a rule, I try phoning several times, hoping to catch the DM at the desk. If I encounter an answering machine, I hang up these first few times without leaving my name, as I would rather catch the DM directly. If it becomes clear that the DM isn't likely to answer, then I go ahead and leave my name and number, and maybe a suggested time to catch me in. On the first attempt, I would not identify my company or reason for calling. If I don't get a call back, then I try again, identifying myself, and giving a short "hot-button" reason for calling me back. (This message normally should not run more than a couple of sentences. For possible hot buttons, see chapter 6.)
- Don't "wing" your messages. Decide just what message you want to leave, then boil it down so that it gets quickly to the point. Rehearse your message until you can say it confidently and with a smile in your voice.
- Then, before leaving your first message on a prospect's voice mail, call your own and leave the same message. Then go back and revise and rehearse it again until it is right.
- Whether to identify your company, or your reason for calling, is something for you to work out, with experience. A DM who thinks you are a potential buyer of his or her services will be more likely to return the call than

one who knows that you are selling. On the other hand, a busy DM may not bother returning calls that lack information. *Definitely do not try to make the sale, or even describe your product, over voice mail.* Just say who you are, maybe identify your company, and give your phone number. If you are out a lot, you could suggest ideal times for calling you back. ("I am generally at my desk each day from ___ to ___.")

SUMMARY

Cold calling—that is, arriving cold at the prospect's office—is usually not a productive way of using your time. In most situations, it will be worth the investment of effort to set up at least a few definite sales appointments each day. (If you have spare time around scheduled appointments, you can use that for cold calling.)

When you phone for an appointment, you may find that the person who actually has Authority, Need, and Dollars is surrounded by a "secretarial Screen" who makes it hard to get through and ask for an appointment.

To get through the Screen, convince him that you are bringing the organization something of significant value. Methods for accomplishing this include

1. Using referrals from satisfied clients who have recommended you to this organization and this decision maker.
2. Making the Screen your ally by outlining in conceptual terms how you may be able to help the organization.
3. Preselling the Screen. But speak only in broad concepts. Do not become drawn into the details. You can only *lose* the sale over the phone; you cannot *make* the sale.

If possible, get the Screen to put you on the Decision Maker's calendar without your having to talk to her at this time.

If the Screen continues to block you, try more creative methods of getting through to the DM:

4. If necessary, ask questions you expect the Screen won't be able to answer.
5. Call when the Screen is away, perhaps before or after the normal working hours, in hopes of catching the Decision Maker directly.

PLAYING THE PERCENTAGES

When you call the Screen, and at every other point in the selling process, you risk hearing "no." Nobody likes to hear no, not even long-time professional salespeople. But you need to look at the noes you hear in perspective:

- Selling is a percentage game. It would be unrealistic to expect that every attempt would result in a sale. But there *are* sales out there waiting to be discovered. Success in selling is, to a large extent, getting through the noes to find the yes responses.
- "No" is useful feedback, from which you can build a sale. The key is to probe that no, so that you know precisely what it means here and now, in this specific situation, coming from this unique individual. Very often, once you know that, you can overcome it, using methods we'll examine later in this book.

Chapter 5

Cold Calling—When You Must

For the reasons discussed in the previous chapter, cold calling—dropping in on prospects without an appointment—is usually not a good use of your time. You can waste a lot of productive time waiting for an opening to see the Decision Maker. Besides, that kind of willingness to wait for an opening might be interpreted by the DM as an indication that you don't have anything better to do with your time.

But there *are* certain situations in which cold calling is appropriate.

1. Cold calling is appropriate for follow-up calls on existing customers, when you drop by to make sure all is going well with your product. (We'll examine follow-up customer-care calls more in Chapter 30.)

2. Cold calling may be a productive use of time if you find yourself with time to spare between other appointments. If you're already in an area, prospecting for new leads there is a good use of that open time. Cold calling is ideal for seeing what other opportunities there are in that part of your territory.

   In some cases, you may just get lucky and stumble upon a qualified Decision Maker who is interested in meeting right then. If so, seize the opportunity. (If the DM is interested but doesn't have the time then, at least move at that point to set up an appointment for another day or time.)

3. Cold calling can be useful as a tool for conducting some kinds of preliminary research and scouting for prospects. To quickly survey the potential for your product or service among the tenants of an office building or industrial park, the best way may be to quickly "sweep" from office to office, gathering information.

   This third use of cold calling is the focus of this chapter.

Cold Calling as a Research Method

Earlier, in Chapter 1, we looked briefly at "smokestacking" and "sweeping" buildings in order to rapidly find potential prospects. In those sweeps, you speak briefly with the receptionist or secretary to make a quick determination of whether it is worth calling back to see the Decision Maker.

Just what information you are looking for at this early stage will vary with your product and the market. The checklist below is a starting point; adapt it to your own uses.

> *Note: As you meet with people during these initial sweeps for information, the tone should be that of a conversation, not an interrogation. Be friendly. Don't put them on the spot with a barrage of questions.*

If someone is reluctant to talk, it could be that he is only a temporary employee and doesn't want to admit it. Or it may be that he doesn't want to give away too much information without knowing why you're there and what you're going to do with this information. To overcome this, put yourself clearly in context without getting into much detail (you don't want to be drawn into making your sales call to this person, who can say no, but not yes). Here are some ways of setting context:

- You could say that you have an innovative product that you think may be able to help this firm, but you need to get some preliminary information to determine whether to ask the Decision Maker for some time.
- Or, you could mention that you are planning a "VIP Seminar" or exhibition. You want to send an invitation to the DM in this organization, but you need to "confirm" some things to make sure that her attendance would be appropriate.

The Kinds of Information You Are Looking For in Cold Calling

1. *What the organization does.* Not every company or agency name is clear. "Automatex" may not give a clue to whether or not the firm can use your product. Government agencies can be even more obscure: Did you ever pass the local "Human Services Center" and get an image of humans up on racks getting their oil changed? (Would that be corn oil or codfish oil?)
2. *How large the organization is* may be relevant in some situations.
3. *Whether this is the headquarters or a branch operation* of another organization. Depending on your product and its cost, buying decisions might be made only at the headquarters office.
4. *If possible, the name of the key Decision Maker.* The guard or receptionist may or may not know.
5. *The exact address and phone number* of this office, so that you can easily check back later. (There may be a stack of the Decision Maker's business cards on the front counter. Grab one, as that gives the details you need, including the spelling of the DM's name.)

Some How-To's

When you arrive at the building or office park, begin by checking the tenant directory. If you already have a list, such as from the Chamber of Commerce, check it against the tenant directory to make sure the addresses are still current. Also, jot down the office number of any other companies with names that hint that they might be particularly worth calling on. (You don't want to pass those offices by as you move through.)

Work systematically as you sweep the area. In a building, start at the top and work downward. (That way, you can easily walk down between floors, and save the time of waiting for the elevator.)

Some buildings will have security guards. If you're in business attire, you shouldn't have a problem if you walk briskly, projecting that you're there on an appointment.

Some buildings have special security, and will let you in only if you have a confirmed appointment. To get around that, some salespeople set up one appointment, then sweep the rest of the building on the way out. The security people may not be pleased, but it may be your only way in.

1. *Make sure there's a friendly smile on your face as you enter each door.* (Granted, this can be hard at the start, when you're on edge wondering what lurks behind these strange doors.) First impressions count, and a smile can put even the most hard-bitten security guards and receptionists at ease.

   Project yourself into the guard or receptionist's shoes; he's sitting there all day, with not much happening. He may not even have a window. You—a salesperson coming through that door—may be the most exciting thing that has happened in the past hour, so bring some sunshine with you.

2. *Keep your eyes open.* Even before you enter the building, a glance at the place and the vehicles outside can tell you a lot. Once you are inside a particular office, the kind of equipment and furnishings can give helpful clues. Does the place look prosperous? Is there a hum of energy in the air? Are there product samples in the reception area, or advertising posters framed on the wall that give you a quick reading of what the operation is about?

3. *Make a mental note of the receptionist's name.* It will smooth the present conversation, and it will be helpful if you phone back later for an appointment. Then you can say, "Mrs. Wilkins, this is Rhonda Prost. We talked the other day..."

   As soon as you leave each office, take a few moments to transfer your mental notes of names, impressions, and facts onto paper. Otherwise, by the end of the day, all will be a blur.

4. *Begin in a low-key way* by saying something on the order of, "I wonder if you can help me?" There's something about asking for help: You immediately become less threatening. After all, most people like to help.

   When the person says, "Sure, I'll try to help," respond with something on the order of, "I was in the building for another meeting, and I was intrigued by your company name. What does Automatex do?"

   At this point, the guard or receptionist doesn't know who you are or why you're there. You could be a potential client of the firm, and so he will generally tell you enough to enable you to determine whether it is worth pursuing further.

   If you sense that you have arrived at a bad time—because things seem to be in crisis with a deadline or the like—apologize, and offer to come back another time. Before leaving, ask when would be a good time to stop in again.

5. *If the organization looks promising*, ask for the name of the person who is likely to be the Decision Maker for your product: "I don't want to see him or her now, but can you tell me who's in charge of _____."

6. *Chances are the receptionist will tell you without any hesitation.* But at about this point, the receptionist may begin asking you some questions about who you are and why you're there. Your best response is, "I'm in the _____ industry, and I may want to contact Ms. Decision Maker with some ideas."

   Notice that when you say you're in the ________ industry, you don't flag yourself as a salesperson. You're just "in the industry." The receptionist may still be thinking that you are a potential customer, and since you're not asking for any of the Decision Maker's time now, you'll probably get the name and information you ask for.

7. *If you don't have any idea of who the Decision Maker* for your product area might be—such as the kind of job title that would probably be appropriate—you can probe the receptionist. "Can you tell me, who here is responsible for __________?"

   It can be difficult to put into words just what person or job title you're looking for. It may help to speak of the general area of the need your product can fill.

8. *After the receptionist suggests a name, echo that name, and ask what the person's title is.* This is a way to double check, in case the receptionist has directed you to the user of the product, rather than the actual Decision Maker.

   When you have that name and title, take it up one more step "And who does Mr. Simpson report to?" Then ask for that person's title.

   The receptionist may not know the formal titles ("I don't know his actual title, but he's in charge of _____"). Whatever you get is at least a start, and will be useful later when you phone back either to ask for an appointment or to probe further to find just where Authority, Need, and Dollars reside.

9. *Note that in this approach, you have not mentioned your name or firm.* That is intentional. It's generally best not to volunteer your firm name yet, as that might flag that you are there hoping to sell, not to buy.

10. *If the organization still looks promising, try to collect literature to review later for further leads and clues.* If you see a business-card dispenser on the counter, take one. Ask the receptionist if you might have a brochure or other company literature, such as an annual report to shareholders. Materials like these can be helpful sources of information, giving you an idea of what the organization is about, what the key themes are, and perhaps even who's who in the management structure.

11. *If the chemistry of this initial call went particularly well, it may be productive for you to leave your business card.* That will serve as a preintroduction later. On the other hand, if you had a difficult time with the receptionist, try to avoid leaving the card, or even your name. That way, you can let a couple of weeks pass before phoning back, and you may not even be remembered. Or a different person may be on the front desk.

12. *Be prepared for good luck.* Even though you are not looking to make your presentation now, things can happen. The DM may be within earshot as you talk with the receptionist and come out to find out what's happening. Or the receptionist may not feel comfortable answering questions, and may ring someone up the organizational ladder to come out.

    Even though you are planning only to do a quick sweep, carry your usual sales essentials of note pad, order blanks, and whatever literature or samples you need.

13. *Nobody likes rejection*, but it can happen that the guard or receptionist will refuse to tell you much. Don't take it personally; he or she was probably just as nasty to the last person who called. (Or maybe somebody else just gave him or her a hard time.) Move on. There are other prospects. And there are other ways of getting the information from this organization, *despite* that receptionist.

Sample Script

Here's an outline of a sample script you can adapt, to get you started. (It's useful as a model for cold calling both in person and over the phone.)

(SR is Sales Rep; REC is receptionist, guard, etc.)

SR: "Hello. I wonder if perhaps you could help me?"

REC: "Sure. What do you need?"

SR: "I noticed your firm's name on the building directory, and I was intrigued. I'm interested in finding out what field you're working in."

REC: (Explains briefly, and SR recognizes that this may be promising.)

SR: "Is this the main headquarters of the company, or a branch location?"

REC: "This is all there is."

SR: "Is all of the firm's data processing [or whatever your field is] done here?"

REC: "So far as I know."

SR: "That's the business I'm in—data processing. Can you tell me who's responsible for it here?"

REC: "That would be Mr. Simmons."

SR: "Mr. Simmons. And what's his title?"

REC: "Supervisor of data processing."

SR: (Recognizes that the supervisor of DP is probably not going to be the Decision Maker with Authority, Need, and Dollars. The appropriate DM will be further up the organizational chart.) "Who does Mr. Simmons report to?"

REC: "His boss would be Ms. Jane Whitely."

SR: "And her title?"

REC: "Vice president of operations. She reports to Dr. Grafton, our president."

SR: "I'd like to give Ms. Whitely a call sometime, because I think we may have some areas of mutual interest. What would her phone extension be? Do you happen to have her business card handy?"

REC: "Of course."

SR: "Thank you for the help. I'd like to leave you my card, as I'll probably be calling in the next few days. And, by the way, do you have a company brochure I could have? Or any other literature that might help me get a sense of the organization?"

If Building Security Prevents Sweeps

Some buildings discourage sweeping or canvassing. Here's how one marketer gets the job done, regardless:*

1. Find out the major firms or best prospects for your product in advance. Even if the security guard won't let you wander through the building, there should be no problem with letting you see the directory.
2. Phone these best prospects and ask for the phone number of their fax machine.
3. Drive to the building, fire up your laptop computer and your cellular phone, and zap an introductory letter to the appropriate manager in each of these firms. (It will be a standard letter, prepared in advance, onto which you plug address information.) In the letter, say you will be phoning them within the next two hours.
4. When the first batch of letters is off, begin phoning the people to whom you sent the letters. Say something to this effect: "I faxed you a letter a few minutes ago explaining who I am. I'm in the area now, and would like to come by to introduce myself briefly, and to learn about you and your organization. I'd expect the meeting should take about ten minutes at the most. Would right now be good, or would it be better to meet in, say, an hour or two?"
5. Don't be surprised if some of the prospects want to come and meet you at your car to check out your system!

If a car fax and cellular phone are not practical for you, you can fax the letters overnight, then call from a pay phone in the lobby.

* Adapted from an article in *Success,* May 1994, page 45, on a technique used by Orlando sales training consultant Gordie Allen.

Chapter 6

Convincing the Decision Maker to Meet with You

Once you get through the Screen and have the Decision Maker on the phone, you have one crucial objective: to persuade that DM to invest time in meeting face to face with you. Time is money to effective Decision Makers, and they are not inclined to waste it in either long phone calls or unproductive meetings.

When you speak with the DM, be friendly *but get to the point.* This is not the time to chat about the weather or how the day is going. Nor is it the time to talk in detail about what your product is, or your background.

"Call Up, Fix Up, Hang Up."

Sales professionals think of this first phone contact as the "call up, fix up, hang up" phase. The point is to make the call, arrange a meeting, then get off the line without getting bogged down.

You don't want to seem brusque during the conversation, but you also don't want to get into a long conversation at this point. For busy Decision Makers, phone calls are, by nature, interruptions, and so the shorter and the more to the point the interruption is, the better.

Another reason for being succinct now:

- You can *lose* the chance to meet with the DM if you talk too much, but...
- No matter what you say, you cannot *make* the sale over the phone.

Once the DM picks up the phone, you have two crucial tasks to accomplish in perhaps thirty seconds or less... that is, before the DM's interest flags, or before another incoming call takes priority. In these opening seconds, you need to:

1. *Introduce yourself and your company* (if you operate under a company name).
2. *Present concise reasons* for your phone call, as well as for why the Decision Maker should invest time in meeting with you.

That may seem a lot to accomplish in thirty seconds, but it can be done, as in this model script. Adapt it to your situation.

> "Mr. Robinson, this is Tom Gibbons of Productivity Services. I'm calling because I believe we can increase your firm's profitability by reducing

office overhead—perhaps by as much as 20 percent in the first year. I'd like to meet with you for about a half hour to explore the possibilities. Would later this week be convenient, or would early next week be better for you?"

Useful Hot Buttons in This First Phone Contact

Before you dial the call, try to have at least one of these classic hot buttons ready to lead with, and another in reserve.

You are following up on a personal referral from someone the DM knows and respects.

This tends to be a very powerful door-opener. But be sure to pronounce the referral's name and organization clearly, so that the DM makes the connection quickly. Here's a model to adapt:

> "My firm has recently completed a project with Lucas Industries, and Mr. Lucas suggested that we contact you. He felt that we may have areas of mutual interest. Perhaps he has already talked to you about this?"

Highlight key relevant cases from your successful track record.

Again, be succinct. Talk bottom line. That is, emphasize what these cases imply you can *do for* the DM's organization, not the technical details of the product or service you offer.

These first models are appropriate if you already have experience that is directly on target.

> "We've been able to help a number of other law firms in the area reduce their overhead costs. This translates into an average of 10 percent greater profitability. I'd like to meet with you to explain how we may be able to help your firm, as well."

Or,

> "As an art consultant, I work with several other people in the Great Falls area who are interested in art for both aesthetic and investment reasons. In about fifteen minutes together we can determine whether this is appropriate for you."

Or,

> "I design training programs, and I have recently worked with two large banks in the Midwest. As a consultant to these banks, I developed teller training that increased the productivity of tellers by over 15 percent. I believe I can do the same for your bank. I'd like to meet with you for a half-hour to explore the possibilities."

But suppose you don't yet have independent experience to refer to. That is, what if all your work has been as an employee, not as a consultant or a self-employed person? One approach is to modify your lead-in. Thus you could rephrase the last model above as

> "When I was at BigBank, I headed a team that developed teller training that increased productivity by..."

Alternatively, if you have just set up your business and don't yet have successes to refer to, you can suggest a potential need area, leaving it to the DM to *infer* that you have the necessary capability for meeting it successfully:

> "As you know, one of the most troublesome problems facing most law firms is how to store and access key data. We can offer you a solution that will both save your firm a significant amount of money the first year *and* increase your access to this information."

Or,

> "I'm an art consultant. I believe it would be worth your time to meet with me for a half-hour at your convenience to discuss a program I offer, as I think it may have significant investment potential for you."

***Briefly* outline what you believe you can do for this organization.**
Again, to capture the DM's interest, emphasize what you can *do for* the DM's organization, not the details of what you do.

This must be a concise, "netted-out" statement, usually not more than two or three sentences. You will lose the DM's attention if you are too long-winded. Here's a model to adapt:

> "I'm calling because I have ideas to share on how my firm may be able to reduce your turnaround time on receivables."

Notice how this model script is designed to intrigue the potential client through a mention of an area of interest—how you can speed up payments, and hence improve cash flow and profitability. It does *not* get into the technical wizardry of the software program you have developed and hope to install.

Your earlier homework in researching the organization may trigger some initial ideas on ways in which you may be able to help:

> "My readings on the difficulties your firm is having in keeping up with demand for your products indicated to me that..."

Or, raise suggestions from your experience of how organizations like this *may* need help:

> "I've been able to help a number of emerging firms like yours, and it's been my experience that you may be experiencing certain typical difficulties in this stage of your growth."

Do not get bogged down at this point in the details of *how* you will do what you propose to do; leave that for the face-to-face meeting.

Explain that you are calling to provide information that the DM requested earlier.
If you are calling in response to the DM's request for information, that clearly is a door-opener. But as you lead with it, be sure to make the point clearly that you *are* following up on a request, and identify the context in which that request was made:

> "We met following my talk last week before the local BOE Association, and you asked me if I had ever heard of the method being applied to

your industry. The question intrigued me, and I researched it, and came up with some interesting results. I'd like to meet with you to share these findings. Would an hour on an afternoon later this week or early next week be convenient?"

If the DM Asks for More Detail

But what if the DM asks for more detail on just what it is that you do, or how your approach differs from that of your competition?

In the first place, you want to avoid getting drawn into too much detail, since you can't *make* the sale over the phone, but you can *lose* it. Yet you can't very well refuse to answer the question, as the DM would then be likely to refuse to see you.

The key is to speak in terms of overall concepts—especially end results—without getting into the technical details. Here's one model for handling it without offending the DM:

> "Ultimately I'm a problem solver. What I suggested a moment ago is only one of a variety of ways in which I may be able to help your organization. Based on my research, I'm willing to come to your office and invest a half-hour of my time to explore these areas of need together. Are mornings or afternoons better for you?"

However, the DM may be asking for additional details with the idea of distinguishing you from your competitors. If this is the case, you will generally sense it from the nature of the questions asked. The more sophisticated the questions, the greater the likelihood that one of your competitors has already "educated" this DM. If that's the case, then respond *succinctly*, highlighting the advantages of your approach.

As much as possible, focus on the positive *"bottom-line" benefits of* your approach—greater ease of use, or improved productivity, efficiency, or profitability—rather than the technical nuances. What matters to the DM, remember, is not so much what your product *is* as what it *does* for him and his situation.

Setting a Time for the Meeting

Sometimes, of course, you'll have to take whatever time slot the DM offers. But with a little preplanning, you can usually nudge the time into a slot that is convenient for both the DM and you.

By planning ahead and having convenient times ready to suggest, you can group several meetings in the same geographic area, and hence avoid running in circles to meetings all over town.

In suggesting a meeting time, experienced salespeople generally offer the DM a choice of alternatives, asking her to select between options. This usually proves to be an efficient way of settling on a mutually convenient time.

Some models for phrasing the choices:

- "Would you prefer to meet late this week or early next?"
- "Are mornings or afternoons generally better for you?"
- "Would Tuesday morning or Wednesday afternoon be more convenient?"

Try to offer a range of choices, such as the morning one day and the afternoon another day, or late one week versus early the next.

If there seems to be no mutually convenient time, suggest the noon hour. Many Decision Makers choose to eat at the desk, in order to gain a quiet time that is relatively free from incoming phone calls and other interruptions.

If the Decision Maker seems interested but is still unable to fit you into her schedule, ask, "What time do you come in in the morning?" and offer to meet then. (Although you could also suggest meeting after the normal hours, it's usually not as good a time, as both of you may be tired at the end of the day.)

"Should Anyone Else Be Present?"

Despite your earlier efforts to ensure that you have contacted the appropriate DM—that is, the person or team with the appropriate Authority, Need, and Dollars—it's nonetheless possible that you have come in at the wrong level.

A subtle way of testing whether this really is the ultimate decision maker is to ask, after you've settled on a time to meet, "Is there anyone else who should be present?"

The question reminds the person to think whether someone from the next level up should be present to bring either Authority or Dollars, or whether the actual user, perhaps a subordinate, should also be invited to attend.

It's not likely to happen, but if this apparent Decision Maker takes offense at your question, as seeming to doubt his authority, you can explain that you want to be sure to bring enough materials, or that you like to get a sense of how large a group you'll be talking with.

Closing the Call

Once you have the appointment, get off the phone as quickly as you can without seeming brusque. The longer you linger, the greater the risk that the Decision Maker may change his mind about seeing you.

But there are three matters that should be attended to before you hang up.

Make sure that the Decision Maker actually records this appointment in his book. You don't want to arrive and find that he forgot the appointment and has left for the day. One subtle way of accomplishing that: Repeat the date and time of the appointment, to confirm that you're both in agreement, then say, "I'm jotting it in my appointment book now. Tuesday, March second at ten." By mentioning that, you cue the DM to do the same.

Also, *make sure that the Decision Maker has your phone number*, so that he can contact you in case something comes up. While this does create a risk that the DM could call to cancel, it reduces the risk of your wasting time on a useless trip across town.

If you need *detailed directions* to the office, suggest that the DM transfer you to the secretary or receptionist; he will appreciate your not taking up his time.

If You Are Not Sure about This Firm or Decision Maker

In this chapter, we've been working on the assumption that you are sure that this firm is a good prospect, and that this is the right Decision Maker. But what if you're not sure? If the call is convenient—in terms of location, travel, etc.—it may be best to take your chances and see how it works out.

But in-person sales calls are expensive in terms of the time and travel invested. If you can't make this call easily while you're in the area for another, then it's worth asking some screening questions before you push for the appointment. What those questions are will depend on your particular product and industry. This script will give you some ideas on how to approach the issue. (SR is Sales Rep, and DM this potential Decision Maker.)

SR: "Mr. Hopkins? This is Tina Rogers of TGR Associates. I'm calling because I believe we can increase your firm's productivity by reducing office overhead—perhaps by as much as 20 percent in the first year. But at this point, I'm frankly not sure if there is an appropriate mesh between our services and your needs. I'd like to ask you a few very brief questions. It'll take about two minutes. Is this a good time, or would it be better if I called back later?"

DM: "Now is fine, provided it's just a couple of minutes."

SR: "I have done some initial research. Let me begin by confirming some of the things I've learned, just to be sure they are accurate. I understand that you're the managing partner at your firm, and that part of your area of responsibility is to oversee all expenditures relating to the operation of the office. Is that basically right?"

DM: "Basically. There are some aspects I would clear with the management board."

SR: "If the firm were to upgrade computer systems, would that be your area of responsibility?"

DM: "That would depend. If it's software relating to office operations, that's my area—things such as accounting systems, word processing, and the like. But when it comes to the software on the professional side, such as specialized design software, then that would be handled by the partner in charge of professional operations."

SR: "I see. Well, I think that may be the person I need to talk to. That's the partner in charge of professional operations—is that the actual title? And can you give me that person's name?"

Notice that in probing for information, you do open yourself up to more questions from the person you're talking to. There is the risk that that person may hear enough to decide that she doesn't want to meet with you, even though you find that you do want to meet with her, after all. But that's the chance you take, and perhaps it is better to risk losing some over the phone than to waste time on sales calls that may not be appropriate.

Summary

When you get through the Decision Maker's secretarial Screen, you come into the "call up, fix up, hang up" phase. This is the time to briefly introduce yourself and ask for an appointment to meet. It is *not* the time to get into prolonged explanations, or to try to make the sale over the phone.

To quickly spark the DM's interest to the point of granting an appointment, you can

1. Explain that you are following up on a *personal referral* from someone the DM knows.
2. Briefly *highlight your successes* with other clients.
3. Briefly sketch what you believe you may be able to do for the DM's organization, based on your *related experience*.
4. Explain that you are calling to *provide information* that the DM requested earlier.

Avoid getting drawn into a detailed explanation of your product or what it costs. To do this, try to remain focused on what it can do for the DM's organization at the *overall conceptual level.*

When you call, be prepared to suggest to the DM a choice of alternative times. This simplifies the scheduling process. It also allows you to group your calls for greater efficiency.

If you're not sure whether you should be meeting with this person or organization, ask questions, and maybe even tell a little more about your product or service than you normally would, as a way of screening out those on whom a face-to-face call would not prove worthwhile.

Chapter 7

Organizing and Learning from Your Phone Calls

Particularly at the start, you're going to spend a good many hours on the phone as you get your selling effort rolling. Time on the phone getting appointments is time well spent, as one confirmed appointment is worth a day of driving in circles and sitting in reception areas trying to find someone who's in the office with time to hear you out.

The phone work will get easier and quicker as you refine your approach, but at the start you are moving up several steep learning curves, all at the same time. You are learning

- How to convey your message quickly and persuasively on the phone.
- What "hot buttons" work for your product or service (or how to adapt your product or service so that it does have hot buttons; after all, what you learn from your early marketing efforts may send you back to the drawing board to redesign your product, or may force you to modify your marketing approach).
- How to organize yourself and the data you get from prospects so that you can travel efficiently through your territory.

In this chapter, we address the first of these learning curves: improving your telephone technique.

The second type of learning, adapting from customer feedback, is up to you, as only you know your product and market.

The third learning curve, organizing and managing yourself as a salesperson, is covered in Chapter 34.

Listening to Yourself

When you begin phoning for appointments, keep a small tape recorder on your desk, and record yourself as you make your calls for appointments. (*Do not* try to tape the other person's side of the call, as it may be illegal to tape someone else on the phone unless you tell them you are doing so and get their permission, and that would distract from your selling message. But there is no law against taping yourself.)

After you hang up, play back your end of the conversation and assess how you sounded. Here's a checklist of things to listen for. Add your own ideas as well.

1. Overall, did you come across as professional? Enthusiastic? Knowledgeable about your product and the market?
2. Did you sound natural? Did you sound like one human being phoning another, or did you come across like one of those automated telephone marketing machines that talk on and on, incapable of listening or varying the discussion?
3. Did you sound as if you were reading from a script? That's not good. (It's a good idea to have an outline of key talking points in front of you, but a full script is a bad idea, as very few people can read from a script and sound natural.)
4. How did your voice sound? For both men and women, the deeper and more resonant, the better. When under stress, the voices of both men and women rise and become more shrill. ("Deep" and "resonant" are relative terms. The point is to sound natural and confident.)
5. Could you hear a smile in your voice? Even though the DM can't see you over the phone, she can still hear a smile. The best way to get this is to speak with a smile literally on your face. A smile affects your mood and shapes the way your voice projects.
6. Was your pronunciation clear? If *you* found that some of the words were mumbled, think what it was like for the stranger on the other end of the line.
7. Were your pace and tempo appropriate? There is a middle ground between being so slow that the other person wishes you'd just get on with it, and being so fast that it sounds like you're mumbling a script you've said a thousand times before.

   Be ready to adjust your rate of speech to the listener. Listen for little things like "Uh huh, yeah, I understand," or "Yeah, yeah, yeah," which are subtle clues to move faster. Be alert also to clues that you may be moving too fast, such as a DM asking you to repeat or explain, or even the kind of silence that indicates that the other person is not quite tracking with you.
8. Did you personalize the conversation, so that it sounded like a *conversation*, rather than you talking at the other person? Did you use the person's name a few times to make her feel that you were talking to her personally? Did you use "joint" words like "we" and "our" to convey that you and the DM are sharing the call?
9. Was your choice of language positive? Was it clear? We'll be looking in more detail at projecting positive expectations through your words. Basically, this involves using phrases such as "when we meet," not "if we meet."

   Also, be careful about using too much insider jargon or being too technical at this point. If you are calling an appropriate Decision Maker, with Authority, Need, and Dollars, she may not know (or need or want to know) the difference between megabytes, megahertz, and megaphones. A DM is interested in bottom-line effect, and the technical aspects matter only as a means to an end. You don't want to lose the DM before you get the chance to meet face-to-face to make your case.

10. Did you handle any questions or objections confidently and persuasively?
    Keep a record of the questions and objections that come up repeatedly. Figure out the best response for each, outline it on paper, then rehearse it until the words flow smoothly and confidently.
    Try to boil down your responses to the minimum number of words needed to make the point. Remember, time on the phone is precious, and you don't want to get bogged down in "perfect" answers that cause the DM to tune you out.
11. Ultimately, did you sound persuasive? Were you successful in getting the appointment? Why? If not, why not? What could you have done better?

Part Three
Helping the Decision Maker Recognize a Need for Your Product

The core question addressed in this part is, How can I get this Decision Maker excited enough to buy my product or service?

In Part 1, we worked through the early steps in the selling process: first researching to locate priority prospects, then finding the key Decision Maker within the organizations you target.

Remember: For our purposes, the Decision Maker is the person (or team) with *positive decision-making authority*—that is, who has the Authority, Need, and Dollars to say yes to what you are offering.

In Part 2, we worked through making the first contacts with that DM: phoning for an appointment, getting through the secretarial Screen, and persuading the DM to meet with you. We also examined how to open the sales call effectively.

Now the preliminaries are out of the way. In Part 3, we get to the core of the persuasive process. First, we examine some productive ways of opening the face-to-face meeting with the Decision Maker. Then we move on through the various ways of convincing the Decision Maker to sign an order (or take some other kind of buying action, such as agreeing to attend your product demonstration).

Why People Buy, and How You Can Help Them Want to Buy

Before getting to the how-to, we need to put it into perspective. Why do people buy? More specifically, why would they buy the product or service you are offering?

Organizations, and the Decision Makers within them, buy only when they arrive at solid "yes" answers to four fundamental questions:

1. Do we face a need?

We buy if and only if we feel a need. Without the pull of that need, all the bells and whistles, and all the price discounts and special offers, are powerless to bring about the sale.

2. Is that need significant enough to justify our spending some money to fill it?

We all face a variety of needs, more needs than we could ever hope to fill, and so only the needs we perceive as truly significant get priority.

Therefore, one of your most important tasks as you sell is to help the potential customer not only *become aware of a need* that can be filled by your product or service, but also *become enthusiastic about filling it.* That is, you should work to develop the awareness of the need if none exists, or to *enhance* this awareness if it is already present in the Decision Maker's mind.

3. Will this product or service actually fill that need?

Only after the need and its importance are clear to the DM is it appropriate to begin talking about your product and what it can do for the customer. After all, the DM is *not* interested in buying your product for its own sake. What the DM *is* interested in is finding a way of filling this need that now seems important. Your product is of interest only insofar as it is a useful means of filling that need.

Therefore, to make the sale, you'll need to make clear the link between the specific needs of the customer (as you have explored them together) and the specific ways in which your product can fill those needs. (We'll examine ways of making this linkage clear in Chapter 13.)

4. Will it fill the need better or more cost-effectively than other approaches?

To conclude the sale, you'll need to deal with the issue of cost. But as we'll see, price is rarely as important as you think. What really matters is not what your product costs, but its cost-effectiveness—that is, what the customer gets in return for the money spent. The key is to show how the $1.00 spent for your product brings back $1.01—or, even better, $1.25. (We'll examine ways of accomplishing this in Chapter 14.)

These "other approaches" are, basically, your competition. The competition may take the form of other vendors like yourself. Or the "competition" may be the tendency to do nothing, and hence continue the status quo.

As a general strategy, when you're speaking with the Decision Maker, it's best to ignore the competition *until* the DM raises these other possibilities through a question or objection. *Then* you can distinguish your approach from the competing approaches, showing why yours is best.

The core of the selling process, then, is guiding the Decision Maker in looking at the situation to determine whether yes answers to these four questions are appropriate. Yes to these four questions should lead naturally to yes to the overall question of "Should we buy?"

In Part 3, we look at ways of helping the DM arrive at positive answers to the first two of these questions:

1. Do we face a need?
2. Is that need significant enough to justify our spending some money to fill it?

Part 4 will focus on the two remaining questions.

Chapter 8

Opening the Face-to-Face Meeting with the Decision Maker

Up to this point, our focus has been on locating the appropriate Decision Maker and convincing that DM to meet with you. Now we skip ahead in time to the day of your first meeting with the Decision Maker.

It's a good idea to confirm that the meeting is still on before setting out on the journey to the DM's office. A quick phone call reminds the DM of the meeting, and ensures that she'll be there when you arrive. If she will not be there, you can reschedule.

Your call to confirm has a second benefit: It subtly projects that you value your time. That kind of self-confidence conveys to the DM that you and your product are worth hearing about.

When should you make this confirming call? If your appointment is set for the morning, confirm it the afternoon before. Otherwise, if it's in the afternoon or late morning, check in with a call that morning.

> "This is Jeremy Triplett with QMS Associates. I'm calling to confirm my appointment with Ms. Hardy at two-thirty today. Is that still on schedule? Good. I'll be there at two-thirty this afternoon."

When you make this call to confirm, ask to speak the DM's secretary (whose name you should already know). There's no need to disturb the DM herself when you confirm. The secretary either keeps the DM's appointment book or will check it for you.

Picking Up Clues when You're in the Outer Office

When you arrive, give the receptionist or secretary your business card, and say that the DM is expecting you at this time. (Business cards are cheap advertising; keep a supply in the pocket of your jacket or purse where you can reach them easily.)

As you wait, scan the office for helpful clues:

- Take a quick look at any corporate publications you find in the reception area, such as internal newsletters, capability statements or brochures, annual reports, or scrapbooks of news clippings. These often suggest what themes are important there this year. It may be productive to echo them in your presentation.

- Although your research prior to contacting the Decision Maker should have turned up information on these themes, it's still a good idea to check over the data available on-site. What you find in this senior person's waiting area may be a lot more informative than what you saw out in the general reception area.
- Be attuned to the messages conveyed by the office furnishings and tone. For instance, if the furniture looks like World War II salvage, then consider making "economy" and "cost savings" key words in your presentation. Conversely, a sleek, high-tech office with the latest in equipment may suggest that you stress how up-to-date, even ahead of the wave, your work or product is.

Business Cards, Brochures, and Other Sales Aids

It's a good idea to give the DM another business card as you shake hands. That ensures that she has your name and your firm's name in front of her as you talk, and isn't distracted by trying to remember it.

But *do not* give the DM (or the secretary/receptionist) any of your brochures or written materials at this point. If you do, the chances are that the DM will spend the meeting reading through them, and you'll find yourself talking to the top of a head that is bent over reading your literature.

The most effective use of brochures and sales literature is to integrate them into the body of your presentation as selling tools. (See Chapter 16.)

Your Opening: Echo the Hot Button that Worked on the Phone

In your earlier phone contact with the Decision Maker, you had only a few seconds to trigger interest, and convince her to invest time in meeting with you.

But you can't take it for granted that this interest will carry over from that phone conversation to today's meeting. In the days since then, she may have fielded hundreds of other calls, and now she may have only a vague memory of who you are and why it seemed a good idea to invest time in meeting with you. Pressed now with other concerns, she may be looking for a reason to end the meeting quickly and get on to what seem to be more important matters.

For that reason, it's good practice to spend a few moments at the start recapturing her previous interest and setting the stage for a successful call. Here's how.

1. **Review the interest-generating statement you used during the phone conversation.**

What you say now should not be a word-for-word repeat of your phone message, but rather should *echo the essence of that conversation* as a brief reminder of the hot buttons that captured interest earlier. But be brief. This should normally not take more than a couple of sentences:

> "As I mentioned in our phone conversation last week..."

2. **If appropriate, cite a *brief* success story to heighten interest.**

Here's a model you can adapt to fit your situation:

> "We have recently been able to help a number of other engineering firms in this area. For example, we saved Brown and Hennessey nearly a thou-

> sand dollars per month in clerical costs. Stone and Feeney were about to hire an additional secretary, but the productivity gains we developed made that unnecessary—again, a very large savings in direct salary, benefits, and even office space.
>
> "I believe we can be equally helpful to you, so I'd like to begin by asking a few questions to determine where we might best be able to help your organization."

Be Prepared for Possible Last-Minute Hesitations

Sometimes, at about this point at the start of the call, the DM may raise objections like these:

- "You'd be wasting your time."
- "I've decided I'm not interested."
- "My job is to practice law, and I leave decisions about systems to my office manager."
- "We already investigated this idea, and we decided it's not right for us."
- "We don't have any money."

Respond to last-minute hesitations the same way you respond to other objections. In Chapters 20 to 22, we introduce the basic model for responding to questions and objections. In Chapter 23, we examine the specifics of dealing with "early" objections like these.

Icebreakers

The approach recommended here is direct and down-to-business: Introduce yourself, refresh the Decision Maker's recollection of why she agreed to see you, then, if appropriate, briefly cite a relevant success story.

But you should be aware that there is another school of thought on how to open the sales call. Some salespeople prefer to open with "icebreakers," hoping to build rapport before getting down to business. Thus they might first spend some time chatting about the weather or traffic, or about the golf or fishing trophies that they see on the wall.

But put yourself in the DM's shoes, and you'll probably conclude—with me—that icebreakers are not a good idea. The DM invited you for a business purpose, not a social call. Given today's pace of work, few people have time to waste on small talk with strangers.

Besides, if you open the call by talking about golf or trivia, you come across as someone who's not very serious about business. Even worse, you may be perceived as manipulative. The DM knows why you are there, and will appreciate your getting on with things and not wasting valuable business time.

Still, there *are* some circumstances, and some parts of the country, where icebreakers are appropriate. For example, if you already know the DM from another context—perhaps from a church, civic, or professional organization, or from passing on the golf course—a few words are in order. Similarly, in some locales (especially smaller towns, where the pace is slower and people tend to be more interested in others), a little socializing at the start of the call may be appropriate.

If you do choose to open with icebreakers, be alert to signals that the DM is ready to get down to business. Often a shift from a relaxed to an upright position in the chair indicates the shift in interest. Another signal may be a change in expression as the welcoming smile shifts to a more formal expression.

For more guidance on reading the DM's nonverbal signals, see Chapter 29, "Sending and Receiving Nonverbal Messages."

Summary

Get to the DM's office early enough so that you have time to get a sense of the themes that are important in that organization this year.

Don't take it for granted that the DM still recalls why she agreed to meet with you. Spend a few moments introducing yourself and *briefly* recapturing interest. Approaches include

1. Reviewing the interest-generating statement you used during the phone conversation
2. Citing a brief success story to heighten interest

Be prepared to respond to any last-minute reluctance to meet with you.

Normally avoid wasting time at the start with icebreakers. Unless there is a sound reason, such as personal acquaintance with the DM or the custom of the region, respect the DM's time and get on with the purpose of your call.

Chapter 9

Developing/Enhancing the Decision Maker's Awareness of Need

As we examined in the overview to this part, organizations, and the Decision Makers within them, buy only when they arrive, consciously or subconsciously, at solid yes answers to four questions:

1. Do we face a need?
2. Is that need significant enough to justify our spending some money to fill it?
3. Will this product or service actually fill that need?
4. Will it fill the need better or more cost-effectively than other approaches?

In this chapter, we examine the impact of the first two of these questions on how you go about selling your product or service. The point is that before potential clients will buy your services, they must be convinced that they face a problem (or need) that your work can solve for them, *and* that the need is significant enough to be worth investing time and resources to fill.

Typically, the DM will not feel a strong sense of need at the start. The status quo may not be perfect, but it seems adequate. Thus, to make the sale, you will usually have to either *create* (from scratch) or *enhance* (make stronger) that sense of need.

To accomplish that, help the DM understand what those unfilled needs are costing, both directly and indirectly.

In some cases, the Decision Maker will already be aware of the need. But caution: Even if the DM and others in the organization already acknowledge the need, it's nonetheless good practice to take the time to enhance or strengthen that sense of need in order to increase their readiness for what you offer.

In both developing and enhancing the sense of need, three main approaches are generally helpful.

1. Let your product (or work sample) *speak for itself.*

Advantages: There are products that can easily sell themselves, at least if the conditions are right. Ice cream cones and convertibles on sunny spring days fit into this category. They create their own sense of "need"—to see them is to want them. Similarly, if your product (or service) has the good fortune to arrive in a hot market at the right time, it can also sell itself.

Disadvantages: If you rely on the product to sell itself, you risk finding yourself trapped on a one-way street to the exit if the DM's awareness of the need does not blossom of its own accord when he sees your product.

In short, if there's no immediate recognition of need, or if the DM fails to immediately make the connection between the need *as he perceives it* and how your product can fill that need, then you face the DM's response, "Looks nice. Great idea. But so what?" If you encounter that kind of block, it's difficult to get selling momentum going again.

In short, relying on your product or service to sell itself *may* work, but it's a risky strategy. Besides, if your product or service doesn't immediately "click" with the DM, you don't have a foundation to support other attempts. The basic difficulty with expecting the product or service to do your selling for you is that the DM lacks a mental framework for seeing your product or service in its overall context. That is, he sees a solution (your product), but just why he needs that solution may not be apparent.

If at the start of the call is not the time to show your product, then, you may wonder, when *is* the right time? Basically, after the need for it has been established. First get the DM aware of a need and looking for a way of filling that need, *then* show how your product fills that need. (We look at this in Part 4.)

2. Tell the client of the need.

Advantages: If the DM is open to it, *and* if it is done skillfully, this can be a very efficient way of getting to the core of your selling message. You can move more directly into presenting your solution, with no further preliminaries.

Disadvantages: If it is not done with skill, then you risk antagonizing the DM, or bringing out a defensiveness that blocks further progress. People (even chief executives) don't like being told that things are less than perfect in their area of responsibility. They may become defensive and stop listening to what else you're saying.

Clearly, statements such as, "You really need the software I sell because your billing department is a mess," are too direct, and so are likely to antagonize the DM and make him defensive and unwilling to listen further. (Even if you put it less bluntly, the risk of putting the DM on the defensive remains.)

However, if you put these needs in context, or if you manage to depersonalize or generalize them, you may be able to speak of problems and resulting needs without raising defensive hackles and making the DM feel put on the spot. One way to do this is to speak in general terms, without pointing the finger at this organization or DM. For example:

> "We find that many of our clients have had difficulties in [fill in according to your situation]."

Or,

> "It often happens that start-up small business ventures find themselves handicapped by [fill in, according to the need your product or service fills]."

Optionally, if the DM responds with interest, you could go on to ask,

"Have you found that to be the case either in your own firm or with the other small entrepreneurs you know?"

Another approach that can allow you to speak directly of problems and needs without making the DM defensive is to use an informational presentation. For example, a consultant specializing in helping firms comply with government regulations might open sales calls with a presentation giving an overview of the area, pointing out how complex the area is and how costly a failure to comply can be. To make her points more clearly without seeming to point fingers at individuals, she could "show and tell," using visuals such as news clippings on the fines and civil judgments paid by firms that failed to comply. She could then go on to cite the success stories of other clients she has helped. (Caution: Be sure to get clearance before citing clients by name.)

3. Ask the right questions, so that the DM tells *you* of the need.

The easiest time to sell something is immediately after the DM has told you why she needs it—and maybe even told you how your product will help pay for itself in other savings.

There is little you can say to compare in power and credibility with having the DM tell *you* of the need and implications in her own words. Besides, if you nudge the discussion in the right direction, the DM will not only tell you of the need, but also tell you of the dollars-and-cents reasons why it makes sound business sense for the organization to fill that need (and hence buy your product or service) *now*.

Sound too good to be true? Actually, getting the DM to do this for you doesn't take magic or sorcery. You simply need the patience to listen well... *and* the knack of asking the right questions.

Sometimes you may not even need to prompt with questions, particularly if the prospect invited you to come in and make a presentation. In that happy situation, the DM is probably already aware of the need, and is primed to find a way of filling it. Thus all you may need to do is listen to the DM, and sort through the data presented to find the facts that make your case for you.

More often, though, you'll need to take an active role by guiding the DM through a sequenced series of questions. (We'll examine some how-to ideas for those questions in the next chapter.)

Disadvantages: Working through the question-and-answer dialogue takes time. Thus, it may not be practical in selling small-ticket items. Similarly, some decision makers may be too rushed or too impatient to allow you the time to ask all the questions you would like. Thus you must be ready to ask the right questions, but also flexible enough to switch to another approach, if necessary.

Asking the Questions: The Selling Wedge

In your question-and-answer dialogue with the DM, you have two key objectives to accomplish. The first is to educate yourself about the problem and the resulting needs.

The second (equally important) is to "bring the client with you" through your analytical process. You may already be virtually certain, from your experience with other clients, what the DM's answers are likely to be. From that, the needs are clear... but typically only to you.

To make sure that the DM is mentally tracking with you through all the steps of the process, it's important to ask all the questions, and work together through each mental step. Some questions and answers may seem so obvious as hardly to be worth mentioning. But keep in mind that you have been through this analysis before, whereas it's all new to the Decision Maker.

By asking the questions, you get the DM talking—and hence thinking with a fresh perspective. Once the DM has put into her own words sound reasons in favor of your proposal, you can then echo those words later as "authority" supporting your case. What the DM tells you about the need, and the implications flowing from it, is going to carry far more weight than anything you could say.

Besides, even though you may be totally confident that you know what the answers are going to be, you may be surprised by the responses of this unique Decision Maker and organization.

Useful question-and-answer dialogues of the kind that lead to sales don't often happen by chance. It helps to work systematically through a well-planned sequence of questions that brings out the facts of the situation, logically leading to the conclusions you seek.

We address the how-to of selling by asking the right questions in the following chapters.

Summary

If you are to make the sale, the Decision Maker must, first of all, be aware that a need exists, and that the need is significant enough to justify spending money to fill it.

In helping the DM become aware of the need and just how significant it is, you can choose among three main strategies:

1. You can *let your product speak for itself.* Sometimes just showing what you have, or samples of its output, is all that it takes to create the sense of need, and hence make the sale. But these are relatively rare cases. If the product alone doesn't do it, then you may be stranded, with no way of getting the sale going.
2. You can *tell* the client of the need. Sometimes this works. But sometimes it antagonizes the DM and creates a defensiveness that blocks progress.
3. Or, you can *ask the right questions*, and so lead the customer to tell *you* of the need. This seems to take longer than the first two methods. But getting the customer talking is usually a far more productive selling approach, as the DM develops a real sense of the situation and a sense of "ownership" of the solution.

Chapter 10

Selling by Asking Questions: The Selling Wedge

In the previous chapter, we examined the three main ways of developing or enhancing the Decision Maker's awareness Âof the needs that you can fill. You can

1. *Rely on the product to sell itself*, so that the capabilities of the product create the sense of need for it—as the sight of an ice cream cone creates the sense of "need" for one of one's own.
2. *Tell* the client of the needs.
3. *Ask the right questions*, so that the client tells you of the need and its significance.

Approaches 1 and 2, as we saw, have significant disadvantages. When using them, you're basically selling *at* the Decision Maker—that is, pushing your product. The sales call can easily degenerate into a competition pitting you and your product against the customer. By speaking of your product before you really listen to the DM's needs, you subtly convey that you put your own interests first, ahead of those of the customer You *may* get the sale. But then again, you may antagonize the customer, who resents being "sold."

Approach 3 avoids those difficulties. By asking the DM to tell you about the general situation, and then about the needs that have developed, you begin a dialogue. From this dialogue will come a shared awareness of the facts behind the problem and a shared sense of "ownership" of the solution that results. The chances are very good that the DM will develop a sense of trust in you and a feeling of confidence in both your shared diagnosis of the problem and the solution you propose.

As helpful as that question-and-answer dialogue usually is to both you and the customer, there is nothing magical about it. What makes it work are basic commonsense questions that progress from broad context to targeting specific needs.

The pattern of the questions you ask in developing or enhancing need awareness resemble a wedge, broad in scope at the top, and narrowing from that broad, overall perspective to focus on and define the specific needs and consequences. (In practice, it may be helpful to cycle through the questions again to develop several different needs.)

The Selling Wedge

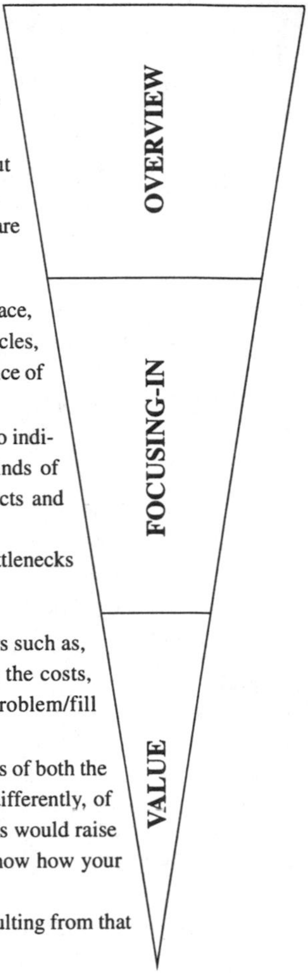

Overview Questions At the broad top of the wedge, your questions focus on broad, overall matters. Basically, your questions are directed toward getting an overview of what goes on, so that you can begin to target the specific areas within the DM's organization that may need your services.

In your overview, you want to learn basic information about the potential user—at least enough to get a sense of the terrain.

Core Overview question: What relevant tasks or activities are performed here? What is the general situation?

Focusing in Questions Once you have the overview in place, you can begin narrowing your focus to the specific obstacles, difficulties, or bottlenecks that provide concrete, specific evidence of a need.

You begin with a sense of the kinds of situations that tend to indicate a need for your product or service. Then you ask the kinds of questions that will lead the DM to become aware of those facts and their implications.

Core Focusing-in question: What obstacles/difficulties/bottlenecks are arising here?

Value Questions Finally, your questions zero in on matters such as, What difficulties are these unfilled needs causing? What are the costs, short and long term? What would it be worth to solve the problem/fill the needs?

To make the sale, it's important to raise the DM's awareness of both the needs that exist, and the value of filling those needs (or, put differently, of what *failing to fill* those needs is costing). Your Value questions would raise those issues, as well as collect data that you can later use to show how your product will help pay for itself in cost savings.

Core Value question: What direct and indirect costs are resulting from that unfilled need? What other effects result?

OVERVIEW

FOCUSING-IN

VALUE

A Second Look at the Questions

The visual above provides an overview look at the Selling Wedge. Now we'll take a closer look at the three types of questions within that Wedge.

Overview Questions

At this stage, you are looking for an overall "map" of broad areas, such as the organization and its work flow. You are also looking for the first indications of potential problem areas that may be worth probing in more detail. (What these problem areas are will depend on what your product is.)

Useful Overview questions develop both background facts and a sense of context. They are usually open-ended, so that the person has considerable freedom and scope in responding. The responses should provide you with an overall map of the terrain.

Here's a model script to adapt for opening the sales call and making the transition into the questions that will lead the customer to talk of needs. (It fits at the very start of the call, as soon as you have settled into your chair.)

> "As I mentioned on the phone, I've been able to help a number of other small manufacturers in the area to increase productivity—on average by 10 percent. I'm here because I believe I can do the same for your firm. To help me better target my presentation to your actual needs, perhaps you could give me a brief overview of how you presently handle the match between orders and output."

In your opening, you can narrow the question by reflecting what you have already learned, as in, "My particular focus is on how you _____."

Generally, the DM's overview will slow within a couple of minutes. Depending on whether it has flagged enough promising leads, you can either extend the overview by asking another broad question or target in to follow up on loose threads. (A "loose thread," as we're using the term here, is any sort of hint of potential trouble in an area that is relevant to your product—that is, a potential area of need for what you will be proposing.)

Caution: Don't be too quick to cut off the DM's overview. As you begin the sales call, it's tempting to jump into a discussion of what you "know" are the needs the customer faces, and the ways your product or service can help. But if you skip to talking of solutions before you establish with the DM a shared understanding of the problem, you will tend to lose the DM's confidence, as you are taking mental leaps that he does not follow.

Typically, if you resist that temptation to jump in, and instead let the DM roll, you will find that several different potential need areas may emerge, as may a number of different aspects of one broad need. For instance, as you listen, you might hear one loose thread relating to the need to speed up a work process in the DM's operation, another relating to excessive labor costs, and a third that might come at the need from the viewpoint of how the client could improve service to its own customers. All three may offer you different approaches for showing how your product can fill the need.

Other typical Overview questions include, What does your unit do here? Can you give me an overview of your operation?

FOCUSING-IN QUESTIONS

As the DM gives you that overview, listen for loose threads that may lead to needs you can fill. With experience, you will develop a sense of the common types of loose threads that are relevant to your product or service. Even more important, with experience you will develop an intuitive sense, or "nose," for relevant trouble areas, even in novel areas of opportunity.

Concentrate on each area in turn. As you follow up each area, *focus in* more closely with your questions to explore whether a problem does in fact exist.

In going back to follow up on a loose thread, you can say something on the order of, "You mentioned that you were experiencing a bottleneck in shipping. Can you tell me more about that?"

What you are looking for here is the DM's statement of facts that provide evidence of the need for your product. Precisely what form this evidence takes will depend on what your product is and what it does to help users. If you sell a software package that simplifies tracking items and consolidating paperwork, then you would listen for hints that the difficulties relate to these areas.

Make notes of this evidence, either mentally or on paper. Try to capture the DM's actual words and data, as you will want to echo them later. There is no better authority than the DM's statements. For example, suppose the DM mentions the need to hire temporary workers one week each month in order to get a certain report out. Hold onto the cost figures for use later, and be attuned to both direct costs (salaries) and indirect costs (such as training each month's team of temporaries).

Later, in making the point that your software package can pay for itself by saving those expenses: "You said that ____. We can help you there, since ____."

So far as possible, let the DM roll, describing the situation in her own words. You may need to probe with additional questions either to get the details you need or to keep the DM on track. But the tone should be that of a conversation, not an interrogation. Try to minimize your interruptions.

Not every loose thread will lead to a need you can fill. Some will turn out to be dead ends as far as providing evidence of the need for your product or service. If that's the case, let the thread go and tug on another thread. "You also mentioned ____. Can we talk about that for a moment?"

If a thread continues to look promising, stay with it. Probe with more questions if necessary in order to get the DM to state clearly why that need is worth filling. Just how significant that need is, and how your product can fill it, may be perfectly obvious to you. But keep in mind that you are an expert on your product and its uses. The DM does not have that kind of familiarity. Thus, if you are to make the sale, it's important for the DM to feel that need as vividly as possible.

One way, as we mentioned earlier, would be to *tell* the DM of the need and its significance. But telling has its disadvantages: Basically, Decision Makers discount what salespeople tell them. Also, some Decision Makers become defensive if anyone seems to be pointing out things they may have done wrong, or problems they have ignored.

That's why it's usually better to continue asking the questions that get the DM to tell you, in his own words, what that unfilled need means: What is it costing while it remains unfilled? These costs, depending on the situation, may be in dollars, inconvenience, distractions, or some other form.

Don't stop listening after just one loose thread. When you have established one clear need for your product, it's tempting to skip ahead to show just how your product can fill that need. However, the more needs there are that you can fill, the better will be your chances of making the sale. Once the first need is established, I tuck it away in my head and move on to establishing the second and third needs. Only after I have all or most of the needs established do I begin to show how my service can fill the most important of those needs. (The third or fifth need may be the most powerful, from a selling perspective.)

Typical Focusing-in questions include, "You mentioned earlier that you sometimes experience bottlenecks when the SMG section gets overloaded. When might that happen? How often does it occur?"

Value Questions

These final questions in the series should test the significance of the problem (or need area) and develop an awareness of the consequences.

The purpose of these final questions is to get the prospect to put into his own words how useful it would be to the organization to fill the need that you have been exploring through your questions.

Once the Decision Maker has articulated just how valuable it would be to fill the need, you can later quote this back to him as a sound justification supporting your recommended solution. ("As you said earlier, Mr. Swenson, your operation is having difficulties with ____.")

At this stage, you would also be asking other specific testing questions on the dollar value of filling the need, as that information will be valuable in a later step, when you show the value of installing your proposal. (We examine the methods for establishing value in Chapter 14.)

Typical Value questions include, "Suppose you were able to eliminate the weekly backups in the SMG section—how would that affect the rest of the assembly line? What are these delays costing you? You said that as a result of the bottlenecks, you sometimes have to run another shift on overtime on the weekend—what does that cost? How is the morale of the employees who have to come in on Saturdays holding up?"

Model Wedge Dialogue

Here's a shortened version of the questions as I might ask them if I were to make a call to sell sales training workshops based on *Selling 101* to a small manufacturer.

Q: (This is an Overview question.) "I notice that a lot of the machines here in the plant are shut down. Are they not in use, or are the workers on break?"

A: "They're not in use now. Things are a little slow here these days."

Q: (Another Overview question.) "May I ask what percentage of capacity you're running at now?"

A: "Sixty-five percent."

Q: (Focusing-in question.) "If you're only at 65 percent, then a lot of capacity must be sitting idle. Is that because sales are below what they should be?"

A: "We're very disappointed in our sales."

Q: (Focusing-in.) "How large is your sales staff? What level of experience?"

A: "Right now just four people. We're looking for a couple more. Actually, to tell the truth, we probably should just go ahead and replace the people we have, except that the new ones would have even less experience."

Q: (Focusing-in.) "Can you tell me some more about the difficulties your salespeople are having?"

A: "Frankly, I'm not really sure what the problem is. We have a good product, and there's a real need for it. But the sales force just doesn't seem to know how to find the right prospects, or how to get orders from those they do find."

Q: (Value.) "You mentioned that the plant is operating at only 65 percent of its potential capacity. What would be the effect on your bottom line if sales went up enough to get up to 70 percent capacity? To 75 percent? To 80 percent?"

A: "Right now, the way things are, we're losing money every day. If we could get up to 70 percent, we'd begin to break even. At 80 percent, we'd have to add some staff, but we'd be making money hand over fist."

Cycle Back through the Wedge to Develop Additional Needs

After you've worked through the Wedge question sequence of Overview, then Focusing-in, then Value to establish the first potential customer need, then you can cycle through the Wedge again to pick up on another clue and carry it through to a second area of need, and then a third, and so forth.

In cycling through for these additional needs, you won't necessarily have to begin with another Overview. Instead, you can cut back to something the DM said, as in, "You mentioned also that _____. I'd like to explore that for a moment. Does it ever happen that _____?"

Summary

While you could let the product speak for itself to do your selling, or come straight out and tell the client of the need for your product, these methods can backfire and alienate the customer.

It's usually better to bring the Decision Maker in as a partner in solving the problem by asking the right questions. These questions get the prospect thinking about the situation in a fresh way, and, if there is a need for your product, putting into his or her own words the indicators that prove that need and the value of filling that need.

The Selling Wedge provides a useful structure for this kind of productive dialogue. Basically, ask common-sense questions that go from the broad situation to targeting specific needs. Begin with broad *Overview* questions, then *Focus-in* for more detail on possible areas of need. Finally, ask questions to collect information on the dollars-and-cents *Value* of filling each of those needs.

Overview Questions

Core Overview question: What relevant tasks or activities are performed here?

Typical/sample Overview questions: "What does your unit do? Can you give me an overview of the operation?"

Focusing-in Questions

Core Focusing-in question: What obstacles/difficulties/bottlenecks are arising here?

Sample Focusing-in questions: "You mentioned earlier that sometimes things go wrong. When? How often? Any idea why?"

VALUE QUESTIONS

Core Value question: What direct and indirect costs result from that unfilled need? What other effects result?

Typical Value questions: "What is this costing you directly, or out-of-pocket? Are there any indirect effects, such as lowered morale or customer dissatisfaction?"

SOME IF-ALL-ELSE-FAILS PROBING QUESTIONS

If I'm in a sales call and find my usual question sequence just doesn't seem to be pulling out any possibilities, I fall back on questions like these:

- "If I could do one thing for your organization as it is today, what would that one thing be?"
- "If I happened to have a magic solution in my briefcase for your most pressing need right now, what form would it take? Can you describe it for me? Can you describe what it would do for you? Why that particular need?"

These are only suggestions to get you started. Experiment to make the questions your own. The wording doesn't matter so much as the idea of giving the prospect a totally open-ended question to follow wherever it leads.

At this point, if the sales call seems to dead-end, you have little to lose, so you can afford to be somewhat whimsical in your approach. In fact, if you can laugh a little as you ask the questions, as in asking about a "magic solution," so much the better, as the Decision Maker will be that much more likely to get into the what-if nature of the exercise.

Chapter 11

Matching the Question to the Situation

The questions you ask are like seeds: It's crucial to give them time to grow. After you ask, be silent, even if it means letting the silence hang in the air. That gives the Decision Maker time to think and respond.

Even though you ask questions at this stage of the call, it should never come across as an interrogation. In the ideal case, you ask just one or a few questions to signal direction, then let the DM go from there in telling the story in her own words.

Ask a question, then let it "grow" in the silence and listen closely to the response. Ask another question only if you must. In some cases, you'll need to rephrase the question so that it's clearer, or to focus the DM's response so that it's more on target. But those are exceptions. As a rule, once you've asked the question, bite your tongue and let the DM talk.

There are other good reasons to ask fewer questions and allow more silence. Constant interruptions to ask new questions may irritate the DM. Besides, if you let the DM go on at her own pace, and in the general direction she thinks best, you may find other potential needs opening up that you wouldn't have anticipated.

Above all, don't be so busy asking questions (and thinking of what your next question will be) that you neglect to listen to the answers you do get.

Do Not Ask the DM about Problems

It's true that you're meeting with the DM in order to find problems that your product can solve. But do not ask about "problems," because good managers do not *have* problems. Or at least they won't *admit to* having any problems in their area. After all, eliminating problems is part of their job as manager, and to admit that problems can exist is about the same as admitting that they haven't been doing their job well.

Besides, *problems are often not recognized as problems*. Instead, situations may be taken for granted; they have always been part of the environment, and so they are assumed to be just a fact of life, not something that can be rectified or improved.

To get around this bind, find other words that you can use in place of "problem" as you get the DM to discuss the situation. The word "need" doesn't carry the same emotional baggage for managers that "problem" does, and you can usually ask, "What needs are you facing here?" without pushing the DM into denial.

Other helpful words include "difficulties," "bottlenecks," and "obstacles." Or you might speak of "areas needing improvement." There may be still other terms that are particularly relevant to your product or industry.

In some cases, it's helpful to approach from the opposite direction—that is, instead of focusing on the negative side (the needs), ask about the positive aspect, such as "goals," "desires," "plans," "proposed improvements," and the like.

Other Ways the Questions Help Your Marketing

We're emphasizing asking questions to get the DM talking about needs. But there is another way in which the questions and answers help: As you work with the DM, her responses may give you very helpful product and market research.

The DM's responses can tell you about

- New products that you could develop, suggested by the prospect's special needs
- Uses for your product that hadn't occurred to you
- Ways in which your existing product or service can be modified or expanded to fill needs you had been unaware of

The DM may even give you helpful advice on your product or your marketing approach. This advice may come as advice, or it may come in the form of questions, comments, or objections. When Hewlett-Packard decided to shift one division from defense work to enter the growing market for professional video equipment, it listened to the customer in a big way. As one H-P manager put it in *Fortune*, "We did no formal training. We bought people airline tickets and books and sent them out to spend a lot of time with customers. They left as microwave engineers and came back as video engineers."

The point is that if Hewlett-Packard can learn from customers' comments and questions, so can small entrepreneurs.

Question Types and Their Uses

Keep in mind that there are three main types of questions:

- Open-ended questions—for example, "What do you know about asking questions?"
- Closed-ended questions—for example, "In what situations would you use questions as selling tools?"
- Yes-no questions—for example, "Do you think you ask enough questions?"

Open-ended questions, as the name implies, give the person who's asked a wide-open range within which to respond. In the first example above, notice how wide a scope is provided by the question, "What do you know about asking questions?" The other person has the freedom to answer with very little, or to give a lecture telling you more than you'd ever want to know.

Closed-ended or targeted questions narrow the range of response. You can use them to collect information (the normal use of questions), or you can use them Socratically, asking the question to get the other person thinking about something he or she might not have thought about, or thinking about it in a new way. For example, I might have asked, "In what situations would you use questions as selling tools?" not because I wanted to hear the response, but instead as a subtle way of making the other person realize that questions *could* be used for nontraditional purposes, such as selling.

Yes-no questions are even narrower: If the other person responds to the question as you asked it, the response will be either yes, or no (with perhaps "I don't know" and "maybe" as possibilities).

For your purposes in selling, it's not particularly important that you remember the names or the definitions of the three types. But it *is* important that you be aware of the different forms of questions that are available and the particular uses of each.

Ask Open-ended questions when you want to get the other person talking. These questions give a lot of freedom, and, in answering them, the person has the scope to go wherever he or she thinks is important. In selling, you would ask Open-ended questions early on with the DM, when you are still learning your way around and want to get the DM to provide you with a map of the operation and some broad areas of potential need.

Ask Closed-ended or Targeted questions once you have a sense of the terrain, and want to focus in on particular areas of interest. Thus, you might ask Open-ended questions at the start of the meeting to get a sense of the DM's operation, then zero in on the details of what you expect will be areas of need for your product, asking Closed-ended questions to draw out the details you need.

Ask Yes-No questions to pin down specific facts, or to check your understanding of what the DM has said: "If I understood correctly, you said that _____. Is that correct?"

Keep these three question types in mind as we move on to take another closer look at the Selling Wedge, introduced in the previous chapter. You will be using these three question types—particularly Open-ended and Closed-ended questions—within the framework of the Selling Wedge.

The Selling Wedge: How-To

It takes a while to acquire the knack of selling by asking questions. The core of the Selling Wedge approach is simple: going from general to particular, bringing the DM with you as you analyze the situation and find needs that you can fill.

But it takes practice to come up with the right questions. It's helpful to do some homework before meeting with your first prospects. Think through in advance some of the questions to ask at each stage, so that you have a mental map to guide you when you're face to face with a Decision Maker.

The following worksheet guides you in developing questions that are useful with the Selling Wedge. You'll find model questions appropriate to each level of the Wedge. Adapt them to your particular product or service or selling situation, and jot

EXAMPLES

OVERVIEW

- I'd appreciate a quick overview of your operation, as it relates to [area covered by my product, service].
- Alternatively: What kind of work goes on here? I know you're part of Amalgamated Airlines' data processing department, but I'm not clear yet on how this unit fits into the overall flow.
- What are the key tasks performed here? What are the most important work outputs or products?
- How many people work in this unit? What are their job titles? (If relevant)
- Where does the work output of this unit go? Who depends on it—other parts of this organization, outside customers, etc.?
- Alternatively, if you're already generally familiar with the operation or industry: I notice that [whatever is relevant to a need for your product or service]. Why is that?
- What upgrades or improvements do you have planned for this year?
- How do the organization's objectives for the year affect your unit? With what effect?

FOCUSING-IN

- Looking at the present situation, and looking ahead to the future, what do you perceive to be your important needs?
- Do you ever have any difficulties with [fill in, appropriate to the needs filled by your product or service]?

  If necessary, amplify what you meant by "difficulties" in a way that is relevant to the needs filled by your product or service. Difficulties might include delays, low quality, crises, or whatever your product or service can help.
- If "difficulties" does not ring a bell with the DM, ask instead: Do any bottlenecks or obstacles ever arise? With what effect?
- If these difficulties/bottlenecks/obstacles occur, what is the result?
- About how often do these difficulties occur? Is there any particular pattern? Are there any times when the difficulties have special impact?
- How does that affect your operation? Other parts of the organization?
- What impact do these difficulties have on your customers or clients? How significant is that to them?
- Would it help you if you could [fill in whatever way the product or service can assist]?
- Useful with the right kind of prospect at the right time: Suppose you could have one wish granted in relation to that difficulty, what would be it be? [But before asking, be reasonably sure it will relate to your product or service.]
- Alternatively, if appropriate: What areas have you investigated or attempted to improve upon in the past? Why there? With what effect?

Continued

VALUE

- When these kinds of difficulties arise, what does it cost?
  * Direct costs, such as wasted time or materials?
  * Indirect costs, such as throwing work schedules off in this unit for days to come? Costs to other units of this organization?
- When the difficulties arise, what is the impact on your clients or customers? Does that cost them out-of-pocket? Has it ever resulted in your losing good customers? How often? With what dollar effect to you?
- Suppose I could [fill in what your product or service might do to help the situation]? How would that help you? In terms of dollars, what effect would that have?
- If you could eliminate the impact of that difficulty, what would it be worth to you? Alternatively: If you could reduce the impact by, for example [10 percent, 30 percent, etc.], what would it be worth?
- To a Decision Maker who says something like, "It would be worth a lot": Follow up with a question like, "Can you translate that to an estimate of dollars and cents?"
  * What about direct savings, such as the cost of labor and materials saved? What kind of dollars would this translate to?
  * What about indirect savings, such as the dollar value of avoiding getting off schedule?
  * What about the real dollar effect with customers and clients, such as maintaining their goodwill and a reputation for delivering on time? What about the dollar effect if you can avoid losing good customers?

down your own questions as a reference for the future. (Use a separate sheet. But do *write* your questions; don't trust your memory. Besides, putting ideas on paper tends to focus them.)

General rules:

- In the Overview phase, ask mostly Open-ended questions to get the DM talking.
- As you get to the Focusing-in and Value phases, ask fewer Open-ended and more Closed-ended questions.
- Use Yes-No questions only when you need to pin down a specific fact. (Yes-No questions tend to close off the discussion.)

As you ask your questions, keep it a conversation, not an interrogation. Let the prospect feel that you want to learn all you can about the situation, so that you can help, *not* that you are there to cross-examine.

Caution: Be sensitive to the possibility that the DM may not want to answer some of your questions for reasons of security. For example, he may be concerned that your questions are getting too close to proprietary information that he doesn't want known outside the company. (These sensitive areas might include work procedures, how heavily they are staffed in certain areas, production costs, potential profitability, and the like.)

Signals may range from nonverbal ones, such as facial expression, to hesitation before answering, to a direct refusal to respond to the question.

If you encounter this reluctance, suggest a reasonable compromise that you can work with for purposes of illustrating your point.

> "I sense that this is an area in which some confidential information is involved, and I respect that. Would it be reasonable, for purposes of illustrating the cost-saving potential of my product, to suggest that a typical hourly cost might be____? If so, then we can use that, and you can plug in your own figures at your convenience. Otherwise, would you like to suggest a figure for us to use?"

Chapter 12

Selling by Asking Questions: The Questions in Action

In the previous chapters, we examined the how-to of using the Selling Wedge as a selling tool. In this chapter, we'll see the Wedge in action in a typical dialogue between a customer and a salesperson. This dialogue between a Salesperson (here SP) and a Decision Maker (DM) will help you get a sense of how the questions in the wedge sequence fit together into a conversational flow.

Notice how in practice the three types of questions tend to flow together in a natural, conversational way. When they are used with skill, the DM does not hear the clanking of gears as the SP shifts from one band of questioning to the next.

In this example, the Salesperson is marketing an improved word-processing system. He is hoping to convince the Decision Maker, here the managing partner in a law firm, to install this equipment in place of an older system that is now in place. This is the seller's first call on this Decision Maker.

Opening Statement/Overview Questions

SP: "As I mentioned when we spoke on the phone last week, we've been able to help a number of other law firms in the area increase their productivity, and hence their profitability. I'm here because I believe that we can do the same for your firm."

DM: "I hope you can. We can certainly use some help."

SP: "So that I can better direct my explanations to your specific needs, perhaps you could give me a brief overview of your firm? I know you have twenty-two partners, but how many associates? How large a support staff? What kinds of practice are you involved in? Is the firm subdivided by specialties?"

The DM answers the questions, and the SP follows by asking if there are any plans for expansion. The DM replies, "None beyond normal growth."

Focusing-in Questions

SP: "You mentioned that the firm does a lot of trial work for insurance companies. That means that you generate a great deal of paper—motions, depositions, briefs, and the like. How does all that get typed?"

DM: "Each partner has a secretary. In addition, there is a word-processing center to work on large projects."

SP: "Does it ever happen that a crush of typing arrives from several cases at once? Is this ever more than your typing staff can handle easily? What happens then? How do you get the work done and still meet your deadlines? Does that crash effort disrupt the other normal flow of work in the office? What effects does that have?"

***Note*: For the sake of brevity, several questions are grouped together here. In practice, of course, the salesperson would ask one question, and wait for the answer before asking the next.**

DM: "This kind of crunch happens frequently. To deal with the volume then, the typists and secretaries have to put in a lot of overtime. The firm also uses temporary typing services, as needed. Other typing gets delayed. Sometimes, if the need is especially pressing, we'll see $200-per-hour lawyers doing their own typing on their personal computers, just to get things out in time. That's very costly to us."

SP: "How do the secretaries and typists feel about this overtime?"

DM: "They get hefty pay for overtime, but they're usually not happy about having to work evenings and weekends. That gets old very quickly. A number of secretaries and typists have left the firm because they were not willing to spend that much time away from their families. In many cases, those that we lost tended to be the best people, burned out by the constant overtime workload."

SP: "We've been hearing a lot lately about secretarial burnout in other firms as well, and they've had a great deal of trouble replacing these people because good legal secretaries and legal typists are so hard to find. Do you have any difficulties in replacing the people who have left?"

DM: "We sure do. Even when we are able to find experienced people, it usually still takes several months before they become fully productive."

Testing Value

SP: "That's expensive. Have you ever put a dollar figure on what it costs to replace a secretary or typist?"

DM: "We've never run the figures, but I'm sure that with all factors taken into account, it costs several thousand dollars each time."

Another Question to Test Value

SP: "You mentioned earlier that your firm used temporary typists to help out with crunch periods. Do you have any idea of what that costs in a typical year?"

DM: "As a matter of fact, I do have a good handle on that, as our accountants break our costs out into categories. It was $13,000 last year."

Focusing-in Questions

Next, the salesperson cycles back to pick up on something said earlier, in order to establish another need or aspect of the need:

SP: "I'd like to backtrack a bit. Have you ever missed a filing deadline because you weren't able to get the typing done in time?"

DM: "Knock on wood, we've never missed a deadline. But it has been close at times. More than once we've ended up chartering a plane to fly papers to other cities in order to meet filing deadlines."

TESTING VALUE

Though the following is a statement rather than a question, it serves the function of a question in drawing out the DM:

SP: "I can imagine how costly it is to charter a plane."

DM: "Sometimes there's no alternative. It's either hire the plane, or lose the case by default and face a suit for malpractice. It's not a cost we can pass on to the client, since the delay was our problem. So we had to swallow the expense ourselves both times."

FOCUSING-IN QUESTIONS

Again cycling back to establish another area of need:

SP: "Going back to something you said earlier, you seem to have quite a high ratio of secretaries and typists to attorneys. Are they busy most of the time, or are many of them 'bench strength' for when you need additional typing help?"

DM: "It's more bench strength than I'd like. I'd estimate that probably 40 percent of their time is spent waiting in reserve. It's hard to predict workflow in this business. That's why we have to overstaff—for reserve capacity when we need it. Yet there are still plenty of occasions when we don't have enough help when we need it."

SP: "Are you saying, then, that as much as 40 percent of your secretarial and typing staff is normally not needed? Is 40 percent of that cost wasted?"

DM: "Probably not the full 40 percent. But it is a fact that a large part of our payroll is wasted in this way."

SP: "Have you ever totaled what that comes to annually?"

DM: "I'm sure it comes to a great deal of money—into six figures."

SP: "Let's do a quick check. As a ballpark figure, I'd estimate that your payroll for secretaries and typists totals around $5,000 per week, or $20,000 per month. Is that a reasonable estimate?"

DM: "It's reasonable."

SP: "Let's work that through. If we assume that just 10 percent of that represents wasted dollars because of overstaffing to be ready for crunch periods—a conservative 10 percent, not the more likely 40 percent—it still comes to $2,000 per month, or $24,000 per year."

DM: "That *is* a good bit of money. I hadn't looked at it that way before. And I agree that 40 percent is more likely, so that means we're wasting nearly $100,000 each year. I really wasn't aware that it amounted to that much!"

SUMMARIZING

Next, the SP summarizes and echoes back some of the key information that the DM has provided. From this, a pattern of needs emerges. This ties loose ends together into conclusions, and prepares the way for the next step, which is introducing the product, and showing how it meets these needs.

SP: "Clearly, getting critical typing done can be inordinately expensive in several ways. You mentioned, first of all, the consequences of overtime—overtime pay, of course, but also the cost of losing your best people to burnout. You estimated that the cost of replacing and training came to several thousand dollars each. You mentioned that your accountant found that the firm spent $13,000 last year for temporary typists, mostly to help out with crunch periods. When the typing got behind and you were pressed to make filing deadlines, you needed to charter planes to deliver the documents—at a cost of several thousand dollars each time. Additionally, by conservative estimate, at least $24,000 in secretarial and typist time are wasted in a typical year because of the need to overstaff to meet crunch periods. Had you realized before today just how much money this is costing the firm?"

DM: "Frankly, I had never put it all together. I've been too busy practicing law to look at it all in context. I'm stunned."

TESTING VALUE

In a transitional question, the SP attempts to get the DM to express overall interest. The question also opens the way for the next phase of the selling process, which is linking the benefits of the product to the DM's needs.

SP: "Suppose I could show you a way of getting all of this typing done on time at crunch periods, while still saving the $13,000 now spent on temporary typists. Would you be interested?"

DM: "We would be very interested."

IF THE DM RESISTS ANSWERING QUESTIONS

If the DM says she feels that your fact-finding questions will be a waste of time, or if she begins showing impatience partway through, that's a sign that you haven't set the context clearly enough in explaining why you need this information.

In that case, tell the DM that you can't yet be sure precisely how you will be able to help her organization, but you feel that the chances justify the investment of a few more minutes. Mention that your experience in similar businesses indicates that there will be a benefit from this effort.

Of course, there is another possible reason for the DM to tire of your questions: From her perspective, the questions may not seem to be leading anywhere. You may need to better focus your questions, or you may need to break off from the questions and give an overview of what you are driving at.

Again, be sensitive to the possibility that the DM may not want to answer certain questions because they touch on proprietary or confidential information. For more on how to handle this, see the end of Chapter 11.

Part Four
Showing How You Can Fill That Need

The core question addressed in this part is, How can I strengthen the value of my product in the Decision Maker's mind?

Recall the basic principle: Organizations, and the Decision Makers within them, buy if and only if they arrive at solid yes answers to four questions:

1. Do we face a need?
2. Is that need significant enough to justify our spending some money to fill it?
3. Will this product or service actually fill that need?
4. Will it fill the need better or more cost-effectively than other approaches?

We examined the how-to behind the first two of these questions in Part 3. Now, in Part 4, we'll be examining the impact of questions 3 and 4 on how you sell.

Chapter 13

Making the Link: Showing How Your Product Will Fill This Prospect's Needs

Once the Decision Maker is aware of the crucial need (or needs), your next two steps follow:

- **To make the link clear between that need (or multiple needs) and precisely how your product or service will fill the need.** (This is the subject of the present chapter.)
- **To deal in a positive way with the issues of cost and value.** (The how-to of this is the subject of the next chapter.)

PRESENTING THE SELLING LOGIC VISUALLY

These two steps are closely tied together, with one leading into the next. In your sales call, you will move back and forth from Needs to Solutions to the Value of filling those needs. The selling logic goes like this:

Need	Solution	Value
We found these needs...	My product can fill these needs in these specific ways...	Even better, it can pay for itself.

That selling logic—Need > Solution > Value—provides the framework for a simple but effective visual aid. You can prepare this selling visual aid on the spot with the DM as you take notes. Or, you can use the framework as a model as you prepare more elaborate visual aids, such as overhead transparencies or flipcharts for a stand-up presentation. You can also adapt the model to form a chart in a letter or written proposal.

Following is a model worksheet, set up as if I were selling a desktop computer system to a physician's office in which computers have never been used. The overall need I uncovered was to reduce the secretarial workload to avoid having to hire another person to do typing and other recordkeeping. (For this illustration, we leave the third column, Value, to address in the next chapter.)

Need	Solution	Value
1. Reduce workload in filling in patient billing data on repetitive insurance forms	Computer holds "boilerplate" information and format, and so only new bits need to be typed in.	
2. Reduce time spent in transcribing doctor's dictated notes.	Computer's spell corrector allows typist to work at 30 percent faster rate without concern for errors.	
3. Allow doctor to edit and correct these notes without imposing heavy extra typing load.	Computer makes it easy to type in changes, as the original is stored in computer memory.	

APPLICATION EXERCISE

A blank worksheet is provided here to give you a chance to think through the Needs-to-Solution linkage on your own product or service before you get in front of an actual prospective buyer. If you have already met with some potential buyers, choose one and work through the process using that situation; if not, make up a fictional customer.

In using this worksheet as a selling tool, it is essential to break the customer's needs into specific units, as was done in the example with the doctor's office. There the overall need was to increase the secretary's productivity. But to be persuasive, it helped to break out specific, concrete instances of that overall need. Then we focused on each of those instances, one by one. Breaking it down that way made the linkage between the features or capabilities of the product and those needs clearer and easier to show.

Suggestions on developing the worksheet:

- In the Needs column, list briefly each of the significant needs that you uncovered in the course of your work with the Decision Maker and others in the organization. Try to list the most important need at the top, the second most important next, and so on.
- Number each of these Needs.
- In the Solutions column, beside each Need, briefly note in a word or short phrase precisely how one aspect or feature of your product or service fills that Need. In this, be specific: Note specific needs, and then note specific features that match that need.

Leave the third column, Value, blank, as we will be addressing it in the following chapter, and will come back to it then.

Need	Solution	Value

Alternative Sequence

In certain cases, you may want to reverse the order, so that you speak of your product's features first, then link them to the customer's needs. (You might choose to speak of your product's features or applications first in situations in which it is especially difficult to get the DM to open up on needs. Once the DM sees what you or your product can do, he may be more creative in seeing what needs to be done.)

In the normal situation, the selling logic is

Need > Solution > Value

In this alternative, it becomes

Application > Needs it can fill > Value

Here's the full selling logic, and the model worksheet (visual aid) that follows:

Basic Application	**Needs This Can Fill**	**Value**
My product can do...	Which can help fill these needs...	And its cost is balanced by these savings, which help it pay for itself.

You can also adapt this approach into a selling worksheet like the one following.

- Begin by breaking out the various features or applications of your product or service, and listing them in the Applications column on the left.
- In developing these applications, look for specific things your product can do, one by one. Thus, in our computer example, applications might include "prepare forms," "assist with doctor's notes," "hold letters," "keep financial records," and the like.
- Then go to the Needs column. For each application, list one or more concrete needs that the application can fill. Try to expand your thinking so that you add new needs and new kinds of prospective buyers.

Application	**Need**	**Value**
1. Can store boilerplate for forms, so that they can be adapted to each patient.	• Reduce typing in doctors' offices. • Reduce typing in other offices where there are a lot of forms, such as law offices, insurance firms, government agencies.	

Summary

1. Once the Decision Maker is aware of a Need, your selling efforts shift to helping the DM clearly see the link between that Need and how your product or service can fill it.

2. In making that link clear, this is the core of the selling logic:

Need	**Solution**	**Value**
We found these needs...	My product can fill these needs in these specific ways...	Even better, it can pay for itself.

3. You can communicate that selling logic (Needs > Solution > Value) through the worksheet/visual aid from this chapter.

4. In some cases, it may be helpful to use this selling logic in reverse, beginning with the Applications of your product, then finding Needs to match (then showing the Value).

   Application > Needs > Value

Chapter 14

Raising the Issues of "Cost" and "Value": Showing How Your Product or Work More than Pays for Itself

Remember the selling logic:

Need	**Solution**	**Value**
We found these needs...	My product can fill these needs in these specific ways...	Even better, it can pay for itself.

In the previous chapter, we focused on ways of making the first linkage clear to the DM—that is, the Need-to-Solution linkage.

Now we bring in the second key part of that linkage: showing how your product can, either partly or totally, pay for itself. This gets us into the issues of *price* (or cost), and *value.* There is a major difference between the concepts of price (or cost) and value:

- *Price* focuses on the dollars spent.
- *Value* puts price in the context of *what is gained in exchange for those dollars.*

Thus "talking value" to customers means showing how they will get back $1.01 or $1.25 or even $2.00 for each dollar they spend with you.

The prospect will naturally want to know the cost (or price) of your product or service, and so you can't avoid providing that cost figure. But if you are an effective salesperson, you won't let things bog down on cost. Instead, quickly move on, shifting the Decision Maker's attention from cost alone to the broader issue of what she gets in return for that price paid.

That broader issue, what is gained in exchange for what we pay, is the concept of Value.

Price is important in selling, of course, but it is rarely the decisive factor in whether or not you make the sale. Generally, what really matters is Value—what the buyer gets in return for the money spent. (Another way of expressing that concept of Value is its "cost-effectiveness.")

Effective Decision Makers will naturally be inclined to look beyond price to the really important issue of overall, long-term value. But not all Decision Makers will start with that kind of vision, and so a major part of your role as salesperson is to educate this type of prospect to look with a different perspective.

THE FOUR-STEP APPROACH TO BUILDING AWARENESS OF VALUE

In talking price with the Decision Maker, the key is *never* to talk price except in context. That is, don't let the customer's focus remain on price alone. Instead, guide the discussion so that the DM views the money spent in the context of what is gained in exchange. In guiding that discussion, it's helpful to work through this Four-Step process.

1. Review the specific needs you uncovered.

Speak not just of needs in general, or of the typical needs of most customers, but rather of the *actual* needs that turned up as you worked with this Decision Maker. For example,

> "In the course of our meeting today, we found that you face two major needs. The first is _____ ."

2. Review the specific ways in which your product will fill each of those needs.

Your review of the specific needs and specific ways will usually be brief—just enough to serve as a quick reminder to the DM of what you discussed earlier. For example,

> "We found that the _______ feature of the GEM 2000 can resolve the first of these needs, by _____ ."

In many cases you can most easily accomplish this review of the needs and ways of filling the need by using the worksheet (from the previous chapter) as a visual selling aid:

Need	Solution	Value
1. Reduce workload in filling in patient billing data on repetitive insurance forms	Computer holds "boilerplate" information and format, and so only new bits need to be typed in.	
2. Reduce time spent in transcribing doctor's dictated notes.	Computer's spell corrector allows typist to work at 30 percent faster rate without concern for errors.	
3. Allow doctor to edit and correct these notes without imposing heavy extra typing load.	Computer makes it easy to type in changes, as the original is stored in computer memory.	

3. Present the price.

There's no reason to be defensive or apologetic about what your product costs. If it's a good product that meets important needs of this organization, then naturally you deserve a fair price for it. If you are defensive on the matter of cost, the DM will sense this. But do not linger on price. Mention it, then move on to item 4.

4. Immediately make the transition from price to the value of the solution you offer.

Price and value naturally flow together, and so the transition should flow easily. One way is to restate the price in a broader context. For example,

> "But let's look at that overall dollar cost in context. For example, you earlier told me that getting this work done using your present method takes 200 working hours each month. You estimated that these 200 hours cost at least $3,000 in direct labor, plus at least that much again in overhead—that is, a total of $6,000 each month.
>
> "By contrast, you can have a GEM 2000 for $500 per month on lease. Add seven hours working time for that one operator at a cost of $100 per month, and the cost will total only $600 per month, instead of the present $6,000 per month. This means a saving of $5,400 every month.
>
> "In other words, a GEM 2000 installation will cost only one-tenth as much as your present system. That's very good value for the money spent, don't you think?"

The worksheet again serves as a helpful visual aid to bring in that final linkage in the Needs-to-Solution-to-Value chain. So as you restate the price in the broader context of value, record the results in the appropriate spot in the third column, matching the need it goes with.

Need	Solution	Value
1. Reduce workload in filling in patient billing data on repetitive insurance forms	Computer holds "boilerplate" information and format, and so only new bits need to be typed in.	Saves 15 min per patient. At $15/hour, means nearly $4 saving for each visit.
2. Reduce time spent in transcribing doctor's dictated notes.	Computer's spell corrector allows typist to work at 30 percent faster rate without concern for errors.	Saves 90 min/day, or $22.50 per day.
3. Allow doctor to edit and correct these notes without imposing heavy extra typing load.	Computer makes it easy to type in changes, as the original is stored in computer memory.	Saves 30 min/day, or $7.50/day.

Note: For this illustration, I have valued the secretary's time at $15 per hour, including overhead. Though these savings of $4 or $22.50 may not seem large, they would be significant when added together over the course of a year. Even relatively minor savings may add up to major factors when they are compounded over time, or when they are compared with the alternative, such as the relatively low cost of the computer I am selling contrasted with the cost of hiring another secretary.

How to Use the Worksheet as a Sales Visual Aid

This worksheet is just a tool to help make the Need > Solution > Value linkage clear. It's definitely not something that you would read word for word at the Decision Maker. That would put him to sleep. Rather, talk from it, pointing out key points in each column.

When to use this worksheet depends:

- If yours is a one-call selling cycle, you could use it on the spot, provided your notes and handwriting or printing are clear.
- If you will be calling back in another step of the cycle, you can clean up the chart, type it, and prepare it as a handout, or as an overhead or flipchart visual in conjunction with your presentation and close.

Application Exercise

At the end of the previous chapter, you worked through an Application Exercise in which you developed the Needs-to-Solution linkage. At that point, you left the Value column blank. Now go back and finish that worksheet, including cost and value figures. (As this is only a practice exercise, it is okay to "guesstimate" reasonable figures if you don't have actual customer numbers at hand.)

Chapter 15

Using Other Methods of Highlighting Value over Cost

A quick review of where we are: helping the prospect move beyond the short-term cost of your product or service to view that price or cost in the context of the ovcrall valuc gained.

Keep this in mind: "Price" focuses the dollars that are spent, while "value" shifts the focus to put cost (that is, the dollars spent) in the context of what is gained. Thus, to make sales, show your prospects how they can get back $1.01 or more in value for each $1.00 they spend on your product or service.

The selling logic for helping the Decision Maker develop a sense of that Need > Solution > Value linkage is expressed in this diagram:

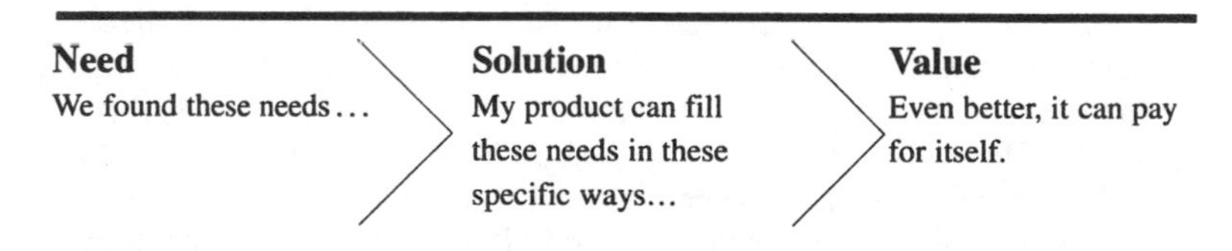

In establishing this linkage, it's helpful to take the DM with you through a four-step process:

1. Review the specific needs you uncovered.
2. Review the specific ways in which your product will fill each of those needs.
3. Present price.
4. Immediately transition from price to the value of the solution you offer.

It may also be helpful, in presenting these ideas to the prospect, to use a worksheet as a visual aid. Here again is the model for that worksheet:

Need	Solution	Value
1. Reduce workload in filling in patient billing data on repetitive insurance forms.	Computer holds "boilerplate" information and format, and so only new bits need to be typed in.	Saves 15 min per patient. At $15/hour, means nearly $4 saving for each visit.
2. Reduce time spent in transcribing doctor's dictated notes.	Computer's spell corrector allows typist to work at 30 percent faster rate without concern for errors.	Saves 90 min/day, or $22.50 per day.
3. Allow doctor to edit and correct these notes without imposing heavy extra typing load.	Computer makes it easy to type in changes, as the original is stored in computer memory.	Saves 30 min/day, or $7.50/day.

The core is simple, so don't let the words get in the way when you're with a prospect: When you present the price or cost of your product, put that cost into the context of the benefits the DM gets for that money spent. That is, show the Value, and that means showing how the DM gets back the equivalent of $1.01 or more for each $1.00 spent.

Alternative Ways of Expressing Value

Basically, value is getting back $1.01 or more for each $1.00 spent. But different customers may have different ideas of what they value. One Decision Maker, for example, may operate with a long-term perspective, and may be looking for the benefits over a one-year span, whereas another may, by the nature of his job, be looking for a shorter-term value. It goes without saying that to be successful, you will need to adapt to the customer's perspective and mindset.

But you need to be flexible in how you approach value. Some prospects will, literally, be looking for a dollars-and-cents kind of value (expressed in dollar terms), whereas others will be looking for their version of "value" not in dollars-and-cents terms, but in intangible forms such as convenience, status, quality, ease of use, assured service, or any of dozens of others.

Therefore, in presenting value, adapt your approach to the actual factors that the specific DM values most. Precisely what she values will vary with the individual, with the situation, and with your product.

How do you know what that individual values? As always in selling, the key is to ask questions and listen well, both to what is said and to what is implied. The DM may have already told you what he values, either overtly or implicitly. For instance, a Decision Maker who speaks repeatedly about the costs and frustrations of a competing product is telling you that he strongly values reliability and good service.

Also, think back to your earlier fact-finding in the organization, before you first met with the DM. What themes and needs revealed themselves? For instance, if you see that the client organization's own sales literature focuses on economy and low cost, take that as a hint to make the case for the ways in which your product or service can lower costs or boost efficiency and productivity.

Other Methods of Highlighting Value over Cost

The four-step process is the basic method for establishing value, but there are some other ways of highlighting value over cost that may be helpful within the four-step framework.

1. Break down the overall cost of your product into more meaningful units.
For example:

> "The cost of the Model III is $4,000. That breaks down to about $16 per week over the normal five-year life of the unit. You'd agree, wouldn't you, that it's well worth about $3 per day for having this kind of convenience ready at hand?"

Or,

> "That cost translates to about $5 per day to gain the advantages of superior quality and service."

Application Exercise

I can't predict the alternative units in which your product or service could be expressed, but with a bit of thought in advance, you may be able to generate some alternatives that would make sense for your clients. Here are some general possibilities to get you started.

Time. For example, if you are selling a product, what is its expected useful life, and how does its cost break down over that expected lifespan? Perhaps you can break it down to a cost per month or per year: "Thus the GEM 2000 would in effect cost only $23.50 per week over its projected five-year useful life. Don't you feel that the benefits of the GEM 2000 are worth far more than $23.50 for each week it would be in use?"

Additional functions filled without any further expense. For example, the computer you're selling might have capabilities that would eliminate the need for separate units for fax, phone modem, and the like. Thus you could start with overall cost, then subtract the cost of the units no longer needed, as here:

Purchase price:		$3,000.00
Minus cost saving re: fax unit	-500.00	
Minus cost saving re: modem	-200.00	
Effective cost of computer now:		$2,300.00

2. Restate the savings that will result in a form that is most attractive to this customer.

In putting cost in context, you can sometimes express the same cost saving in two or more alternative ways. For example, you could point out how installing the computer system you propose would "save the costs of one half-time employee." Alternatively, you could suggest that "it will free half of your secretary's time for other, more creative work."

Or, you could even restate it both ways, for double benefit: "You can use the time savings either to free your secretary for other more important assignments or to reduce the use of overtime."

Application Exercise

Again, look at your product or service, and ask yourself what additional benefits the customer may gain by installing it. Try to generate several broad types of benefits or savings. As you come up with one, see if you can "flip" it into another form, as above we flipped the same benefit to either reduce the secretary's overtime, or free the secretary for more important assignments.

Other Benefits	"Flips," Expressing in Alternative Way

3. Refer to any incidental payoffs that add value.

Earlier, we suggested that you not throw a laundry list of things your product can do at a customer. Instead, focus on only those benefits that match specific identified needs.

Well, now is the time to refer to some of those additional "laundry-list" benefits, since these incidental payoffs, if raised at this point, may add enough extra value to nudge the customer to yes.

If, for instance, you are selling phone equipment, you might find that of the equipment's dozen key benefits, only three or four specifically match the stated needs of this customer. Yet, once you have clearly established how the product will meet those three or four key needs, you may clinch the sale by raising a few more of those unmentioned capabilities as "bonuses."

Think of your own psychology when you're buying something. You finally find a product that precisely meets your needs. You're satisfied and are inclined to buy, but you're still on the fence, not sure you really want to spend the money.

While you're wavering, the salesperson tells you that if you buy today, you'll also get a free bonus (or frequent traveler coupon) thrown in at no extra cost. Very possibly, this something extra just might push you over the edge to buy now—although it would have been only a distraction if the salesperson had mentioned it earlier. While you wouldn't buy *just* to get the "freebie," the reality is that if you were wavering on whether to buy or not, it might be just enough to nudge you to yes.

Application Exercise

List some of the incidental or generally less important benefits to be gained from using your product. Hold these in reserve to use as incidental benefits that you can throw in later in the call in order to give that final nudge in favor of purchase. (Think of these as your own equivalent of frequent flyer miles.)

1.

2.

3.

4. Use the analogy of the telephone.

But suppose the Decision Maker insists that low cost is the one factor that controls her purchasing decisions, and quality of product, ease of use, convenience, and everything else are insignificant to her.

Respond by pointing out that if cost is of such paramount concern, then this organization *could* choose to operate with only a single telephone line and only one telephone instrument. The company could save hundreds of dollars each month if the staff shared that one telephone for all of their incoming and outgoing business calls. Indeed, to save even more on the phone bill, the company could send all employees down to the pay phone on the corner.

Of course, no firm chooses to do this, even though it would lower cash outlays for phone expenses. Instead, most companies wisely invest in extra lines and extra phones so that there is one at every desk, because the value of the employees' time far outweighs the possible cost savings that might be gained from skimping on phones.

Moreover, image and convenience to customers are important factors to be considered: If customers couldn't get through on that pay phone, they would go to another supplier, and the lost sales would quickly dwarf the phone bill.

After you have gotten this message across, make the transition to your specific product, showing how, like phone service, its costs are minimal in comparison with the benefits it brings.

What if the DM Insists on Forcing the Issue to Price Alone?

To repeat the overall point made in this chapter, *most* of the time it is best to try to move the customer's focus from a narrow emphasis on price alone to a broader perspective that encompasses the more important matter of cost-effectiveness. (Cost-effectiveness, remember, can be thought of as another name for value.)

However, there will be times when you have no choice other than to talk price, because "price" seems to be the only word in the customer's vocabulary. Even in those cases, though, you can treat price in a positive rather than a defensive way.

1. Show how your product offers more value (more cost-effectiveness) than does the competing product.

What if your price is significantly higher than the competition's? In that case, you will probably lose *unless* you can educate the customer on the unique benefits of your offering. To do this, shift the discussion back to value, as we have discussed above.

2. Contrast the price with the cost of not filling the need.

In this situation, the customer is saying, "We can't afford it," to which your reply is, "You can't afford to be without it." That is, put price in context with the hidden costs that would result from not having it.

Summary

Price is important, but it rarely is as decisive as you might expect.

More important than price is value. Price focuses on dollars spent, whereas value puts cost in the context of what is gained.

To make sales, show your prospects how they can get back $1.01 or more for each $1.00 spent.

To build the DM's awareness of value, speak of price only in context, never by itself. Generally, that means working through a four-step process:

1. Review the specific needs you uncovered.
2. Review the specific ways in which your product will fill each of those needs.
3. Present price.
4. Immediately make the transition from price to the value of the solution you offer.

Other methods of highlighting value over cost are

1. Restate costs in more meaningful units.
2. Restate cost in an alternative way that is more meaningful to this customer.
3. Refer to any incidental payoffs that add value.
4. Use the analogy of the telephone.

However, there will be times when the customer is determined to look not at overall value, but rather at short-term cost. Even then, treat price in a positive rather than defensive way, such as,

1 Show how your product offers more value (that is, more cost-effectiveness) than any competing product or approach.
2. Speak of price, but then make the transition to a comparison of price with the cost of *not* having what you propose.

Chapter 16

Making Your Sales Points Clearly and Concisely

In making clear the linkage between the customer's *Needs*, the *Solution* you propose, and the *Value* it offers, you can use any of a variety of methods.

1. Use a chart or visual aid to make the need-to-features linkage clear.
A simple chart like the one discussed in the previous chapters can provide helpful structure to that communication, giving the DM a mental framework upon which to see the specific need-to-feature linkages.

Need	Solution	Value
1. Reduce workload in filling in patient billing data on repetitive insurance forms.	Computer holds "boiler-plate" information and format, and so only new bits need to be typed in.	Saves 15 min per patient. At $15/hour, means nearly $4 saving for each visit.
2. Reduce time spent in transcribing doctor's dictated notes.	Computer's spell corrector allows typist to work at 30 percent faster rate without concern for errors.	Saves 90 min/day, or $22.50 per day.

But don't just put a chart in front of the Decision Maker and assume it makes as much sense to her as to you. It's important that the links between the customer's needs, your product, and the value the product gives are totally clear and explicit in the DM's mind. Therefore, don't let the chart stand alone. Instead, use it as a visual aid in talking her through precisely how your product fills the specific needs of this specific buyer. Whenever possible, echo the words the prospect used in telling you of the need:

> "You mentioned earlier that your department was having difficulties in...
> Well, the GEM 2000 can help you overcome that difficulty by..."

Sometimes you will need not only to explain how your product fills the customer's needs, but also to prove it. We examine proof sources in Part 7.

2. Demonstrate your product or samples.

In some cases, it's practical to make the link between need and solution clear simply by showing your product (or the results of the service you perform). For example, if you're marketing your services as a graphic designer, you might demonstrate your ability to fill this customer's needs by showing some relevant samples of the work you've done for other clients.

Similarly, if you are marketing consulting services, this might be the point at which you reach into your briefcase and pull out appropriate samples from other projects you've handled.

In Chapter 9, I discouraged using samples of your product or work to speak for themselves in creating a need in the customer's mind. If you expect the product or samples to create the need, you'll usually be disappointed. Here I'm suggesting a different use for your work samples—that is, using them not in hopes of creating the DM's sense of need, but rather to prove that your product can do what you claim it can.

Once the need is clear to the DM, *then* he'll be interested in determining whether your product can fill that need. It's at that point that samples (or perhaps the item itself) become relevant, as they can often make this clear in a way that words, or even pictures, cannot.

3. Use your sales literature as a tool to make the linkage clear.

Earlier, I suggested that you not hand your brochures or other promotional literature to the DM at the start of the sales call, as he would be distracted by these printed materials, and might not be listening with full attention to your sales presentation.

But now, as you make the link between the customer's need and the capabilities of your product, *may* be a good time to use that literature. However, you can't just hand a brochure over the desk and expect it to make the point.

At the very least, talk the DM through the relevant parts of your literature, pointing out how your features and capabilities mesh with his needs. But make those capabilities explicit; don't take it for granted that the DM will get the point you're making.

> "We concluded that you needed _____ . Well, as you see in this illustration, the GEM 2000 has a [fill in the capability], which can achieve the [fill in the need], which you need."

Getting on the Same Side of the Table

An even better way to use your sales literature: Use the brochure as a tool for positioning yourself and the Decision Maker literally on the same side of the table. Here's what I mean, and how to do it:

A manager's desk is a status symbol, and a barrier between that DM and the rest of the world. The desk or conference table sets up a wall, marking off "us" (this side of the desk) from "them" (those across the desk).

If you can break down or get around that barrier, somehow getting yourself over to the DM's side of the desk or conference table, then you can literally get on the same side, and get your heads together, working jointly to solve the problem.

Your brochure can serve as a ticket around to the DM's side of the desk. When the brochure becomes relevant (as now, when you're making the link), say,

> "There's something I'd like us to look at together. Mind if I bring my chair around?"

Provided there's a reasonable amount of space, the DM can hardly object. Once you get on the DM's side of the desk, you'll usually find that, quite literally, the psychological barrier eases, if not dissolves altogether.

For more on nonverbal communication, positioning yourself and the customer, and related subtleties, see Chapter 29, "Sending and Receiving Nonverbal Messages."

Mark up the brochure as you review it with the DM. Customize it to emphasize the special interests of this prospect by circling or highlighting the key points that are relevant to this prospective client. Draw special diagrams, underline, add highlights, do whatever you need to do to make it clear just how your product fits the DM's needs. After all, it's just a giveaway; there's no reason at all why it should stay pristine, and if your marks help the DM remember your key selling messages, then don't hesitate.

Focus on What Your Product *Does*, Not What It *Is*

One more time: What the customer is ultimately interested in is not what your product *is*, but rather what it *does* to fill his or her specific need.

For example, the Decision Maker's interest will generally not be in technology for its own sake, but rather in the practical results, and particularly in how these results improve the workings of his or her area of responsibility. It's the same with nonbusiness clients: Their interest is in what your product will *do* for them, not in what it is.

Your product may do many things. But in demonstrating it to your prospect, focus only on those aspects that directly relate to that customer's specific needs—that is, the needs that have been clearly identified in your earlier conversation. Do not clutter your message with incidental benefits that are not directly relevant for this Decision Maker and this organization.

People and organizations buy to meet specific, identified needs—that is, they buy to solve identified problems, not to stockpile generic capabilities. A generalized approach that treats all features equally will inevitably miss the important targets: this specific DM's specific needs.

It's not enough simply to throw out some of the things your product can do and hope they stick with the prospect. Nor is it enough to demonstrate the product, or to give the Decision Maker samples, and expect the link between the DM's needs and the capabilities of your product to be obvious.

Your "Half-Minute Messages"

You will quickly develop a sense of the most common kinds of customer needs, and of how the various features or aspects of your product (or service) can fill those needs.

Although each customer's needs may be somewhat unique, they will fall into patterns. Therefore, invest the time to boil down into *short, to-the-point messages* the ways in which specific features or aspects of your product match those common need areas.

Polish these messages. Edit out extraneous words, and simplify the sentences so that you can say them comfortably in not more than thirty seconds, in your normal conversational style. (Tip: Short sentences make points clearly, and are easy to speak in a way that sounds natural and spontaneous.)

Rehearse these half-minute selling messages until they flow smoothly and confidently. Take care that they don't sound rehearsed or "canned." Even though you may have said it hundreds of times, it's all new to this customer, and should sound fresh.

As a rule of thumb, each statement (or selling message) should take you less than a half minute—at most—to say. If you talk longer than that on a topic, the customer's eyes (and mind) are likely to glaze over.

Besides, if you go on for more than about thirty seconds on any single point, you'll tend to begin talking *at* the Decision Maker, rather than carrying on a productive, back-and-forth dialogue.

Netting It Out

In making the link between your product and the customer's needs, *get to the point.* "Net out" your messages. Keep in mind that the object is to make the sale, not to say everything possible about the product.

In speaking of your product and how it fills the customer's needs, be focused. Get to the point. Make your point once, then move on. Don't overwhelm with words. Respect the DM's valuable time. Trust the DM: If she needs to know more, or if you failed to make a point clearly, she'll let you know—either verbally or nonverbally.

Summary

Customers buy to fill needs. Before they will buy, though, they must be consciously aware of these needs, and the needs must seem significant enough to be worth the time, effort, and money it will cost to take action.

If the customer is to buy your product, it must be totally clear to her that your product will in fact fill those needs. Don't assume that what is obvious to you is equally obvious to the customer.

In introducing your product or service, focus on the practical results for the user. Customers, after all, will buy not for what your product *is,* but rather for what it *does.*

As you present your product, emphasize those capabilities that fill the specific needs of this customer. Don't talk about how wonderful your product is in general. Instead, show how its specific capabilities will fill the customer's specific needs.

Thus, relate each capability of your product to one of the specific needs that you identified earlier in your discussion with the decision maker. If possible, echo back her own words as she described the need and what that unfilled need was costing.

Finally, get to the point. "Net out" your messages. Keep in mind that the object is to make the sale, not to say everything you possibly could about the product.

There are three main ways in which you can make a clear, visual linkage between the customer's needs and the capabilities of your product or service that can fill that need:

1. Use a chart or visual aid to make the need-to-features linkage clear.
2. Demonstrate your product or provide samples as a way of proving that the product can do what you claim.
3. Use your sales literature as a tool to make that linkage clear.

Part Five
Convincing the Decision Maker to Act Now!

The core question addressed in this part is, How can I get the Decision Maker to move on this *now,* and not just "think about it"?

By this point in the sales cycle, you've helped the Decision Maker perceive that there is a significant need, and that your product or service can fill that need in a cost-effective way.

Now you need to nudge that DM to take some buying action. Precisely what type of buying action you seek will depend upon the situation.

In Chapters 17 through 19, we examine about a dozen ways of asking the Decision Maker to take buying action. It's helpful to be able to call upon a repertoire of varied approaches so that you can ask and then ask again without coming across as "pushy."

In addition to the actual methods of asking the DM to buy, we also look at some related issues:

- How do you recognize when the DM is ready to take some buying action? That is, what *buying signals* indicate that now is the time to attempt to close the sale? (We look at this in Chapter 17.)
- Also, when you ask the DM to take buying action, just *what kind of actions* can you reasonably ask for? Most of the time, the action will be the obvious one of buying your product or service. But in some cases, it may be too large a step to ask for a purchase initially, and so you may instead ask the DM to take or authorize some intermediate step that must be completed before you can actually conclude the sale. For example, you might ask the DM to attend a demonstration of your product in action, or you might ask for a commitment that if you are able to prove your case through a financial proposal, the DM will buy.

On Hearing No

For people new to selling, asking the DM to buy or take other action may be a little scary. No one likes to hear no. But keep in mind that hearing no is not the worst thing; the worst thing is failing to get the sale you could have had.

Scary as it may be when you're new to selling, taking the risk of asking for the order is essential. By asking for action, you signal that you have made your basic case, and now the next move is up to the DM.

Until you ask the DM to act, nothing—absolutely nothing at all—is likely to happen. If you want something good to happen—that is, for the sale to happen—you have to *ask* for it to happen.

Why No Can Be Good News

When you ask, yes is the ideal answer. But even no is a positive step, as it gives you an opening to probe further, in order to find out what is *really* bothering the DM. Once you hear no, you can get down to the real business of helping the DM change his mind.

If you *must* hear no, then the sooner the better. Once you get the DM to move off the "undecided" square and say either yes or no, the way is opened for you to take the next step. You can either write the order, or openly probe for what specific obstacles are blocking this sale. Once that no is out in the open, you can be more direct in finding what's really keeping the DM from buying. No opens the way to move to yes.

Even in the worst case (when the no just can't be overturned), hearing that no early at least lets you cut your losses sooner, and move on to find more promising prospects.

Why It Pays to Complete the Order Blank Before You Go into the Sales Call

Many of the best salespeople make a practice of filling in the sales order form *before* going into the meeting with the DM. It takes a little time, and some order blanks will get thrown away. But the benefits make it worthwhile.

For one thing, you don't have to stop the sales momentum to collect basic data on such things as address, billing address, and the like. Even more importantly, by completing the form in advance, you project to the DM your confidence that the sale will happen. Expectations are infectious, and a large part of selling is projecting positive expectations.

Precall Planning: Determining What to Close For

In the jargon of professional salespeople, asking for the order or other commitment is "closing." You might "close" the customer, or "close for" the order. You might try several different "closes."

Before going into any sales call, think through your *primary* and *backup* objectives for that call. The range of objectives includes

- **Closing for the order**. In the ideal case, your primary objective will be to close for the sale. That's the ideal, but in some cases it may not be realistic. For example, it's not likely that you will meet with a DM for the first time and walk out of that meeting with a $50,000 order. It could happen, but it's not likely. On the other hand, if yours is a low-cost item, you can't afford to make many callbacks.

- **Closing for the DM's agreement to continue the sales cycle with you.** With some products (and in some price ranges), the typical selling cycle might extend over two or three or a half-dozen calls. The first call might be to introduce yourself and your product, and to make the first cut at assessing needs. Later calls may be for the purpose of conducting more detailed needs analysis and other fact gathering. In still later calls in the cycle, you may introduce proof sources, such as demonstrations or cost proposals.

  In longer sales cycles, you should "close" the DM before proceeding to the next step. It isn't enough for the DM to passively assent to your coming back another time. Instead, you want the DM's clearly expressed commitment that he is interested enough to have you proceed. There is no point in your investing time and effort if the DM is only going through the motions with you.
- **Closing for at least the chance to come back and try again another time.** This is the basic fallback position: If you can't get the DM to say yes now, then at least try to keep the door open so that he agrees that it would be a good idea for you to call back perhaps in a few months, or when conditions have changed, or when your product has been updated to better meet his needs.

It's important to plan in advance what your sequence of objectives will be with this customer, because selling is a fast-breaking game. Things happen that you can't anticipate, and you don't want to find yourself boxed into a corner—or find yourself walking out of the door with no order in hand, and no graceful way to come back later.

By having your sequence of alternative objectives in mind, you can back off from pushing for an action that the customer clearly will not take today. If you see that the way to a sale is closed, you can move to an alternative that makes sense with this particular customer. For example, you could shift from going for the sale to inviting the customer to agree to a demonstration or a free or low-cost trial.

Chapter 17

Recognizing Buying Signals

Back in Chapter 4, we took a look at some of the buying signals you might encounter from the Decision Maker's Screen as you try to set up an initial appointment. These signals, mostly over the phone, included

- Change in manner or tone
- Questions that indicated interest
- Statements that implied that the screen was won over, so that the only real points at issue were the details, such as time and place

But it's not only Screens who give you useful buying signals: An interested Decision Maker will bristle with positive signs that are there to be read. It's important to remain alert to these signals, as they can tell you—even before the Screen or Decision Maker may know it himself—that he is ready, or nearly ready, to buy. Indeed, there will be times when the Decision Maker's buying signals are so strong and positive that there is no break between your presentation and the DM's agreement; it's as if there is one continuous flow to the communication. In those happy cases, you don't really need to ask for the order, as the DM's words or actions make it clear that all that remains is to work out the details.

The actual buying signals will depend to a large extent on the individual's unique mannerisms, and so you'll need to be alert and flexible. To get started, attune yourself to basic areas such as those following.

- *Nonverbal signals.* If the DM is sitting forward in his chair, nodding his head, and muttering words like, "Great! Exactly what we need! Yes, I see how it fits in," then you have strongly positive buying signals. That is probably the point at which you should stop trying to persuade the DM, and instead move on to wrap it up by closing for some kind of buying action.

  See Chapter 29 for more guidance on nonverbal messages in the sales call.
- *Questions and comments.* It's usually a positive signal when the DM begins asking about practical matters, such as, "How soon can you deliver?" or "Is it available in [a certain color or size or other similar detail]?" Questions of this sort imply that the DM has basically made the decision to buy, and now has moved on to settle the details.

- *Certain kinds of objections.* If a DM asks detailed questions about your product or about how it differs from your competition, you probably have a signal of interest. After all, busy people don't get into the details unless they see a good reason to do so. The fact that the DM is interested enough to explore this kind of practical issue signals that the DM is at least testing the what-if of buying. The trend is positive, so be ready to move with that trend.
- *Interest in haggling over details.* The sale is probably yours if the DM initiates tentative negotiating probes over matters that are relevant only if the sale is going through. (The sale is yours, that is, provided you can negotiate mutually agreeable terms.)

  For instance, a DM might say, "You're talking about too long a lead time before you can install. The delay is costing me money." But analyze what she is saying beneath the words, which probably is, "I'm ready to buy, provided you can speed up delivery."

Incidentally, these buying signals by the DM may not be consciously sent, so that it's important for you to look *through* the actual words and gestures to find what is really meant or implied. In this case, the DM may not have actually decided to buy (at least, not on a conscious level), but the interest in delivery times betrays what's really going on in her mind. If you're attuned to that, you can adapt as appropriate.

APPLICATION EXERCISE

It will be helpful for you over the longer term to keep a written record of the buying signals you encounter. Taking a little time to jot them down serves two purposes. First, the notes supplement your memory. Second, the practice brings your analytical powers into action, helping you learn to spot subtle cues and to generalize the meaning of signals (which may vary somewhat from person to person). A worksheet like the one following helps you organize the various aspects.

Cue	**What It May Signal**
Nonverbal signals:	
Verbal signals:	

- Questions/comments

- Interest in details, etc.

- Other

Chapter 18

Asking the Decision Maker to Take Buying Action

There's no single best way of asking for the order or other buying commitment. In this chapter, we examine three of the most widely useful approaches, then in the next chapter we look at eight more methods.

However, before we get into specific ways of asking for the order, it is helpful to focus on two overall strategies that will be useful regardless of how you ask for the order.

Two Basic Strategies in Asking for Action

Later in this chapter, we'll be focusing on specific ways of asking the DM to take buying action. Before we do that, though, we need to examine a pair of strategies that are useful as you ask the DM to take action.

1. Project the assumption that the Decision Maker will naturally agree.

That's a reasonable assumption. After all, you've invested your time and best efforts in working with the DM to diagnose real needs. Then, drawing on your experience and expertise, you've proposed a sound, cost-effective way of filling those needs. Viewed in that context, it makes perfect sense that the DM will naturally choose to implement your recommendations.

But your confidence and enthusiasm must be contagious. Some suggestions on communicating that assumption:

- *Project enthusiasm by energetic body language.* Sit forward in your chair, as people do when they are interested and excited. Talk a little faster and a little louder than normal (unless, of course, you're already notorious for talking too loud and fast).
- *Project confidence and positive expectations verbally.* Avoid tentative expressions that communicate uncertainty. Instead, speak as though the other person has decided in your favor. Say things like "*When* you install our system, not "*If* you install it."
- *Speak clearly and with energy in your voice.* Project the sense that you are enthusiastic about your product or service, and that it is still exciting and new to you—and, hence, that the DM should find it just as exciting. Don't make the mistake of quickly mumbling through your sales message, or of

reciting it mechanically. You may be saying things you have said a hundred times before, but don't let that show: It's all new to the DM.

- *Communicate by the level of investment of your effort.* Subtle things can make significant impressions. For example, by taking the time to fill out the order blank before you arrive at the DM's office, you subtly signal your confidence that the decision will naturally be in your favor.

In the same way, complete a detailed action plan for installing your product. In this action plan, use actual calendar dates such as "August 7," rather than generic formats like "two weeks after ordering."

The DM will be impressed that you bothered to think through the plan specifically for this organization. He may infer that since you invested this level of effort, not only were you confident that the product is right for the firm, but that you can be counted on to be organized, professional, and on time.

2. After asking for action, be silent. Wait for a response. Once you ask, leave it up to the DM to respond—no matter how long the silence lasts.

Once you ask for the order, stop talking. By asking for action, you put the ball in the DM's court. You have asked a question; now let the silence hang heavy while the DM decides how to respond.

Your silence gives the DM time to think. It also adds pressure, because most people find silence uncomfortable. Don't rush in to rescue the DM from this pressure. After all, it is the DM's own delay that is causing this uncomfortable silence. The DM himself has the power to ease that pressure by responding to your question.

The silence and resulting pressure will usually be on your side, as they force the DM to make a decision to end that silence. If your presentation has made sense, then the DM will be pushed to say yes. With the silence hanging, he may find it hard to come up with any good reason to say no.

But even if he does say no, then you can probe to find the reasons. Again, as you ask these probing questions, use the power of silence. Ask a question, then *wait for the answer*—no matter how long it takes. If you butt in with another question to fill the silence, you rescue the DM from making the decision.

Often, too, the pressure of the silence will cause the DM to blurt out the *real* reasons behind his hesitation. These underlying reasons may be quite different from what he has said earlier. For some people, no is just a habit they follow without really thinking. Your silence can break through that habit and force them to focus on the actual situation.

Basic Closing Approaches

1. Simple direct request for the order.

Sometimes the positive signals will be so strong that little needs to be said, and the sale seems to wrap itself up. The simplest close follows this outline:

- *Summarize* the key points made, highlighting the needs raised and the ways in which your product will fill those needs.
- *Check for completeness.* Make sure you have touched upon all matters of importance to the DM by asking something on the order of, "Is there any-

thing else we need to talk about now?" If the DM does raise issues, deal with them, then summarize once again and check for completeness again: "Can you think of anything else we should talk about?"

- *Go on to ask for the order.*

APPLICATION EXERCISE: SIMPLE DIRECT REQUEST

Take the time now, before reading on, to solidify your understanding of this closing approach. Develop at least two different ways of making a simple direct request for the order (or other appropriate buying action).

Put your words down on paper, either in the space below or on a separate sheet. Though you write them for future reference, make sure that they are phrases that you can say comfortably. That is, try saying them aloud, then edit them until the words feel comfortable. Use short, easy-to-say sentences and the kind of vocabulary that feels natural to you.

Version 1:

Version 2:

2. Summary and recommendations.

Briefly summarize both the key needs and the corresponding ways in which your product will fill these needs. Then test for completeness by asking a version of the question, "Is there anything that keeps us from proceeding with this?" (Or simply, "Anything else?" or even, "Anything else we need to discuss/talk about?")

Deal with any additional issues that come up, then ask for the action you need. Here's a model:

> "To sum up, Ms. Barker, we discussed your need to increase productivity in the billing department, and at the same time to cut the expense of hiring temporary clerical workers. The GEM 4000 meets both of these needs. It will increase productivity by at least 20 percent, which will significantly reduce the need for temporary help by an estimated 15 percent. If you approve the plan now, we can have the GEM 4000 in place by the end of the week. Will that be soon enough, or shall I request a priority installation?"

APPLICATION EXERCISE: SUMMARY AND RECOMMENDATIONS

Again, experiment with developing a summary and recommendations close appropriate for your product or service. Using the model above as a guideline, jot down two to four key points that you might want to review with the typical customer, then wrap up your summary with the recommendation to buy. (In your summary, briefly touch on both the customer's needs and how your product or service will fill those needs. Add the issue of cost-effectiveness or value, if appropriate.)

Review Points

	Needs	Solutions	Value
1.			
2.			
3.			

Your recommendation to take buying action:

3. Action plan (or implementation schedule).

Here you again summarize the needs and the corresponding ways in which your product will fill those needs. Then you show how you intend to put your proposals into operation, using a *written action plan* as a visual aid. Advantages of using an action plan (or implementation plan) as a tool for closing include the following:

- *You project your confidence that the purchase makes perfect sense.* The DM will be impressed by the interest you show in going to the trouble of planning this implementation schedule even before the sale is locked in.
- *It is direct, to-the-point, and businesslike.* The DM will respect your professionalism. The schedule shows that you know what you are doing, and that you plan ahead to make sure it will work as promised.
- *It will cause any final or hidden objections to surface now*, so that you can deal with them. After all, acceptance of the action plan implies assent to the purchase, and so it becomes a matter of clarifying the hesitations or living with them.

To use this approach, type out a schedule in advance, using a format similar to the following example but adapted to your specific needs.

Always use actual calendar dates like "April 1" instead of "ten days after signing." Even though you may later change these dates to reflect discussions with the DM, they project your confidence that the order will come through as the natural and inevitable outcome of your sales efforts.

The "Who Is Responsible" column shows that you have thought it through. It clarifies both what you do and what cooperation you will need from the DM's organization. If necessary, include here mention of actions or other support that are needed from the DM's organization, such as approvals, preliminary funding, or other preparation like making space or working area available. (In the model below, SELL Co. is the seller, and BUY Inc. is the potential buyer.)

Task	Who Is Responsible	Date
Train staff in use	SELL Co. conducts training. BUY Inc. provides meeting room, plus 3 staff.	4/23
Ready work area	BUY Inc. has space and electrical outlets ready.	4/30
Deliver, install units	SELL Co. gets 3 units in place and running.	5/1
Initial pilot usage, supervised	BUY Inc. begins usage with 3 operators. SELL Co. has technician standing by for first 2 days.	5/2–5
Adjustments, modifications as needed	SELL Co. makes all adjustments within 24 hours.	5/5–30
Final sign-off	BUY Inc. staff, after review.	6/1

APPLICATION EXERCISE

Experiment with adapting this model to your product. What realistic tasks would be involved, with what time frames? What actions would you need to take in order to install, and what cooperation would you need from the customer?

Task	Who Is Responsible	Date

SUMMARY

In asking the DM to take any kind of buying action, work with these two strategies in mind:

1. Project the assumption that the Decision Maker will naturally agree.
2. After you ask for action, be silent. Wait for a response. Let the Decision Maker respond—no matter how long it takes.

In projecting your confidence that the DM will naturally agree, be attuned to subtle aspects, such as

- Your *body language*: Let your enthusiasm show.
- Your *verbal language*: For instance, say "When you buy," not "If you buy."
- The *level of your effort invested*: Project your confidence that you will get the order. For instance, come in with the customer's name and address already filled in on the order blank.

Be attuned also to the customer's buying signals. Begin by looking for signals in these areas, but be open to other kinds of signals you'll encounter:

- The DM's *body language* and other nonverbal communications as they evidence enthusiasm and interest.
- The DM's *questions and comments,* if they imply readiness to proceed.
- The DM's *interest in discussing or negotiating details* that imply that she may be taking the sale for granted, consciously or subconsciously.

There is no single best way of asking the customer to buy or take other action. But have a repertoire of different approaches ready, so that you can ask again and again without sounding like a broken record. Here are three to get you started, with others explored in the chapter that follows.

1. Simple direct request
2. Summary and recommendations
3. Action plan

Chapter 19

More Ways of Asking the Decision Maker to Take Action

When you are asking the DM to take any kind of buying action, work with two basic strategies in mind:

1. Project the assumption that the Decision Maker will naturally agree.
2. After you ask for action, be silent. Wait for a response. Let the Decision Maker respond—no matter how long it takes.

In Chapter 18, we also addressed the how-to of three key ways of closing the sale and asking the DM to take buying action:

1. Simple direct request
2. Summary and recommendations
3. Action plan

In this chapter, we carry on this process and examine eight additional ways of asking for the sale. You don't need to master them all before your first day of selling. Just get started, and know that they're here for you when you've mastered the basics and are ready to expand your repertoire of methods.

One study among Xerox sales reps found that, on average, it took six attempts by the salesperson to close the sale before the Decision Maker typically agreed to buy. The point is, don't give up if you hear no, or even if you hear no again and again. Keep asking. As one put it, "Each time you hear no means you're that much closer to hearing the ultimate yes."

4. The similar situation technique

Here the similar situation refers to how another organization acted when faced with a situation like that now facing the DM. You can take a negative tack and describe the difficulties that resulted because the other people did not buy your product. Or, usually better, you can take a positive approach and describe the advantages they gained because they *did* buy from you. The positive approach allows the prospect to identify with success.

The similar situation closing approach works best if you can add credibility by citing actual names of organizations and decision makers. It also provides a concrete proof source.

Details on specific points of similarity are useful, as they enable the present prospect to identify more strongly with each benefit. But don't get bogged down on details: A sentence on each should be enough as a start. If the DM is seriously interested in your product and wants to know more, you can count on his letting you know.

> "A small accounting firm like yours installed our software last fall. By their own analysis, it had paid for itself by the end of the first week. The senior partner told me that her only regret was that they hadn't found it a year sooner. We can have it in operation for you fourteen days from today. Will that been soon enough, or should I request special installation?"

Incidentally, it's even better if you can name that other client, but be sure to get clearance before doing so.

APPLICATION EXERCISE

If you're a one-person business, you shouldn't have any difficulty in keeping track of similar situations to which you can refer. Still, it's a good idea to keep an up-to-date log of your installations, so that the similar situation is fresh in your mind a year or three after you have moved on.

It's even more important to keep a formal log if you are working with others, so that everyone knows what the others have done. (Sometimes, in the rush of business, that kind of "collective memory" is overlooked.)

5. Last chance.

Few things put the sense of urgency into a customer like a bargain that is about to slip away. "The sale ends today," or "This is the last one in stock at the old price," or "Our prices will be rising 5 percent effective the first of the month" is a powerful motivator to take action *now*.

APPLICATION EXERCISE

Keep a list of potential "last chance" approaches, gleaned not only from your work, but from the ads you watch and read. How do others, even those in totally noncompetitive fields, create a sense of buying urgency? Can you adapt those approaches to your own situation?

6. Choice of Alternatives

Here you present the DM with two and only two alternatives, phrased so that by choosing either alternative, the DM is by implication saying yes to the basic proposal.

This approach is particularly useful with a DM who may be indecisive by nature, or who seems overwhelmed by the variety of possibilities from which to choose. By narrowing the range, you help him sharpen the focus.

In selecting which pair of alternatives to use, decide whether to focus the customer's choice on central or secondary issues.

- *Central issues.* The alternatives on which you focus go to the heart of the matter: "Do you think Option A or Option B will be best for you?"
- *Secondary issues.* Here you focus the decision on a choice between two less important issues, both of which imply assent to the sale you are proposing. You may have encountered a variation of this the last time you bought a

new car, when the salesperson asked whether you "preferred" Misty Green or Azure Blue.

It is true, as you may have been thinking, that the choice of alternates close can seem a bit manipulative or "high pressure." If you're not comfortable with it, you'd better not use it. On the other hand, if you do try it, you'll be surprised at how easily it accomplishes the purpose without antagonizing customers. Many will respect your self-confidence in assuming that the sale makes such good sense. Others will appreciate your focusing the issues for them, so that they can select more efficiently between alternatives.

Application Exercise

When you are using an alternative choice close, it's important that you sound comfortable presenting the choices. For that to happen, you need to prepare the choices in advance, so that you're not winging the alternatives on the spot.

Jot down some of the possible alternatives you might present to customers, then practice saying them aloud until they feel comfortable. Develop at least two of each type.

Central issue alternatives:

1.

2.

Secondary issue alternatives:

1.

2.

7. The order-blank request

For this to work well, you need to plan for it from the start of the call. As soon as you sit down with the DM, take out a fresh order blank and put it in plain view. As you collect information on the customer's needs, print it on the form. (Remember: *Before* going in to the DM's office, fill in the basic customer data such as the firm's name and address.)

At the end of your selling message, you do not ask the DM to buy. Instead, you ask a question that implies that the sale has been agreed to, such as "Will I need a purchase order?" or "Will you want it shipped here to 2210 Waverly?"

Similarly, when the order blank is complete, don't ask the DM to "sign" it. Instead, ask him to "authorize" or "okay" it.

APPLICATION EXERCISE

Jot down, then edit and practice until you can ask comfortably, at least two different questions to which a yes answer to the question would imply a yes to the purchase. Then practice how you would phrase asking the DM to "authorize" or "okay" it, or any other similar words that imply approving the purchase.

1.

2.

8. The "sharp angle" request

Suppose the DM asks a question about your product, such as whether it can be in place by the end of the month or whether it can be obtained in a color that will coordinate with the other office equipment.

Instead of immediately saying, "Yes, of course," respond with another question that puts a condition on your yes. To do this, you might respond, "So you'd want it, provided it's available in that shade of blue?"

Having your reply seem conditional makes your response more valuable to the customer. Then your response becomes not just Yes, but "Yes, I'll meet your request, *provided* you can reassure me that you are serious enough about this issue to be willing to buy if I supply what you are asking for."

Once the DM has assured you that he would indeed want it in blue (or whatever), then you can explain that you can indeed supply it as requested. Then immediately move to the details of delivery, payment, or the like, *without* pausing to ask whether he does want to buy. (After all, you can rightly assume that he does in fact want to buy, given that he was interested enough to ask, and, further interested enough to select a color.)

An incidental benefit: The conditional question is also useful in sorting out those who are serious prospects from those who are only chatting with you to fill up the time until they can retire.

This works, naturally enough, only if you can say yes to the DM's inquiry. If you know you can't supply what the DM wants, do not say no. Instead, probe to find out why that is important to the DM. It may turn out to be unimportant, and you can move on from it. If it is important, your probing may open up alternatives that can supply what the customer is *ultimately* after. (For example, you might find that he doesn't care so much about getting the product in blue as about having a change from the color now in place.)

APPLICATION EXERCISE

What are some questions that prospects might ask that you could then turn around as sharp angle closes? Look particularly for possible customer questions on details of the product, delivery schedules, and the like.

Jot down some of these possible requests on the worksheet that follows, then briefly outline how you would use a sharp angle or conditional response. Even though your actual reply might be a simple, "Yes, of course we can do it," in this closing approach your objective is to project the impression that you are willing to make a special effort to comply with the customer's request, as that request is implied in the question. You make your response conditional, as you want to be sure that the customer really does want the product if you go to that "extra effort" to supply it.

(Granted, this is tricky and somewhat manipulative. Certainly use it if you actually do have to invest extra effort to meet the request; otherwise, be careful, as you could antagonize a customer.)

Possible Customer Requests or Questions	How You Will Condition Your Response

9. The balance sheet

This is especially helpful when you're working with an indecisive prospect, or one whose responses are so vague that you can't quite focus on any specific objection to get your teeth into.

Take out a sheet of paper, and draw a line down the middle. At the top of one column, print "Reasons Favoring." Print "Reasons Opposing" at the top of the second column.

Reasons Favoring	Reasons Opposing
1.	1.
2.	2.
3.	3.

Then state the issue in a form like this: "It seems to me that the question you're facing is whether to go with the GEM 4000. Do you agree?"

Once the question has been defined in that way, focus on the reasons *favoring* the purchase. The prospect will already be able to list some of those reasons. Jot them down in the appropriate column. Suggest any other reasons favoring the purchase that she overlooked.

When the positive list is complete, move on to work with the DM in coming up with the reasons against the purchase. Since they are *her* reasons for not wanting to buy, you shouldn't feel any need to provide additional help here.

When you're finished, the list of reasons favoring will probably be much longer than the list of reasons opposing. Point out that difference in the length of the lists, and ask for the order by saying, "The right choice seems obvious, doesn't it?"

What if the DM still hesitates? At least now you have a clear statement of the reasons that are holding her back, because she has listed them for you in the Reasons Opposing column. Go over these one by one, eliminating each, using the four-step process for handling objections that you'll meet in Part 6.

Salvage Tools

The closing methods in this last group are primarily useful in salvaging the situation when nothing else seems to work, and you feel the sale is slipping away.

10. The "final" objection

This is based on the four-step process for responding to objections that we cover in Part 6. You'll find the how-to at the end of Chapter 24.

11. The lost sale, or "Columbo"

The approach gets its name from the old TV series with Detective Columbo of the shaggy raincoat. Columbo interrogates a suspect, but gets nowhere. He pulls himself to his feet and shuffles to the door, apparently defeated. The suspects relaxes, thinking that it's over, the pressure is off. Then, halfway out the door, Columbo pokes his head back in with one final question—the question that's at the core of it all. The suspect, caught off guard, makes a fatal admission.

Use this when everything else has failed: The customer has given a final, definite no, and the sale seems lost. Pack up your briefcase, stand, start to leave. But just before going out the door, pause and say, as if it's an afterthought, "I feel I should apologize."

The DM, will probably be surprised, and ask why you feel that way. Respond, "Because somehow or somewhere I've obviously failed to make the benefits clear to you. I'm certain that if I'd done a better job, you'd see the value, and there'd be no doubt in your mind. I wonder, would you mind telling me where I went wrong? What could I have done better? Did I leave some questions unanswered?"

The DM may say, "Get on out of here," but more often he will be pleased to give you some advice.

Listen attentively, and look through the words to what is really being said. For instance, if the DM says it was simply a matter of lack of funds, it may be that you failed to explain alternative financing plans, or that you lacked a low-cost introductory offer.

Or, if the DM says that the company prefers to buy from well-established firms, the real problem is that you failed to establish your credentials clearly enough. As a consequence, the prospect failed to look past the lack of a known name tag to recognize the quality of your product, or the commitment of your company to stay in the marketplace.

Again, listen well, as this is valuable feedback. Learn from it before you make sales calls on other customers. But if you're really deft, you may also be able to use this feedback in one final attempt to salvage this "lost" sale: "I appreciate your giving me this feedback. I can see that, as you say, the cost factors were the key sticking point. And I apologize: I let you down. I neglected to make clear that we offer an extended payment plan that would let you install our product for an initial payment of only $_____ ."

Application Exercise

It's important to be completely comfortable with this approach in order to use it effectively. Any awkwardness would be fatal. That means a lot of practice before trying it. Rehearse (out loud, or at least in your mind) not only the words but your movements as well, until it flows with a natural feel.

Summary

Nothing—absolutely nothing at all—is likely to happen until you actually take the step of asking for the order (or closing for the order, to use sales-reps' jargon). When you ask, you risk hearing no. But it's best to hear that no early, while you can still turn things around.

In asking for the order (or other buying commitment), follow these two basic principles:

1. **As you ask, project the assumption that the Decision Maker will *naturally* say yes, since your proposal makes such perfect sense.**
2. **After asking, be silent. Wait for the Decision Maker's response before you say another word—no matter how long that takes.**

Among the most effective ways of asking for the DM's buying commitment are these:

Covered in Chapter 18:

1. Simple direct request
2. Summary and recommendations
3. Action plan

Covered in this chapter:

4. Similar situation
5. Last chance
6. Choice of alternatives
7. Order-blank request
8. Sharp angle request
9. Balance sheet
10. "Final" objection (for how-to, see Chapter 24)
11. Lost sale, or "Columbo"

Part Six
Coping with Questions, Objections, and Hesitations

The core question addressed in this part is, What's the best way in this situation of responding to the Decision Maker's questions and objections, so that the sale doesn't become blocked?

It's a fact of selling life that most of the time you'll hear either no or a strong reason not to buy the first time (and maybe even the second and third time) you ask for the order. (Recall the Xerox study I mentioned earlier that found that the typical sale came through only on the salesperson's sixth attempt to close.)

But it's also a fact that much—if not most—of the time, the tough objections you encounter, or even the flat no, are intended only as trial balloons.

Consciously or subconsciously, the Decision Maker may be thinking, "The easiest thing is to say no. No preserves the status quo; there's less risk that way. Besides, if this salesperson accepts my no, then obviously she can't believe very strongly in her product. If she's not enthusiastic enough to be willing to fight for it, then why should I buy?"

An objection such as "We can't afford it" or "We already deal with your competitor" may sound like a reason for saying no. But in fact the objection may be a question in disguise, intended to draw you out so that the DM can hear how you handle it. Even a flat no may be meant as a subtle, noncommittal way of asking you to provide more reasons in support of what you're offering.

In short, the apparent objection you hear may be saying,

- "Give me more information on which to base my decision."
- "Tell me how to handle this objection, because I know I'm going to hear it from others."
- "I'm almost convinced, but I need one more reason to justify my saying yes."
- "Give me a little more proof that your product really will fill my needs."

By the same token, just as objections are often a sign of interest, what sounds like a question may in fact be an objection in disguise. For example, a customer who asks, "Can your computer do...?" may in effect be objecting, "I think your competitor's product is better, *because* it can do this. I'm asking the question to give you a chance to prove my assumption wrong."

Chapter 20

Determining What Is Behind the Question or Objection

People who are new to selling are sometimes tempted to ignore customer objections, or to try to sweep them under the rug with some sort of quick response, as if getting them out of sight will somehow also get them out of the Decision Maker's mind.

But that's a mistake. You may be able to change the subject away from the Decision Maker's concerns, but the concerns will still be there, and probably stronger than ever because you seemed to be unwilling or unable to deal with them. In this chapter we look at a better way of responding to the Decision Maker's objections.

The Four-Step Process for Responding to Objections and Questions

Some questions and objections are so easy that you can respond to them quickly and directly, and move on.

For our meaning here, an "easy" question or objection is one that is in an area in which your product or service is strong, or that raises issues that you can handle quickly without raising secondary concerns. For example, if the objection relates to a misunderstanding on price that you can set right by pointing to a catalog, do that and move on:

> "The answer is yes, we do guarantee our installations for three years, the longest in the industry, according to this survey in *Industry Times*. I'll leave a copy with you. Now, moving on to the issue of..."

In handling more difficult objections and questions, it's helpful to work systematically through what we will be referring to in this book as the Four-Step process:

1. *Probe*. Basically, you get the DM talking about why he is hesitating.
2. *Restate*. Then you sum up your understanding of the DM's concerns, and ask the DM to confirm whether that is a fair restatement.
3. If it is, then you *Respond Positively* to that concern, showing how your product or service overcomes that concern.
4. Then you *Move On* to another matter, without getting bogged down on this single issue.

We'll examine the first step, Probe, in this chapter, and the how-to of the other three steps in the next chapter.

PROBE TO FIND THE REAL POINT OF THE OBJECTION

When the DM raises an objection or says no, you can't afford to assume that you know what's behind it. The reason this customer is saying no is not necessarily the same reason you've been hearing all week from others.

Often enough, the DM will volunteer a reason. That stated reason may or may not be the real reason, but at least it is a start. (Often the Decision Maker himself may not understand what is really behind his hesitation.)

Sometimes, too, when you ask for buying action, the DM will respond with a question or comment, instead of giving a clear yes or no. That may be a stall, to gain thinking time, or it may be setting up an implied condition.

For example, if you ask the DM to buy, and the DM counters by asking whether you provide service in another area, the DM may be signaling interest in buying, but only if you give that service. Therefore, it's important for you to know what's behind the DM's response: Just why is the DM asking a question now, instead of responding to your close?

Similarly, if the DM raises a question or objection, hold off responding to it until you are certain you know precisely why this is a concern to this unique individual. Even though you may have heard this general type of objection many times before, the point that this person is making may be subtly different, perhaps because of some special circumstances of which you are not aware.

Suppose, for example, the Decision Maker says, "We can't afford it." An unskilled salesperson's first response might be to try to salvage the sale with a quick offer of a discount. But that's grasping at straws, because you don't really know what the DM means; "can't afford it" may have any of several meanings. In order to respond effectively, you must know which of them is operating here.

- "Can't afford it" may mean, "We don't have money left in this year's budget." If that's the case, then there's no point in offering a price discount—at least, not until you have determined exactly what "can't afford it" means to this customer, at this time.

  If you go ahead and offer a price break without knowing what's in the customer's mind, you unnecessarily cheapen your product. You give away profit you might have had. In any case, this year's cut price will be the starting point for next year's negotiations. Yet, even so, the discount may not be what's actually needed to swing the sale now.
- From another Decision Maker, "can't afford it" might mean, "You haven't yet convinced me of the value of your product. You have failed to show me why your product is worth more money than your competitor's." In this case, a price break might help, but probably not as much as pointing out the additional ways in which your product is better than the competition's.

Situations like this show how important it is to Probe in order to get the Decision Maker talking. The more the DM tells you, the better your chances of finding the core objection, and hence of arriving at the best selling response.

Another response you might hear is that your product is "too expensive." But until you probe to find out what this DM means by "too expensive," you'll be operating in the dark. When you do probe, you may find that in fact this DM thinks your product is fairly priced. She meant something else by "too expensive": It's too expensive in the sense that your product, in the form you offer it, costs $12,000, whereas this DM has a $10,000 limit for purchasing on her own authority. Anything costing over $10,000 needs to be approved by a higher level. So, for this DM, $12,000 is "too expensive" to buy on her own, without a lengthy approval process, but a pair of $6,000 purchases would be no problem.

Once you learn exactly what this DM's "too expensive" means, you can make it possible for her to buy today simply by changing the terms of your offer from the package deal to a proposal for two separate items, each costing less than $10,000.

"Let Me Think About It"

"I need to think about it before I can sign" is a common DM response. That seems reasonable enough, and you might be inclined to back off now and offer to come back another day. At first glance, that sounds fair, but it's usually a bad idea. The trouble is, "I need to think" is usually an excuse to *avoid* thinking. It's often used, consciously or not, as a procrastination device to avoid making a decision that should be made on the spot.

Treat it as you would any other objection. Begin by Probing: "Perhaps I can help? Just what aspect is it you need to think more about?" The DM may tell you a specific concern, and you can go on to respond to it.

But then again, the DM's response may be vague—usually because he's not really clear himself on just what he does want to think about. In that situation, it's helpful to probe more specifically. To do that, suggest one possible area, as in, "Is it a cost factor you need to think about?"

If the DM says "Yes, cost is something I need to think about," then focus on that as the objection. Probe it in more detail, then handle it as an objection (that is, Restate, Respond Positively, Move On).

If the DM says, "No, it's not cost I need to think about," respond by raising another possible concern, such as, "Then is it a concern about warranty?" If that's not it, then move on, suggesting one possibility after another until you have exhausted all the reasonable possibilities (not more than four or five).

At that point, after you have worked through these four or five significant possibilities, say something to the effect,

> "We've determined that your reason for hesitating now is *not* cost, *not* warranty, *not* delivery schedules, *not* financing. From my experience, I've found that these are the main concerns that customers have, but none of them apply here. Tell me, Mr. Lewis, is there any real reason not to sign today? Can we go ahead and write up the order now?"

Phantom Objections

Sometimes the real concern will be hidden behind one or more "phantom objections." For example, a customer may raise an objection that seems to concern price, but that is actually a cover to disguise the fact that she does not feel a need strong enough to justify buying.

Or "too expensive" may be this DM's way of saying that you have not yet proved that your product will in fact fill those needs. Thus it seems too expensive because it's a gamble whether he will get value for his investment.

Sometimes a price objection or other phantom objection is a smokescreen to hide the fact that the person you have been dealing with does not have the level of spending authority he earlier claimed. Now he's embarrassed to admit that he misled you, and so he hides behind a phantom objection.

Perhaps you can fit within his authority limits by restructuring your deal into segments. If that's not feasible, you can take this person with you as you move up a step or two on the organizational ladder to find the person with actual decision making capability.

Incidentally, if you do try to move up the organizational ladder, make an effort to bring the present person with you. Even though this person is not in fact the Decision Maker, he still may be a significant Decision Influencer, and so can help you make the sale. Besides, you don't want to antagonize this person by going over his head.

Probing the DM's Questions to Find and Address the Real Concern

You can also greatly increase your sales effectiveness by using the Four-Step approach as you respond to the questions that the DM raises. In the first place, questions are often disguised objections.

Second, by finding what is *behind* the question, you gain the opportunity to more closely target or customize your selling message to the particular concerns of this specific prospect. *What* the DM asks is important, but even more important is *why* the DM is asking it.

Suppose the DM asks if your product is available in green. Or asks how soon you can deliver. Or asks whether you can start immediately on a consulting project. The answer to any of these questions may be, "Yes, of course." But don't be too quick to say it. Instead, Probe to find out why the DM asked. Is it a real concern, just a passing thought, or a way to procrastinate on making the decision?

Thus you could respond, "Why would green be helpful to you?" Or, "How soon would you need delivery?" Or, "In what ways would it be helpful if I could start immediately?"

If the DM answers, "Well, on second thought, I guess it doesn't matter at all," then you can move on and not waste time. But if she says, "Green equipment is part of our corporate image, and we had to turn down your competitor because they didn't have a green model," then you know you have a key selling point, provided you can supply it. (If not, you can probe some more to explore whether it may be worthwhile to develop a customized color in order to clinch the sale.)

Besides, skillful probing may lead the DM to express in his own words just how serious the problem is, and what it's costing. Make notes of these DM statements so that you can echo them back later as evidence to help establish the value of your services, or to convince the DM to take action now.

Probing as a Way of Making Your Response Seem More Valuable

By delaying your answer to probe the reason behind the question, you can target your response. You can also condition your response, which may make it seem more valuable.

By pausing to Probe why that question is important, you project the impression of attaching a condition to your response, which may have the psychological effect of giving greater value to your agreement. Thus, you can say, "From what you tell me, I can see why you need this help immediately. I'll find a way to arrange my schedule so I can begin on it tomorrow." Or, "Yes, I can see why green is obviously important to you. I can arrange to have the model available for you in green."

When the DM Offers Shifting Reasons

Sometimes, when you probe the prospect's questions or objections, you get a different response with each probe you ask, one after the other. As soon as you deal with one, another comes. Shifting reasons or shifting objections usually means that you have not gotten to the core concern. Keep probing. You might even deal directly with it, saying,

> "You've raised several different reasons why you're hesitating in buying. From my experience, that usually means there's an even deeper reason. Sometimes the person may not even be consciously aware of just what that deeper concern is. Can we talk about that?"

Or,

> "What, ultimately, is holding you back from signing today?"

The Simplest Probe

The point of probing is to get the DM talking, so that you can find out what is preventing the sale from taking place. You can turn that situation around and use it as your probe:

> "Tell me, what would it take to make this sale happen?"

Incidentally, this kind of question, where you put it in the buyer's court, can be extremely useful, both in probing to the core of the difficulty, and in eliciting fresh thinking from the DM. Helpful variations might include,

> "What could we change to make it more helpful to you?"

Or,

> "I'd appreciate your input: If you were in my shoes, what modifications would you make to the product (the pricing, etc.) in order to make it more useful to organizations like yours?"

Or,

> "What do you think would meet your needs for the upcoming year?"

Application Exercise: Developing Your Own Probes

As you probe the DM's no (or hesitations or objections), your basic questions will be in the nature of "Why?" or "Why not?" or "Why do you feel that way?"

But sometimes those will seem too blunt, and may risk making the DM feel that you are interrogating him, or pushing him into a corner. One way to avoid that is to stay attuned to how you look and sound as you probe. Develop a sensitivity to your voice tone and volume, as well as your vocabulary. Think of yourself as a consultant working with the DM to analyze a problem, not as a trial lawyer cross-examining a hostile witness.

Another way of avoiding coming across as a pushy interrogator is to develop a repertoire of alternative questions that you can ask in order to probe more gently, or to vary your approach. Here are some that I find helpful; add others that are appropriate to your product and your personal style.

- "Not for you? Why do you feel that?"
- "You say you're not interested because of _____ . Tell me, why is ______ important to you?"
- "I understand what you're asking, but I sense that there's a deeper concern behind it. Can we talk about that?"

Chapter 21

Restating, Responding, and Moving On from Objections

In the previous chapter, we examined the basic approaches for responding to the objections and questions raised by prospects.

With easy questions and objections, respond directly and quickly, then move on. (Easy objections are those in areas in which your product is strong, and in which your response isn't likely to open up other complications.)

For more difficult objections and questions, it's helpful to work through the Four-Step process:

1. *Probe,* to get the DM talking more about his concerns or why he is hesitating.
2. *Restate;* that is, sum up your understanding of the DM's concerns, and ask the DM to confirm if that fairly restates his position.
3. If it does, *Respond Positively* to that concern, showing how your product or service overcomes it.
4. *Move On* to another matter, without getting bogged down on this single issue.

In the previous chapter, we looked at the first of those steps, *Probe.* Now we examine the how-to of the three remaining steps.

Restate the Concern as You Understand It

In this Restate phase, your overall objective is to

- Narrow the issue as much as possible, so that you have a clear, manageable target to respond to.
- Put that specific concern in context, so that the DM can see that, at worst, it is only a minor issue.

In Restating, sum up your understanding of the core of the DM's question or objection. Try to boil it down into a sentence or two.

As you Restate, it usually helps to rephrase the concern in the form of a question, as questions tend to be clear and succinct. For example, you might say,

> "Let me make sure I understand your concern. You tell me that you find the new warranty program that Competitor X has introduced to be a very important factor in the decision to buy. I think the unspoken question is

whether my company would be willing to match it. Is that a fair understanding of your concern?"

Restating, particularly in question form, may seem unnecessary effort, but it generally more than pays off. First, the paraphrase forces both you and the prospect to attend more closely to what was actually said, and to what was actually *meant*. That kind of close attention probably won't be given if you merely parrot back the DM's words.

Second, as you rephrase the objection, you may be able to "disarm" it. For example, if the customer objects that your product is "too expensive," your restatement question can be, "Let me make sure I understand the point you're making. Are you suggesting that the product seems too costly in relation to the benefits it brings?"

If the customer agrees, "Yes, that is what I meant," then you have created an opening to review the value of your proposal, showing how the dollar costs are outweighed by the benefits.

Alternatively, the DM may respond that you haven't quite understood his point: "No, what I meant was that it seems too expensive in comparison with your competition." From that point, you can move in any of several directions. For one approach, you might try to Restate your understanding again, refining it.

For a second approach, you can go back and Probe some more to get a sense of which competitors are most important to the DM, or of precisely how the DM is measuring the cost of those competing products. If you do that, then Probe also to find out whether that method actually compares oranges with oranges. For example, is the DM looking only at out-of-pocket expenses, and perhaps overlooking the combined effect of both direct and indirect factors?

Another example: Suppose the Decision Maker says, "I've heard through the grapevine that your products don't hold up well under steady use."

You could rephrase this—and at the same time disarm it—by saying, "Your underlying concern, as I understand it, is this: Does my company offer a solid warranty, and do we have service people who can give you immediate assistance if anything should happen to our units? The answer to both is very definitely yes."

As you Restate, make it clear to the DM what you are doing, and why. Here are some helpful "signal" phrases to put your Restating in context; add to the list others that feel comfortable to you.

- "Let me make sure I understand your concern: Is it that . . . ?"
- "What I'm understanding from your question is that . . . "
- "So that we're both in accord, what I'm hearing from you is that . . . "

If appropriate, you can also Restate not just the actual words used, but the *impression* you pick up: "What I'm sensing (or picking up) is that you tend to feel ____."

Respond Positively to That Concern

You might think that between your Probing and Restating, you would be spending too much time before even getting into dealing with the objection itself. In fact, it normally shouldn't take that long to clarify the customer's point. In any case, it's worth the time, as by clarifying the issue and gaining the DM's agreement on what is the precise concern, you gain the advantage of a clear—and narrow—target.

Trying to respond to a vague, open-ended objection such as, "Your product is too expensive" is a lost cause because the objection is so broad that you can't really get a handle on it. Does this customer's "too expensive" mean that it costs more than your competition? That it doesn't seem worth the money? That she doesn't have the money? Or is "too expensive" just a negotiating ploy to get you to offer a discount?

The more precisely focused the DM's concern is, the more specific you can be in your response. That's where first Probing, then Restating to further define the real issue proves helpful. If you can narrow "too expensive" to something more manageable, like, "Your product costs 10 percent more than a comparable item from another vendor," or "It costs $1,000 more than my purchasing authorization allows," then you can Respond Positively to this narrow concern.

Once you have a clear idea of what the customer's core concern really is, respond to it directly. Deal with the concern fairly, *but don't get bogged down*. Give a clear response, deal with the objection, then move on.

Responding Positively

However, as you Respond to the prospect's questions or objections, it's important that your response be Positive. It's a mistake to respond in a defensive way, projecting the sense that, "Well, there is a problem with my product, and there's not much I can do about it, but maybe you'll buy anyway." (Even if the words weren't that defensive, one's voice tone and nonverbal communication might have that effect.)

To develop the habit of Responding Positively, first *do your homework*. Anticipate the kinds of objections that might be raised, and develop clear, succinct responses. If your product is good, be prepared to explain how it is good in this area. If it does have a weakness in this particular area, be able to put that weakness into perspective against all of the things it does well.

Second, pay attention to the subtle messages you project by your expectations, and by your mannerisms as you respond. When a question or objection is raised, answer it with the positive assumption that the DM will easily accept your response. Develop the mindset that your product is so basically sound that any objection, product criticism, or question can be raising only a minor point that you can deal with easily and then move on.

Still another aspect of Responding Positively is to *become aware of the subtle signals you project,* through your voice tone, body language, facial expression, and energy and enthusiasm. These are just habits, and with awareness of what they are, plus some effort, you can change.

Here's how: Observe yourself when you are "in flow," and isolate the tones and mannerisms that come naturally to you then. Define what they are, and even try to describe them on paper. Then make a conscious effort to repeat these mannerisms at a time when you don't naturally feel confident. (True, it's acting, at least at first. Then the new, more positive patterns will become your normal way.)

Move On

Normally the best way to Move On after Responding Positively to the objection or question is to ask for a buying commitment. Proceed on the assumption that your response to the objection cleared up any lingering doubts. Therefore, it's only logical for you to ask for the order as soon as you have dealt with the objection.

Thus if the DM agrees that you have satisfied his concern, you might respond, "Excellent. I can schedule you for installation early next week. Will that be soon enough?"

Don't be compulsive about working through every point you had planned to cover. If the DM is ready to buy now, give her the opportunity. Don't talk so much that you keep her from saying yes. Respond to the concern without any excess words, then ask for the order.

There's always a risk of talking yourself out of sales by saying too much, particularly if you manage to blow a minor issue into a major block by responding to it at great length. It may have been only a passing thought to the DM, and you don't want to dignify it by paying it too much respect. Give a brief, to-the-point response, then move on.

Knowing When It's Okay to Move On from an Objection

How do you know whether you have dealt adequately with the objection? First, be sensitive to the DM's signals, verbal and nonverbal. (For some ideas on this, see Chapter 29, "Sending and Receiving Nonverbal Messages.")

Second, test your response by asking the customer a variation of, "Does that answer your question?"

The DM's response then gives you the feedback you need. If you have not dealt adequately with the concern, she will say no—or at least hesitate. Treat that hesitation as an objection, and repeat the cycle of Probe, Restate, and Respond Positively, backing up to cover the points you skipped over. Then Move On, usually by closing for the sale or other buying action.

The object of the exercise is to get the order, *not* to give a comprehensive sales presentation. The presentation is only a means to an end.

Questions as Buying Signals

Sometimes, when you look through a prospect's question, or even what appears to be an objection, you find that the prospect is subconsciously signaling a readiness to buy.

For example, you may encounter the question, "How soon could you install?" Or you could run up against the apparent objection, "It just won't do us any good. It's too close to our busy season to take a chance on something new."

Very possibly, both the question and the objection are signaling a message to the effect, "I'm interested in buying, but can you get it up and running quickly, without any bugs or glitches? High season is coming up, and I can't afford any downtime."

As a salesperson, it's tempting to respond immediately to the concern as it is expressed: "Sure, we can help, even though your season is under way." But that can lock you into a dead end.

It's better to Probe before trying to deal with the concern. If the DM's question is, "How soon can you begin?" Probe by asking, "How soon do you need it?" For one thing, that forces the prospect to focus what probably had been just a final vague concern before signing the order.

Similarly, to the objection, "You've got a good product, but we can't think of buying now, because it's too close to our busy season to try something new," Probe to define the specific concerns, using questions such as, "When does your busy season begin?" and "In what specific ways would you think this new approach could affect the work now?" As you push the prospect to be specific, you'll probably encounter one of two responses:

- The DM will come up with a tangible concern that you can deal with.
- The DM will in effect admit that the question/objection was a disguised buying signal; he is all set to buy, provided you can dissolve this last vague doubt.

Mastering the Four-Step Process

This Four-Step process—Probe, Restate, Respond Positively, Move On—provides the overall strategy for dealing with objections or questions at every stage, from those you may encounter from the Decision Maker's secretarial screen through the final objections before the Decision Maker signs the order.

But the four steps must become automatic. To make the process second nature, mentally rehearse it with imaginary customer scenarios.

For guidance in handling early objections, see Chapter 23. For guidance on responding to later or core objections, see Chapter 24.

Chapter 22

Applying the Four-Step Process

Quick review: Questions and even objections show that the customer is at least somewhat interested—perhaps not yet persuaded, but at least sufficiently interested to want to explore your product or service further. An objection may be a question in disguise. Even no may be a test to see how you will react: Do you have faith enough in your product to keep plugging?

In handling objections and all but the simplest questions, the Four-Step process will help you turn around the customer's thinking better than would a direct rebuttal:

1. *Probe* to find the real point of the objection or question. Similarly, if you hear a flat no, Probe by asking "Why?" or "Why not?" Don't assume that you know why this individual is saying no, and don't assume that he is raising the objection for the same reason that the last customer did.
2. *Restate the Concern* as you understand it. Restating forces both you and the Decision Maker to pay close attention to what you are each saying. Also, in restating it, you may be able to disarm the objection and move into areas in which you have an especially strong response.
3. *Respond Positively to that concern.* Respond to the concern with a clear, convincing answer. Don't get bogged down on one issue or one objection and let the sale stall. Respond, then move on.
4. *Move On.* Generally, the best way of moving on is by asking the DM to take a buying action.

In short, make sure you know the real reason the DM says no. If you encounter a string of different reasons for the no, keep probing until you get to the core reason. (Conversely, make sure that the DM is saying yes for the right reasons, as otherwise you may lose out on longer-term potential.)

Application Exercise

Focus on a few of the most significant (or common) objections you encounter from prospects. (If you haven't yet begun selling, try to anticipate what these will be in your situation.) Chances are, three basic objections will be among them, though the precise wording may vary:

A. "Your product is too expensive."
B. "We've always used (a specific competitor's product)."
C. "There are many similar products on the market. What makes yours special?"

Over the next few pages, we'll work together in running three typical objections through the Four-Step process. For each, I'll provide my model for handling it through the phases of the Four-Step process.

In the space provided, adapt that model to fit your particular product or situation. Then *take the time to mentally rehearse* your response, so that the words flow easily, and you can move confidently from one step to the next.

A. Objection: "Your product is too expensive for us."

Probe:

My model: "When you say it's too expensive, in what sense do you mean 'expensive?'" (If necessary, probe by offering some alternatives, such as, "Do you mean more expensive compared to other competitors?")

Your Adaptation:

Restate:

My model: "Just to make sure we're in accord, you're saying that my product costs $____ more per unit than your present supplier charges you. Is that your concern?"

Your Adaptation:

Respond Positively:

My model: "Let me respond to that with two points. First, if you buy five or more at a time, I can match that price. Second, earlier in our discussion, we found that my product fills your primary need, which your present supplier also does. But we go beyond that and fill the additional need of ______, which the item you're presently using cannot do."

Your Adaptation:

Move On:

My model: "In short, we accomplish significantly more than the present product, plus we can be totally competitive on price if you buy in quantities of at least five at a time. If you buy ten at a a time, I can offer a further discount, so that they would cost you just $90 each. Which would be better for you now, five at $100 each, or ten at $90?"

Your Adaptation:

B. Objection: "We've always used (a specific competitor's product)."
Probe:

My model: "In what ways do you feel the XYZ is better for you?" (If necessary, probe more specifically, as in, "Is it better regarding size? Ease of use?")

Your Adaptation:

Restate:

My model: "Let me check my understanding of your key concern: You're inclined to buy the XYZ over our model because you believe the XYZ has lower maintenance costs. Is that basically it?"

Your Adaptation:

Respond Positively:

My model: "I'd like to show you two ways in which we can guarantee that long-term maintenance costs are 20 percent lower with our product than with the XYZ. First, we offer a maintenance contract, with costs guaranteed for a year at a time, at a rate of $________. Second..."

Your Adaptation:

Move On:

My model: "Given these facts, I think the choice is clear. My product does the job for you, and saves $____ per month in direct operating costs. Also, with a maintenance contract, your upkeep costs are guaranteed within agreed-upon limits. It makes good business sense to install my product. We can have it in place and running by the fifteenth. Would that be soon enough?"

Your Adaptation:

C. Objection: "There are many similar products on the market. What makes yours special?"
Probe:

My model: "If you were to choose one of these competitors, which would you be most inclined to select?" (After the DM responds) "Why? What is it about that one that you find particularly interesting or appropriate?"

Your Adaptation:

Restate:

My model: "Feeding back what I understand, what appeals to you about the Gen X are two main factors: the two-year warranty and the low operating cost, which you understand to be under $100 per month. Is that a fair restatement of your feelings?"

Your Adaptation:

Respond Positively:

My model: "Well, I'm very pleased to tell you that my product, the DYNA-15, also comes with a standard two-year warranty, which I can show you in a moment is significantly better than the Gen X warranty. In addition, an optional service contract is available for a further five years, at low cost. Wouldn't you agree that the combination of warranty plus optional extended contract, which would protect you for seven years, not just two, puts us way ahead of Gen X?" (If the response is yes, you could try to close for the order at that point. Or, if it seems more appropriate, you could move on to the second point before closing.)

"There's something else. You said that low operating cost is important to you. We have recently run a study of actual customer operating costs with our DYNA-15. The findings? Operating costs average less than $980.00 per month, which is a full 20 percent below the advertised operating costs of the Gen X. That 20 percent saving would be very significant to your operation, wouldn't it?"

Your Adaptation:

Move On:

My model: "Given these facts, the overall quality of the DYNA-15, plus the way it exceeds the Gen X on the two key matters of warranty and operating cost, the DYNA-15 seems ideal for your use. Would you want that with the basic two-year warranty, or would you rather protect yourself for the next seven years with the service contract?"

Your Adaptation:

COMMENT

Notice that in responding to the objections, we didn't get bogged down in the details, such as precisely why the warranty for the DYNA-15 is better than that of the Gen X. It's important to work through the Four Steps relatively quickly, so that the DM moves with the flow of the response.

Then, if the DM wants to know more in detail about the warranty (or other elements) treat that as a request for proof. We deal with the use of proof sources in Part 7.

Chapter 23

Responding to Early Objections and Concerns

Objections, concerns, and questions are normal parts of life in selling, so don't back away when you encounter them. The key is to listen well to what the client is *really* saying, respond in a positive way, then move on.

Refresher: The Four-Step Process

Recall the basic Four-Step process for responding to questions and objections:

1. *Probe* to find the real point of the objection.
2. *Restate* the concern as you understand it, normally in question form. (*Note*: In some cases, particularly if the prospect seems hurried or distracted, it may be necessary to skip the Restate step.)
3. *Respond in a Positive way* to the concern as you now understand it.
4. *Move On* without getting bogged down. Generally, the best way of moving on is to ask the DM to take some form of buying action.

In this chapter, we'll be building from that basic framework by looking at some of the specific objections that you're likely to encounter *early* in your contacts with either the Screen or the DM. (You may encounter these either in your initial phone conversation with the DM or at the start of the face-to-face meeting.)

For suggestions on dealing with the later or core objections, see Chapter 24.

1. "You'd only be wasting your time."

As in dealing with any objection, use the Four-Step process. Probe to find out why the DM believes you'd be wasting your time. She may be merely trying to scare you off. Then again, she may be raising a serious concern, such as:

- She is not the appropriate Decision Maker, as she lacks Authority, Need, or Dollars. Or you have mistaken the role of this department, and she has no involvement at all in buying the kind of services you provide.
- She has no money to spend, perhaps because of temporary cash flow problems or because this is the wrong time in the budget cycle.
- The organization has recently purchased a competitive product.

If these are true, then it may not in fact be worth your while to proceed—at least not now. But don't give up too easily, as these may only be phantom objections—the DM's proven excuses for brushing off all salespeople. Test the DM's firmness, as in this model:

> "I realize that your budget is particularly tight this year, but I'm confident that what I have to offer will be worth your investment of time. I'll be happy to meet with you at your convenience. Are mornings or afternoons generally better for you?"

2. "I'm not interested."

Probe and Restate to determine why this lack of interest, then Respond Positively, and Move On before you become bogged down on this single issue. In responding positively, you may strengthen your statement of benefits or cite additional successes with other clients.

Often, your probing will uncover that "not interested" really means "not interested in spending time with salespeople." Then you can say,

> "Frankly, Mr. Jordan, most of the lawyers I meet with are just as reluctant as you to spend time. For a professional person, time is money. But it's precisely *because* your time is valuable that I'm calling. I mentioned a moment ago that we were able to save Bell and Haupt five hundred dollars a month in secretarial time. What I didn't mention was how much of the lawyers' time was *also* saved—in the range of several dozen hours per month. Are you willing to invest a half-hour now in order to save dozens of hours each month in the future?"

Or,

> "I understand how you may feel, Mr. Graham. I certainly wouldn't expect you to be interested until I've explained what we have available, and to discuss the many things it will do for you. That's why I think it'll be very productive for us to meet. Would tomorrow or the next day be better?"

3. "You're calling the wrong person."

Probe to find out why the DM is saying this. It may be that you really have come to the wrong person. Perhaps there are two Mr. Robinsons in the company, and this Robinson has nothing at all to do with your specialty.

More often, this will be a case of a senior manager referring you down the chain of command to a subordinate who is more closely involved in the technical details. Thus the DM's response may be phrased as, "My job is to practice law (or run a factory), and I leave decisions about equipment to the office manager."

We address how to deal with this in the following item.

4. "Talk to my subordinate about this."

Keep in mind why you contacted this DM, rather than the subordinate: because your research led you to the conclusion that Authority, Need, and Dollars resided here. Perhaps your information was wrong; perhaps sufficient Authority, Need, and Dollars do rest with the subordinate.

Before moving on, take a moment to check this with your present contact:

> "I'd be pleased to meet with Mr. Bates. But tell me: If he finds a need for what I'm offering, is he cleared to sign on his own authority? Does he have his own budget for this type of work?"

If yes, then it's easy: Move on to the subordinate, as in this case Mr. Bates appears to be a Decision Maker with Authority, Need, and Dollars.

But if the present DM is retaining final control over the decision, then do whatever you reasonably can to keep your own direct link back to him. One of the most frustrating situations you can get into as a marketer occurs when you lose control over your sale, so that you find yourself having to rely on a third party to carry your sales message.

Remember that the subordinate is someone who has only the power to say no—or to carry your message as he interprets it. Your chances of making the sale are slim if you permit yourself to be cut out of the communication loop, so that your only access to the real Decision Maker is indirectly, through the subordinate.

But you can't openly refuse if the DM tries to pass you down to a subordinate. Instead, ask questions: Probe to find out why the DM thinks it best to move your level of contact down lower on the organization chart.

It may be that she is assuming that the subordinate is more appropriate because he is more closely involved in the technical side, and so would have a better sense of the Need for your services.

But without Authority or Dollars, the subordinate can be only a Decision Influencer. Decision Influencers with direct, hands-on awareness of the needs are good to have along as members of the team. But for you to be able to conclude the sale successfully, you *must* have continuing access to the Decision Maker who controls Authority and Dollars in this matter.

Here's a model for making that point and making the case for this DM to remain personally and directly involved:

> "Very frankly, Ms. Haynes, the reason I'm calling on you is because we've found that senior executives in your position tend to be more in tune with the overall needs of the company. Their broader perspective enables them to see how this work can provide a broad, cross-functional impact in several departments. While I agree that Mr. Kraft should be present, I also strongly suggest that you remain personally involved, as well."

When you put it in this context, the DM is likely to agree. That gives you access on a continuing basis. But if the DM won't agree to that, push for at least final access back to the DM, so that it is you, and not the subordinate, who comes back to the DM to summarize the findings and make the recommendations.

> "If Mr. Kraft and I make any significant findings, I would like clearance to come back to you directly, so that we can review our progress and discuss any recommendations that I may find appropriate. Is that agreeable with you? Could we set a tentative time for this follow-up meeting with you? Perhaps two weeks from today?"

By gaining this kind of commitment from the DM at the start, before you move down the line, you safeguard yourself in a number of ways.

First, you test whether this referral downward is just a way of getting rid of you. By pushing for access back to the DM, you force the issue. If the DM is hiding behind a subordinate because he can't say no, it's better to find that out now, before you've wasted time and energy on a lost cause.

Further, by retaining your own channel back to the senior person, you gain "clout" with the subordinate. That subordinate will be far less likely to brush you off or to put you at the bottom of his priority list if he knows that you will be reporting directly back to the DM.

Keep this channel to the DM open as the work progresses by occasional brief phone calls or letters that both keep him informed and remind him of the commitment. For example, it may be appropriate to "copy in" the senior person as memos or written findings are developed. (But don't overwhelm the DM with trivia.)

By keeping that continuing channel active, you'll find it easier to reestablish full contact when you are ready to make a demonstration of the product, or to present a written proposal.

If the DM Won't Agree to Your Continuing Direct Contact

Don't assume you know the real reason. Probe to tap in on the DM's thinking. Perhaps, without saying so explicitly, the DM is implicitly delegating full buying power to the subordinate. But don't take this delegation for granted. Test it by asking something on the order of

> "If Ms. Rigsbee finds our product useful, what will be the purchasing procedure? Will she be able to sign off on her own authority?"

If the answer is yes, then move on to Ms. Rigsbee. If not, try again to set up at least a tentative time to make your presentation to this DM after your work with Ms. Rigsbee has finished.

> "I'll phone Ms. Rigsbee for an appointment as soon as I leave your office. After she has had the chance to see my product, I'd like the opportunity to come back with her as we report our findings to you. Can we set a tentative time to meet with you now? Perhaps two weeks from today—would that be convenient?"

If the DM still says no—both to giving a firm commitment to meet with you later and to delegating purchasing power to the subordinate—then you had better give some serious thought to whether it's likely to prove worth your while to proceed any further.

A Decision Maker's unwillingness to commit to a follow-up meeting with you usually means one of three things, none of them promising. He may be indicating that he's just not very interested in your product or service. Or he may be implicitly admitting that he's afraid to make the decision, and would rather pass the responsibility on to the subordinate—though still keeping control of the Authority and Dollars. Or, he is implicitly admitting that he doesn't want to say no to your face, and is hoping that either you take the hint and go away or the subordinate will do the dirty work for him.

None of these are positive signs that your investment of time and effort in meeting with the subordinate will pay off for you.

So, given that situation, should you go ahead anyway and make your pitch to the subordinate, in the hope that he'll do as good a job of carrying your message to the

DM as you can? Of course there is always hope, but the odds of that are so slim that rarely will it be worth your while. No one else can do half the sales job that you can, so why waste your time? It's probably better to use that time finding a better prospect.

5. "I'm too busy."

Probe to find what's really behind this "too busy." Perhaps what the DM really means is that she is temporarily pressed for time. If so, respond,

> "I recognize that I may have caught you at a very hectic time. Perhaps it would be more convenient if I called you back. Perhaps the middle of next week, or would two weeks be better?"

Offering the alternative choice here is essential; otherwise the DM is likely to say, "I'll give you a call as soon as things settle down." Odds on, that call will never come. Never let control over timing of callbacks slip out of your hands.

On the other hand, perhaps the DM is permanently overwhelmed by an unending workflow. This gives you a superb opening if what you're selling offers a way of easing that burden:

> "I appreciate that you are busy. Most successful executives are extremely busy. In fact, it's specifically to help you ease some of this pressure that I want to meet with you. I can show you how you can free yourself from routine tasks that are eating up your productive work time. I'm asking you to invest a half-hour of your time now in order to save many times that in the longer term. That makes a lot of sense, don't you think?"

6. "Are you trying to sell me something?"

This is a bluff used to scare away weak salespeople. Don't be put off. There's nothing illegal or immoral about trying to make a sale.

But the question does put you in a bind. You can't very well deny that you are trying to make a sale, when in fact that is precisely why you are calling. One good way of countering the question is,

> "Frankly, it would be very premature to propose a sale at this time. What I first recommend is that we meet personally and discuss your present situation, and how our capabilities may benefit your organization."

Or,

> "Yes, I am trying to sell you something. I'm trying to sell you increased profitability."

Note the unexpected effect here, as you propose to sell not a "thing," but rather a result. Who could reasonably refuse to talk about a way of increasing profits? Or of reducing costs or overhead?

7. "Tell me what you have over the phone. Tell me how much it costs."

Since the Decision Maker can't sign the order over the phone, you obviously can't *make* the sale. But you *can* lose it if the DM hears just enough to decide not to meet with you.

The request puts you in a bind. Clearly, you can't directly refuse to talk, as the DM in turn would refuse to meet. Here are a couple of models for finessing it:

Telemarketing as a Selling Strategy

This caution—never try to sell over the phone—is meant for a product or service that needs face-to-face contact to be sold effectively.

But there are items that can be sold successfully over the phone—and others that can be sold successfully *only* that way.

In the right situations, telephone marketing (or "telemarketing") can be a very productive and cost-effective strategy. It may be the best approach for you. My caution here is against trying to sell over the phone when a face-to-face approach is needed.

If your product or service is one that can be sold by phone, then use that route; it will usually be far cheaper than making face-to-face calls. (Telemarketing tends to be appropriate for low-cost items, or generic items where your main sales message is that you are less expensive than your competition.)

But if your product or service needs face-to-face contact, then you can only *lose* the sale, but not *make* it, over the phone.

> "Mr. Welch, we're in the business of solving problems for our clients, rather than pushing hardware. Until I've met with you, and discussed your interests and needs, I have no way of knowing what we may recommend, or what it might cost."

Or,

> "We're a consulting firm, and most of our recommendations involve the use of data processing equipment, but in a variety of contexts. I would need to see you and discuss your needs before I can be more precise."

8. "Send me some information on this in the mail. Then we'll talk."

Some Decision Makers prefer to read before meeting with salespeople, in the belief that will make the face-to-face discussion more productive. That's understandable from their point of view.

But keep in mind that you are ultimately selling not products or services, but rather the solutions to problems. It's all but impossible for a brochure to make that point as clearly as you can. Brochures can't ask the questions that open fresh possibilities.

Your brochure can only help the DM see what the product (or service) *is*; few brochures are as able as you to help him see what the product can *do*.

> "I understand your position, Mr. Thompson, and it is possible for me to mail you a brochure. But the services we offer are targeted to the client's specific needs, and so I believe it would be more effective if we were to meet in person. This would give me the chance to analyze your areas of specific need. When we meet, I can leave you a brochure. More important, I can provide you some additional ideas targeted to your specific interests."

Then add, without pausing for his reply,

> "I can drop off the brochure and meet with you on Tuesday morning or Thursday right after lunch. Which would be more convenient?"

Or,

> "Checking my calendar, I see I'll be in your area on Tuesday afternoon. If we can meet for a few minutes then, I'll drop the brochure off person-

> ally. That will be faster than the mail, and I'll be able to answer any questions that you may have."

If the DM's response remains, "Send it first," don't close the door by pushing too hard. Agree to mail what she requests, but make it clear that you will be following it up soon:

> "I'll be happy to send the information today, then I'll check back with you later in the week, after you've had a chance to look it over."

It's crucial to make it clear from the start that you *will* be following up on the material you mail. Some people use "send literature" as a way of brushing off salespeople. By making it clear from the start that you will be actively following up soon, you sort out those who are genuinely interested from those who are interested only in getting rid of you. You don't want to turn anyone off, yet there is no point in wasting postage because the supposed Decision Maker can't make a decision.

9. "We already tried something like your product, and we're just not interested."

Probe to find what that "similar" product was, and the precise reasons why they decided against it.

Once you know the reasons, treat them as objections, Restating and Responding Positively to each point. Show either how your product is totally different from the other product, or how it avoids the difficulties the DM encountered previously.

When you probe regarding that other time the DM's organization tried something, you may find that the DM's responses are vague. It may be that he does not have a clear memory of just what went wrong before. Or it may be that he is throwing out "already tried it" as a way of shooing you off.

If the DM has no clear answers when you ask why the previous trial was unsatisfactory, take a further step: Ask leading questions covering the most likely reasons, then rebut them.

You might ask, "Was it cost that put you off [the competing product]?"

The DM might answer, "You bet. It was just too expensive."

Respond, "Then you'll be interested to know that our new Model Ten costs 30 percent less, and typically pays for itself within the first year, through increased productivity."

If You Get a Series of Objections, One after Another

Probe each of these objections. But if you keep getting a new objection as soon as you resolve the last, something is wrong. A customer might have two or three, or occasionally even five objections or concerns. To get more than that indicates that something deeper is going on.

You can address the issue directly:

> "We've discussed a number of your concerns, and I think I've dealt satisfactorily with each of them. But when I encounter this many objections, that's usually a signal to me that there's a deeper concern operating. Can you help me with what that might be?"

That may spur the DM to open up and raise the deeper issue. But sometimes the string of objections is used to disguise something that he's perhaps embarrassed to talk about. It could be that, despite what he said earlier, he doesn't have the Authority, Need, or Dollars. Or maybe there has been a reshuffling in the organization and his position has suddenly become insecure, and he doesn't feel free to buy anything, yet doesn't want to talk about it.

Summary

In this chapter we focused on responding to early objections—ones that you will generally hear early in the call, even as early as when you phone for an appointment.

The basic framework for dealing with objections is Probe, Restate, Respond Positively, then Move On. (Though each step is important, don't be compulsive about the process: for example, if the Decision Maker is impatient, you might cut the Restate step to move things on more in keeping with his tempo.)

Specific early objections to be prepared for are:

1. "You'd only be wasting your time."
2. "I'm not interested."
3. "You're calling the wrong person."
4. "Talk to my subordinate about this."
5. "I'm too busy."
6. "Are you trying to sell me something?"
7. "Tell me what you have over the phone. Tell me how much it costs."
8. "Send me some information by mail. Then we'll talk."
9. "We already tried something like your product, and we're just not interested."

Application Exercise

Focus on a few of these early objections, emphasizing those that are likely to be most important to you. Reread the model scripts provided, and "translate" them to wording appropriate to your product or service and to your own way of speaking.

Rehearse these responses, both mentally and speaking aloud, so that they come quickly to mind, and so that you can say them easily and comfortably.

Chapter 24

Handling Core Objections

In Chapter 22, we examined the basic model for reacting to objections and difficult questions: Probe, Restate, Respond Positively, Move On. Then in Chapter 23 we focused on ways of responding to specific early objections—the kind of roadblocks the Decision Maker or Screen may throw up to avoid meeting with you.

In this chapter, we shift to methods of dealing with late or core objections. These are the objections or hesitations that focus on the heart of the matter—that is, on the fundamental question of whether or not the DM will buy.

Although you can encounter these core objections at any time during the sales process, they most commonly arise after you have asked the DM to buy, or to make some other kind of buying commitment.

Though here we discuss specific strategies for coping with the objections, keep in mind that your response should always be within the overall Four-Step response framework: Probe, Restate, Respond Positively, Move On.

The wording the DM uses in expressing the core objection will vary. Sometimes the objection is expressed more by nonverbal indicators than by the words used. In the items following, you'll find some of these indicators, but be open to other cues that you encounter.

1. The customer's sense of need for what you offer is not strong enough to motivate her to sign the order.

Indicators: No apparent interest, or only lukewarm enthusiasm, expressed in phrases such as, "Well, I don't know," or, "Maybe later, but right now we have more pressing needs."

Low enthusiasm may also be expressed by nonverbal signals, such as minimal eye contact, low energy in the voice, apparent boredom or distraction, slumping back in the chair, or general diffidence in manner.

Other indicators include absence of any questions or comments, minimal or indifferent response to the questions you ask, and a general "ho-hum, so-what" demeanor.

Remedy: Use the Four-Step process to define the real objection—Probe, Restate, Respond Positively, Move On. If a specific objection comes out, react to it.

If no clear problem emerges, recycle back to the Selling Wedge sequence of questions (Chapter 10), and try again to develop or enhance the DM's sense of need for your product. In doing this, you may try to develop the DM's awareness in greater depth of the practical implications of the needs that you already discussed. Alternatively, you may look for additional needs.

2. The customer is not convinced that your product offers good value.

Indicators: Phrases such as, "I don't think we can justify the cost," or, "Too expensive," or, "I frankly don't think it's worth the money to us."

Remedy: Cycle back to the wedge sequence of selling questions (Chapter 10) to further develop the Decision Maker's awareness of the various types of value offered by your product or service as it would help this specific organization.

3. Although the DM recognizes that a need does exist, she is not convinced that what you offer can in fact fill that need.

Indicators: Phrases such as, "It's an attractive package, but I'm not sure it can do the job for us," or, "How can I be sure it'll do what you say?"

Other indicators include a series of technical questions that focus on specific details of what you propose. These signal that the prospect is testing whether your product has the capability of fulfilling all you promise.

Remedy: Use the Four-Step process—Probe, Restate, Respond Positively, Move On—to find the specific area of doubt. Then offer a proof source that is appropriate to that concern.

What type of proof source to use will vary with both the circumstances and the kinds of concerns the DM is expressing:

- One proof source might be a demonstration of your product in action to show how it works, or how it will fill the specific need.
- Or you may demonstrate sample products.
- Or the appropriate proof source might be a written proposal showing how you arrived at the cost savings you promise.
- References from similar organizations that have successfully used your product or services to solve related needs can also serve as very effective proof sources.

Part 7 provides guidance on the major kinds of proof sources available, and when and how to use them.

4. Although the DM recognizes that significant needs exist, he is not convinced that your product is the best available way of filling those needs.

Indicators: Phrases such as, "In my mind, Microsoft has always been the standard of the marketplace, and I'm reluctant to change" or, "We've been looking at the Remco Whizzer. How does your product differ from that?"

Additionally, a series of technical questions may indicate that the customer is comparing your product with that of others she has studied—which means that she is exploring the idea of buying a product like yours. So apparently the need is clear to the DM, and what is now at issue is whether your product is the one that can best and most cost-effectively fill that Need.

Remedy: Subtly Probe to find which of your competitors are also on the DM's short list, and why. That information gives you some clues as to what capabilities are of particular interest.

Target your responses accordingly. Restate your understanding. Respond Positively by detailing the specific ways in which your product is better than the competing product the DM is most interested in.

As you Respond Positively, avoid going to either extreme, speaking only in generalities, without offering any evidence to back up what you say, or becoming bogged down in technical details, without establishing the overall context.

In presenting your proof, set the context with a general statement, then offer back-up detail to prove your general statement. Here's a model:

> "The GEM 4000 provides a 30 percent higher output than the Remco Whizzer. For example, in an independent lab study comparing the two units, the GEM 4000 turned out an average of 130 widgets per hour over an eight-hour span, while the Remco Whizzer, which advertises 100 per hour, actually averaged only 80 per hour. In addition, the Whizzer broke down three times during the test period."

5. The DM seems both to recognize the need and to like your product, but claims that no money is available.

Lack of money or insufficient cash flow can be a real concern. But "no dough" is often used as a phantom objection either to hide a deeper concern or to brush you off. Use the Four-Step process (Probe, Restate, Respond Positively, Move On) to determine which is the case here. Useful questions in probing this issue include

- "Would it change things if we could arrange a lease in order to reduce the front-end payment?"
- "We do have an economy model, which I'd be pleased to demonstrate at your convenience. Perhaps tomorrow at this same time?"

If nothing else seems to break through, you might try this: "Suppose for the moment that it were possible for me to cut the price in half—would you buy in that case?" (This is useful as a way of probing for a suspected phantom objection. But make it clear from the start that this is a "just suppose." You don't want the DM to think that you are actually offering this large a reduction.)

6. The customer says in effect, "I like it. But not now."

There are situations when the present is truly not a good time to buy. But more frequently, "not now" is a phantom objection that you need to dissolve in order to find out what's really behind the DM's reluctance.

In probing here, ask questions on the order of

> "We've explored the facts, and found that this improvement can save your company over $2,000 per month. With savings like this possible, how can you hesitate when each passing month means another $2,000 slipping away?"

There may be genuine reasons why no purchasing decision can be made at this time, such as low cash flow or the fact that you have arrived at the wrong phase of the annual purchasing cycle. If that's the case, at least keep the door open to future business by agreeing on a callback date.

7. The "final" objection.

Sometimes you'll find that as soon as you handle one question or objection, the prospect raises another. A few objections are to be expected, but an endless stream of them usually means that the DM is dancing away. Here's a way of taking one of those objections and making it the DM's *final* objection.

Basically you use a modified form of the Four-Step process for responding to objections: Probe to find the core concern, then Restate that concern in your own words "so that you can better understand it."

As you restate this objection, make a point of agreeing with the DM on the importance of the objection. You might even reinforce the significance of the point by saying something on the order of, "I can understand the importance of this concern. I agree that the equipment would not be of much value to you unless it could [whatever is relevant to your product]."

Then go on to say, "In fact, that's probably the only thing standing between us, isn't it? If my equipment could do [whatever the objection relates to], then you would probably buy—right?" The DM will usually agree.

Next, carry the point further by asking the DM to explain the point of his concern. "Just to clarify my thinking, why is this particular capability so important to you?"

Your point here is to determine if this is the real, most basic objection. You will probably get one of three kinds of responses:

- *He will explain why this issue is of particular importance* to him. In this case, he becomes committed to the position. Respond to it using the Four-Step process, and conclude by asking for the order. It's only natural for you to ask for the order, since the DM has already admitted that he would buy if you could show that your product can overcome the difficulty.
- Or, while he is trying to explain the importance of his concern, *he will touch on the real objection.* He may not even have been consciously aware of it until that point, so listen carefully both to what is said and to what is implied, so that you can spot this buried objection. Then use the Four-Step process to respond to that objection.
- Or, in the course of explaining why it is important to him, *he will realize that the concern sounds silly when put into words,* and drop the point. Move On, probably by closing for the order or other kind of buying action.

Keeping Yourself and Your Product in the DM's Mind

If wait you must, look for ways of reminding the DM over the succeeding weeks and months that you still exist and want the business. For example, in the course of your travels, you may come upon a news clipping in an out-of-town publication that the DM may not have seen and that is relevant to his business or industry. Send it, along with your business card and a short note: "For Your Information" or, "Thought you might find this of interest."

Also, be sure to send the DM a copy of your newest brochure or catalog when it comes off the press, along with a short personal note. The note need not be long, just something on the order of, "Here's our new brochure. As you will notice, we have introduced several new features since we talked in October. I recall your mentioning then that planning for your upcoming fiscal year begins in June, and I will be in contact with you then."

SUMMARY

The basic framework for dealing with objections and tough questions is Probe, Restate, Respond Positively, Move On. Keep that in mind as the basic model. Using that framework, along with the specific responses addressed in this chapter, be prepared for common core objections, such as these:

1. The customer's sense of need for what you offer is not strong enough to motivate her to sign.
2. The customer is not convinced that the product is a good value for the money.
3. Although the customer recognizes that a need does exist, she is not convinced that what you offer can truly fill that need.
4. The DM recognizes that the need exists, but is not convinced that you are offering the best possible solution.
5. The DM seems to be in favor of what you offer, but claims that no money is available.
6. The customer says in effect, "I like it. But I don't want to buy now."

APPLICATION EXERCISE

First task: Again focus on the two or three of these core objections that are likely to be most significant to you. Adapt the model responses provided in the sections above to your own product and personal style. Rehearse your responses, so that you can say them comfortably and with conviction.

Second task: As you sell, make a practice of jotting down the key indicators—both verbal and nonverbal—of these and other objections. Also, as you encounter other objections, jot them down as well, then develop your own model responses.

Chapter 25

Dealing with Other Problems with the Decision Maker

Although the "other problems" that we'll be looking at in this chapter are not objections in the normal sense of the word, the same Four-Step process (Probe, Restate, Respond Positively, then Move On) helps in getting to the core of the difficulty.

1. You hear an endless string of objections.

It seems that as soon as you demolish one objection, the prospect raises another, and then another. A string of relatively insignificant objections, thrown out one after the other, usually signals that there is a deeper underlying problem that you have not dealt with.

Before you can make any progress, you *must* break out of the pattern of reacting to these one by one, and Probe to the core of the root difficulty. (Often, the DM herself is not consciously aware of just what that ultimate difficulty is, but has a vague feeling of unease about the situation.)

Sometimes the customer may throw up this string of objections because she's embarrassed to admit that she doesn't have as much buying authority as she had claimed, or that the rules of the game in the organization have changed since you first talked, so that her authority has been diminished.

Or it may be that although she does have Authority, Need, and Dollars, she is worried about the economic climate over the next few months.

How do you deal with the string of objections? As always, Probe, Restate, Respond Positively, then Move On.

But in this case, you'll need to be flexible and creative in how you probe. For example, you could begin by confronting the hesitation head on, in hopes of unblocking the DM's root concerns:

> "You're raising a variety of issues, but I sense that there's a deeper concern that's troubling you."

If that doesn't break through, draw on a combination of intuition and experience, and say something on the order of, "I sense that behind your hesitation may be some concerns about which way the economy is heading. Could that be at the core of it?"

If the customer concedes that yes, what you suggest is indeed the root cause, then Respond Positively to it. Do not slip into a defensive mode.

Thus, if the concern is the economic climate, you could respond by showing how the savings resulting from installing your product will more than pay for the out-of-pocket expense. Thus the purchase would make sense regardless of the direction the economy takes.

2. You realize, after encountering a series of phantom objections, that this person does not in fact have the necessary Authority, Need, or Dollars.

Indicators: You make your presentation and feel that there is interest on the DM's part. But then you encounter a string of weak objections, one after another.

Look through the objections to what is being said underneath. Perhaps the person is ultimately saying, "I can't really make that decision" or "I can't make it alone." Sometimes Decision Makers suddenly find that they don't have as much authority as they assumed they had. Perhaps your proposal surprised them by coming in above their purchasing limit. Or perhaps they have picked up on changing political undercurrents in the organization, and realize that it's prudent to get higher-level sign-offs to cover themselves.

Remedy: If you find out fairly late in the sales cycle that your contact really does not have full Authority, Need, or Dollars, you have two main choices:

1. You can withdraw from the call at this point, and attempt to reestablish your contact with the organization at a higher level.

   But if you leapfrog over your present contact, his feelings may be hurt by your going over his head, and you may lose a friend. It may turn out that although he's not the Decision Maker, he may be a significant *influencer* of the final decision. Or you may come back a few months from now to find that the person you cut around is now sitting in the Decision Maker's chair.

2. It usually works out better to try to move upward to the appropriate level, *while taking this person with you.* That gives you the chance to make your case directly to the DM, and at the same time gives the present contact an opportunity to gain favorable exposure to a senior manager in a way that he might not otherwise have been able to arrange on his own.

   To accomplish this shift, you might say,

   > "I agree with you, and I'd be very pleased to meet with Mr. Jackson. I'd like you to come with me when I make that call. Shall I set up an appointment with Mr. Jackson, or would you prefer to do it for us?"

   If the present contact agrees to set up the appointment with the senior manager, set a time to check back with him to confirm the date. The knowledge that you will be checking back reduces the likelihood of procrastination.

   However, if you do try back a couple of times with this contact, and each time you find that he still has not made the call, step in and offer to make the call yourself.

3. For some reason, you and the DM seem to grate on each other's nerves.

You may be able to defuse this hostility simply by articulating what you are picking up:

DON'T DELEGATE THE SALE

When the sale moves up to a higher level within the organization, make sure that you move up with it.

You can count on your message being garbled if you let someone else try to do your selling for you. No matter how enthusiastic this other person is, the reality is that he does not know your product and its capabilities the way you do. He simply won't be able to handle the senior manager's questions and objections.

Besides, a lower-level manager will tend not to be very aggressive in following through, or in pushing for a yes decision. After all, naturally enough, his main objective is to keep his job, not to make a sale for you.

> "Mr. Roberts, I sense that for some reason you and I got off on the wrong foot. I don't know why this happened, but I'd like to try to overcome it."

It may well be that the DM's tension has nothing to do with you at all. Perhaps you walked in just after a rough session with his supervisor.

If you can't salvage the situation reasonably quickly, then it may be best to cut your losses and move on—either to a different prospect organization or to another person within this present organization.

Sometimes all it takes is to come back and make a fresh start another day.

4. It appears that the DM is displeased with or hostile to your organization, or is concerned about the risks of dealing with a small entrepreneur.

If doubts exist, there's no point hiding your head in the sand. Probe to find the root cause of the customer's doubts. Bring them out in the open so that you can deal with them. Use the Four-Step process: Probe, Restate Positively, Respond, then Move On.

5. You realize that this individual is psychologically incapable of making a decision.

There's no easy solution to this one. When possible, you can attempt to maneuver the decision to a higher level in the organization by helping the indecisive person find someone to whom he can pass the buck—perhaps his boss, or a committee or task force.

The DM may even be open to delegating the decision downward to a subordinate who is strong enough to step in and fill the vacuum.

6. You discover that the organization actually has no need for what you offer.

If you're certain of this, admit it as soon as you know it. This saves both your own and the Decision Maker's valuable time.

Even more important, it projects your professionalism. The gesture builds goodwill and credibility with the customer—useful currency if you should want to call again in the future when your product or their needs change.

In any case, *keep the door open for later callbacks*. Leave product literature for their files. Offer to put them on your mailing list for any new product announcements, special offers, and the like.

And, as always, ask for referrals—people or organizations that the DM thinks may have a need for your product.

SUMMARY

Although, strictly speaking, they are neither questions nor objections, these special problems that arise in your relationship with the DM can usually be defused by using the four-step process: Probe, Restate, Respond Positively, Move On.

1. You hear an endless string of objections.
2. You realize, after encountering a series of phantom objections, that this person does not in fact have the necessary Authority, Need or Dollars.
3. For some reason, you and the DM seem to grate on each other's nerves.
4. It appears that the DM is displeased with or hostile to your organization, or is concerned about the risks of dealing with a small entrepreneur.
5. You realize that this individual is psychologically incapable of making a decision.
6. You discover that the organization actually has no need for what you offer.

Part Seven
Presenting Your Proof

In Part 7, we focus on using "proof sources." What is a proof source? Basically, anything that's helpful to you in proving any part of the case you made to the Decision Maker.

Precisely what it is that you need to prove will depend on what came up in the course of your discussions with the DM and others. Recall the point made earlier: Organizations, and the Decision Makers within them, buy only when they arrive at solid yes answers to four questions:

1. **Do we face a need?**
2. **Is that need significant enough to justify our spending some money to fill it?**
3. **Will this product or service actually fill that need?**
4. **Will it fill the need better or more cost-effectively than other approaches?**

The DM may be ready to sign immediately, requiring no further proof. Alternatively, the DM may articulate precisely what does need to be proved. But if the DM can't spell that out, then these four questions, turned around, suggest the corresponding areas which may require more proof. Thus you may need to prove,

1. That there is a *need.*
2. That the need is *significant enough* to justify spending money to fill it.
3. That what you are offering will *fill that need* (or needs).
4. That it will *fill the need better* and more cost-effectively than any other approach, either within the organization or through your competitors.

But there is usually another point that may also need to be proven before the sale can be made:

5. That you and your organization are reliable, experienced, professional, trustworthy, and likely to remain in business at least long enough to fulfill your obligations under this sale.

To ascertain which of these (or other matters) are at issue, talk with the DM, ask questions and listen well, attending to both the spoken and unspoken concerns to isolate what is still at issue and needing proof. Then select a proof source that can effectively back up your case. Among the more generally helpful sources of proof are these:

- *Samples* of your work, or of the output produced by your product or service
- *Demonstrations* of your product (or yourself) in action
- *Case studies of successful projects and references* from satisfied customers, most often evidencing your reliability
- *Written proposals*, most often to document costs or cost savings, or to put in writing assurances about timing, warranty, and the like

In the chapters in this part, we'll focus on the when-to and how-to of the most common proof sources: presentations, demonstrations, and proposals. Use the same basic approach when you're using other kinds of proof sources.

Crucial First Step before Developing Any Proof: Obtaining a "Gentleperson's Agreement"

Before you invest time or effort in developing any kind of proof source, be sure to get agreement from the key Decision Maker on three key points:

First, that the key people, especially the Decision Maker, will be present for your personal delivery of the agreed-upon proof. That may mean committing to attend your formal presentation or demonstration, or reviewing work samples or trials.

Second, precisely what the proof source (whatever form it takes) needs to prove. There is no point in your proving A if the DM's concern is whether the product can accomplish B.

Third, that you have a "Gentleperson's Agreement" that if you do prove certain agreed-upon points, the Decision Maker will be prepared to sign an order.

It is true that by asking for these three commitments up front, you are asking a lot in advance from the DM; there is a risk that the DM may not agree to these points.

On the other hand, developing a proof source (such as writing a proposal) involves a considerable investment of time and energy on your part. It also involves "opportunity cost"—the time you spend developing this proof for this prospect is time taken away from working with other potential clients. The Decision Maker can't reasonably expect you to make this investment of time and opportunity cost unless he is seriously interested, and ready to commit.

For these reasons, it's only fair that the DM should *commit in advance* to these three very reasonable conditions:

- *to be personally involved—and physically present*, not just through a subordinate—for the review of the proof you present, whether that is to be a demonstration, presentation of a proposal, or whatever else is agreed upon; and,
- *to define clearly in advance just what needs to be proven*; and,
- *to agree to buy if you do prove these agreed-upon factors.*

What if the DM Won't Commit to the "Gentleperson's Agreement?"

What if the DM is not willing to agree to these conditions? Then it's better to be realistic from the start: if the DM is unwilling to make that commitment, ask yourself if there is any real point in proceeding with the proof... at least until you have addressed the underlying reasons for his unwillingness to make that agreement.

Insisting on that Gentleperson's Agreement is a subtle but effective way of ensuring that the person is serious about having you proceed, *and* of ensuring that he has the level of Authority, Need, and Dollars that he claims to have.

If the DM balks at this agreement, Probe to determine why. If it is something that you can deal with, do so.

But if you hear only a variety of nebulous excuses, then it's usually best to cut your losses and move on. True, you will have wasted your effort up to this point. But without this kind of agreement, the chances are that you will only waste more time and effort on a lost-cause, dead-end effort.

Some salespeople are reluctant to push for this kind of Gentleperson's Agreement, believing that it is better not to ask the customer for anything at all until they finally ask for the order. I think that's not a wise strategy. For one thing, it projects low confidence in the value of your product or service. If what you're selling's good, you don't have to give it away.

Besides, if you fail to get a commitment from the DM, then the risk is all on your side: you invest time, energy, and your opportunity cost, while the DM invests nothing, not even committing to be on hand for the hour it would take for you to present your proof source. People tend to value that which costs: if all the cost is on your part, then the DM probably won't value the result as much as if he had to invest some of the cost as well. Don't commit yourself unless you get a commitment from the DM in return.

Chapter 26

Your Presentation as a Proof Source

It's a waste of an opportunity to merely mail a proposal or other proof source, or simply drop it off at the Decision Maker's office and hope it will work its magic. If you do that, chances are that it will get pushed to the bottom of the pile, and nothing will happen.

By personally "presenting" your proposal, work sample, or other kind of proof source, you ensure that the Decision Maker attends to it on a guaranteed date, while it is still relevant. You'll generally get a speedier response. Further, by retaining control, you ensure that you *will* get a response—it won't just get buried under other mail.

You also gain the opportunity to test the atmosphere during your presentation, to clear up any difficulties, and, if necessary, to negotiate any final issues that stand in the way of the sale.

But a "presentation," in the sense we're using the word here, means a great deal more than merely walking in and handing the proposal to the DM. *Your presentation is a key selling opportunity*, as it gives you the chance to summarize for the Decision Maker and key Decision Influencers the core messages of your proposal, and to respond to their concerns.

Here are some tips for ensuring that your presentation becomes a strong selling tool.

1. "Touch base" early with the key Decision Influencers.

"Decision Influencers," as we examined in Chapter 3, are people who, while they don't have the final yes authority, still have significant input on how the actual Decision Maker calls it.

Precisely who the Decision Influencers are will vary with the organization and situation. They will usually include the heads of the departments that actually use your product, and perhaps some of the hands-on users of the product, as well. The DI's may also include the DM's key financial adviser, the firm's most experienced technical specialist in this area, or the DM's trusted secretary.

While Decision Influencers are usually below the Decision Maker on the organization chart, they *can* be higher-level people, such as the DM's mentor.

Therefore, as your proposal nears completion, phone these Decision Influencers, especially department heads and others who have been helpful, and briefly outline some of your findings. Do this both as a courtesy to them and as a way of eliciting helpful feedback. If they have concerns, it is generally better to deal with the issues now, while you can still amend or correct the proposal, than to be caught off-guard in front of the Decision Maker.

A further advantage can be gained by bringing Decision Influencers in at this point: You give them a sense of *shared ownership* of the end product. As a result, you develop allies who may be helpful when the big day comes.

However, the final call on whether to invite these Decision Influencers to the presentation is the Decision Maker's. You can discreetly sound out whether the influencers would be free to attend a meeting on certain dates, but don't overstep by inviting them on your own.

2. Get a specific appointment from the DM for presenting the proposal.

Earlier, as part of the precommitment you gained from the DM before starting the proposal, you got the DM to agree to set aside uninterrupted time for this presentation. (On this, see the introduction to this part.)

Now, when the proposal is ready (or is nearing completion), call the DM to settle on a time for this appointment. How long to ask for will vary. But, as a rule, try to work within the range of twenty to forty-five minutes, depending on the dollars involved and the complexity of the situation. In estimating the time you need, be sure to allow for questions and discussion.

When you call for the appointment, make clear from the start that you will need a block of uninterrupted time, free from phone calls and other interruptions:

> "This meeting should take about thirty minutes. I'd very much appreciate it if you can arrange to have your phone calls held for that time. Will that be possible?"

Be ready in case the DM responds, "Oh, it's not necessary for us to meet. Just mail me the proposal and I'll look it over and get back to you shortly."

Don't believe it. You have invested significant time and effort in preparing the proposal; make sure you get the benefit by personally presenting it. Even though the Decision Maker may have the best intentions of reading it later, it never works out as planned, as other calls and crises intervene.

However, getting into a "But you promised to be present" mode is counterproductive. Instead, try to finesse it in a tactful way. For example, you might explain that there are some options that you need to raise with the key people. Or that in the course of developing the proposal (or the survey on which the data was based), you came up with some broader recommendations beyond the scope of the proposal. (Obviously, promise only what you can deliver.)

Before concluding the call, find out from the DM precisely who will be present at that meeting.

The DM herself—that is, the person (or group) with Authority, Need, and Dollars—*must* be present. *Do not* give the presentation until this Decision Maker (or DM team) will commit to being present—even if that means waiting a month or more.

Though the choice of who to invite is the DM's, you can suggest that some of the Decision Influencers who were helpful (and who seem to be supporters of your proposal) also be present. Mention their names, as "they contributed some extremely helpful ideas."

3. In your preparation, focus on key selling messages.

When you're planning the presentation, decide what are the few really crucial points you want to make. These are the "hot buttons" to get the buyers excited, and the items you want them to leave remembering. Concentrate on these. It's far better to present a few core messages clearly than to spread yourself too thin, sowing confusion.

Prepare to the point where you can talk through the key messages. In the meeting room, you want to project that you are fully in control of your material. If *you* can't remember your key points without reading or looking at your notes, how can you expect the DM and DIs to remember what you have said?

4. "Own" your block of time.

You have invested your time and expertise in addressing a problem on behalf of this organization. You obtained the DM's "Gentleperson's Agreement" to set aside this time, in exchange for your investment of effort.

This block of time, therefore, *belongs to you. Act like you own it,* not as if the DM and others are doing you a favor by listening.

The first step to "owning" your time comes as you arrive for the presentation: Remind the Decision Maker that she will want to have all calls held.

Next, control the copies of the proposal and other handouts. Hand out the written proposal only after you have talked through the overview and other key points. If you give out the proposal too early, you'll find yourself talking to a sea of scalps as the attendees focus on reading the handouts, ignoring what you're saying.

It's crucial for you to control the group's attention focus, so that they all attend to your central messages at the same time. For one thing, keep the copies of the proposal in your briefcase, out of sight. If you stack them on the table, one of the early arrivals will pick up a copy and start flipping through the pages. One by one, the others will do the same. At that point, you will have lost them, and the DM will wonder why you made such an issue of asking for presentation time, since you obviously only meant to get everyone together to do a group reading.

Prepare visual aids to focus your key messages. Consider using overhead transparencies if a large group will be present. With smaller groups, such as three or four people sitting around a conference table, a simple notebook-size A-frame may be ideal.

In deciding whether to use overheads or other media, call the DM's secretary a few days ahead to find out how large the meeting room will be, and to get a final count of how many people will be present.

If you use handouts, use them with caution. Make them outlines only; otherwise, you'll find your audience reading the text, ignoring what you're saying.

5. Stay within your agreed-upon time frame.

If the Decision Maker gave you the uninterrupted time you asked for, then fulfill your part of the bargain by finishing on time.

But what if there are significant interruptions? Very likely, the Decision Maker will signal flexibility in giving extra time to compensate for the minutes you lost.

If he does not, and if you really do need the time, ask the Decision Maker's permission to make up the time: "I had structured this around a thirty-minute period, but we did lose about ten minutes. With your permission I'll finish and still hold within my overall limit of thirty minutes. Is that agreeable?"

6. Close with a close.

Closing by asking for what you want is the natural punctuation mark concluding your presentation. You'll find that unless you *do* conclude with a close, the presentation will have an unfinished feeling. You'll generally sense the Decision Maker and others floundering, with a feeling of "Where do we go from here? What do we do now? What do you want from us?"

In most cases, the best way of closing at the end of a presentation is to introduce the Action Plan you propose for implementing your recommendations. (For details, see item 3 in Chapter 18, "Asking the Decision Maker to Take Buying Action.")

If you close with an Action Plan, your final visual aid should outline your proposed installation plan, detailing the steps you will take and the steps to be taken by the client. Use "real-time" dates specific to this prospect (e.g., "June 11"), not generic timelines (like "twenty-one days after signing").

Be prepared to negotiate dates and action steps. It's probably a buying signal if the DM or other key members of the customer team begin discussing or negotiating dates and other details. That indicates that they have "bought" the basic concept and are now only fine-tuning the implementation details.

SUMMARY

If you agree to invest time and effort to develop a report or proposal, get agreement up front that the DM will be personally present for your presentation of it. A presentation is a brief oral summary that gives you the chance to test the climate, to emphasize the key points, and to respond to any questions, concerns, or objections.

1. Keep in contact with the key Decision Influencers and others who have contributed to your effort. They can be allies when it comes to selling the conclusions. By keeping them "in the loop" as you put your findings together, you help them feel a sense of ownership of the solution that has evolved.
2. Get a specific appointment for your presentation. Be prepared if the DM asks you to forgo the presentation and instead mail the report or proposal. Don't let that happen. Have a response ready, perhaps that there are options to be weighed, or that some new ideas or broader issues came up.
3. Focus on your key selling messages. Target what is really important, and concentrate on that. If the DM wants to know more, she will ask.
4. Project ownership of your block of time. At the start, suggest that the DM have phone calls held. Control distribution of the copies of your handouts.
5. Stay within the time agreed upon. But if the DM breaks up the time by taking a phone call or stepping out of the room to deal with a crisis, don't hesitate to ask for additional time at the end to make it up.
6. Close with a close. Don't just talk of your findings. Strike while interest is high and ask for the order. Until you ask, *nothing* is likely to happen.

Chapter 27

Using Demonstrations as Proof Sources

Keep in mind that you use proof sources such as demonstrations, proposals, and formal presentations, for only one reason: to prove that what you are selling can meet the needs that are of prime importance to the customer.

Your product (or service) may do many things, but probably only certain of those capabilities will really matter to this customer. Normally, those will directly tie in with the needs that turned out to be of particular importance during your earlier sales work with the DM.

Thus if the DM agreed that certain needs were vital, then your demonstration should prove how your product can fill those needs, both effectively and cost-effectively. (You would lock this in as part of the Gentleperson's Agreement we discussed in the introduction to this part.)

A reminder: As proof sources, demonstrations are to *demonstrate*—that is, to *show*. Don't let your words get in the way. Let the product or work sample do most of the talking.

The Six Key Phases of a Demo or Formal Presentation

As we begin this chapter, we assume that you have finished all the preliminaries, and that the day of your demonstration (or presentation) is here.

Demos and formal presentations are much alike in many ways, so what we say here applies to both. The key difference is that in a demo you are demonstrating how something works or looks, whereas in a presentation you are typically leading the group through a proposal or other documentation, such as a report or study results.

Once the Decision Maker and her team of Decision Influencers are in place, you have six key phases to work through. (Think of these as gates to go through, rather than as a rigid series of steps. Be flexible; sometimes you may be able to combine the functions of a couple of the gates into one.)

1. Set the context with an opening benefits statement.

A benefits statement is a brief, "netted-out" summary of what you intend to prove, and of what the product ultimately *does* for the organization.

A model benefits statement follows. Note that it's direct and to the point. Note also that it speaks in terms of what the product *does* for the client, not of what it *is* or of technical details.

> "I'm here today to demonstrate the GEM 4000 business mini-computer... specifically, to show how it can increase your unit's productivity in turning

out the monthly ABC report, as well as in balancing the weekly output totals."

2. State and confirm the objectives. Check for completeness. If appropriate, add any others suggested.

Here's a model you can adapt:

"On the basis of our earlier discussion, I believe that these are the three major objectives of greatest importance to you. First..."

Whenever possible, print these agreed-upon objectives *in advance* on a flip chart or other visual aid, so that you can point to them to buttress your words.

Then ask of the group, "Are there any others that should be added?" If there are, print them on the visual so that you can tick them off as you cover each point (see step 4, below).

Generally, any additional objectives suggested by the group will be refinements of ones earlier agreed upon, or at least objectives that you can adapt to.

However, listen carefully as they are suggested, as you probably don't want to commit to something new that you have not prepared for, or that is outside the scope of your demonstration. If that happens, be direct: "That's raising a wholly new issue, beyond what we had earlier agreed upon as essential to be covered in today's product demonstration." The DM may intervene on your behalf, saying in effect that the sale can go through without that item.

But suppose the DM herself raises that new objective, or determines that it is important, after all. You could stand on your rights under the precommitment. But there are obvious risks to that approach.

A better approach is to pause at that point and treat the proposed new objective as you would an objection; that is, Probe, Restate, Respond Positively, then Move On.

In your Probing, begin by finding out why that new objective suddenly seems important to the DM.

Perhaps you can show how the same end can be accomplished in other ways through your product. If the new objective is not something you can easily deal with, Probe to find how important it really is. You may well find that it's only an afterthought or a "nice-to-have," not a "must-have."

You may be able to point that out to the group. Indeed, your questions may well defuse the issue: As you probe to find how important it is, the issue may deflate itself.

In any case, deal with it and move on. If you can solve it, say so. If you can't, say that, too. Then get the demo back on track showing how your product does fill the agreed-upon objectives.

Don't let yourself get bogged down on this or any other question, objection, or side issue. Deal with it, then move on.

3. Confirm the precommitment obtained earlier.

"We agreed earlier that if I can prove to your satisfaction that the GEM 4000 can meet these objectives, you would be prepared to order it now for your use. Are we still in accord?"

The answer will normally be yes, since you obtained the commitment before scheduling this demo. But if the answer is no, probe to find what is holding back a decision, and deal with it before proceeding.

But, as always in dealing with objections or hesitations, don't let yourself get bogged down. If you get back on track and move on, chances are that these minor concerns will be forgotten. But if you let them take over, the sale will be lost.

4. Conduct the body of the demonstration.

The objectives you negotiated earlier with the DM (as part of the Gentleperson's Agreement) will normally serve as topic headings in structuring your coverage. Resist the temptation to take the DM on a guided tour of every aspect and capability of your product.

Instead, structure your coverage to show how each of the agreed-upon objectives can be accomplished.

As you finish your coverage of each objective, pause and ask the DM and others on the team to confirm that they understand the points you have made. Make sure they understand how this aspect of your product fills the specified need.

If their understanding does not seem to be clear, or if they hesitate or disagree, pause to find their root concerns and deal with them before moving on to the next objective.

Be direct in comparing your proposed method and their present system (if one is in place):

> "Presently, getting the monthly ABC report out takes, by your estimate, an average of 170 working hours, and effectively stops all other work being done in the section for the final week of each month. When you install the GEM 4000, the same report will be produced with 25 clerical hours, plus 10 hours of management time—a tremendous saving in time."

When you have the agreement of the DM and her team that you have proven your product's ability to meet one of the objectives, *check it off* on your visual aid (to make a clear signal that you have met that standard), then move on to focus on the next objective.

Tip: Treat your product with extreme respect. Handle it with the loving care that you would a priceless family heirloom. Treat your samples with equal reverence: If the samples are paper, don't just toss them onto the table; instead, handle the sheets as if they were fragile medieval parchments of incomparable value.

5. Deal with questions, comments, and objections.

In dealing with objections and questions, use the approach we have covered earlier. The core is always Probe, Restate, Respond Positively. Then Move On without getting bogged down. For the how-to of responding to core objections, see Chapter 24.

Very likely, some of the people who have worked with you (Decision Influencers) will make favorable comments. Don't let those positive comments slip away into the air. Pick up on them, support them, amplify them as appropriate, as in this model following. For example, a department head may say,

> "This is what we've needed for a long time, to deal with that backlog in [whatever it is]."
>
> "Absolutely right, Mr. Jones," you respond. "You and I talked about that need when we met. You pointed out how__________."

6. Close for the sale or next appropriate action.

Closing here is asking the DM to take the action agreed upon in your precommitment Gentleperson's Agreement. Normally the action will be to buy your product.

However, in some cases, the action may be an agreement to proceed to another step, such as to cooperate with you in working up a formal cost proposal for a multiunit order.

To lead up to this request for action, briefly review the objectives agreed upon earlier. Pause at each objective to gain the DM's agreement that your demo satisfied it:

> "As I showed you a few minutes ago, the GEM 4000 will meet this first objective by _____. Are we in accord that it did accomplish that objective?"

When the DM nods agreement that each objective has been accomplished, put another check mark (for completion) beside that item on the flip chart.

In the same summary manner, work quickly through all of the specified objectives, showing how your product can meet them. Once you have done that, it's only logical that the DM will be ready to sign the order; thus, you can proceed on the assumption that the sale has been made, and that all that remains is to wrap up the details. (Assuming the sale has been made is acting on the premise that since buying makes such perfect sense, the DM will *naturally* agree.)

One of the best ways of projecting your assumptive confidence that the DM will naturally buy is to move on to your suggested action plan or implementation plan. (Set this up perhaps on a wall chart or overhead transparency, as appropriate to the setting.)

For additional ideas on closing for the sale, see Chapter 19, "More Ways of Asking the Decision Maker to Take Action."

But suppose you find that the DM is reluctant to sign the order, even though she agrees that you proved that each of the objectives settled upon in the earlier Gentleperson's Agreement has been accomplished. By her reluctance to sign, the Decision Maker is now, by implication, saying that you have not yet proven—to her complete satisfaction—that you can accomplish one or more of the specified objectives.

Deal with that reluctance as an objection. Probe, Restate, Respond Positively, then Move On. Probe to find out precisely what point the DM is hung up on, and focus on it. Do not let other issues intrude now.

SUMMARY

The purpose of a demo is not to show everything your product or service can do, but rather to prove to the customer that what you are selling can meet the needs that are of special importance to this customer.

Demonstrations are *to demonstrate*—that is, to show. Don't let your words get in the way. Let the product (or sample) do most of the talking.

There are six key phases, or gates, that you need to pass through in a demo or formal presentation:

1. Set the context with an opening benefits statement.
2. State and confirm the objectives agreed upon earlier. Check for completeness. If appropriate, add others the DM suggests.
3. Confirm the DM's precommitment you obtained earlier.
4. Conduct the body of the demonstration.
5. Deal with questions, comments, and objections. But don't get bogged down. Probe, Restate, Respond Positively—then Move On.
6. Close for the sale or next appropriate action.

Chapter 28

Using Written Proposals as Proof Sources

A sales proposal may be hundreds of pages long, or it may be as short as a one-page letter. In deciding on the length, on the approach, and on what to cover, the key is to keep in mind what a proposal is: a *proof source.*

Therefore, your proposal needs to be long enough and detailed enough to prove what needs to be proven to the Decision Maker—and (at least in theory) not a paragraph longer.

Gaining the DM's Precommitment

In preparing a sales proposal, begin by determining precisely what the proposal is to prove. Effective proposals—that is, proposals that *persuade*—are specific, not generic. They speak to the needs and interests of *this specific prospect*, not those of average, typical, or generalized clients.

There's no need to guess about where the focus should be in a proposal. Talk it over with the DM to clarify and negotiate what specific matters need to be supported by written proof.

Recall the three key elements that must be part of the explicit Gentleperson's Agreement that you should obtain before beginning work on the proposal:

> **First, that the key people, especially the Decision Maker, will attend your formal presentation of the proposal**
>
> **Second, precisely what the proposal needs to prove**
>
> **Third, the core of the Gentleperson's Agreement—that if you do prove these agreed-upon points, the Decision Maker will be prepared to sign an order**

The Skeleton of the Proposal

As we pointed out at the start of this part, what you need to prove will typically involve one or more of these five factors:

1. That *there is a need*
2. That *the need is significant enough* to justify spending money to fill it
3. That what you are offering *will fill that need* (or needs)

4. That it will fill the need *better and more cost-effectively* than any alternative approach, either within the organization or through your competitors
5. That *you and your organization are reliable*, trustworthy, professional, experienced, competent, and likely to be in business at least long enough to fulfill your obligations under this sale

Successful proposals typically address these concerns within a three-point structure:

- **The customer's Problem (or needs)**
- **Your proposed Solution**
- **The Value of your solution to the customer**

There may be other specific elements to be included, but these three usually provide the overall framework. Problem, Solution, and Value may form the headings on a short letter proposal, or they may be repeated several times as you cycle through multiple need areas in longer proposals. Omit any of the three and your proposal loses impact.

Elements to Include within that Skeleton

These three concerns—Problem, Solution, and Value—are the core of your message in the proposal, and provide the overall structure of your proof logic.

Within the framework of Problem, Solution, and Value, you string together the nuts and bolts of the physical proposal. Most formal proposals should include certain elements, which usually form separate sections or topic headings. (For our purposes here, "formal proposal" refers to anything beyond a short letter proposal of about five pages.)

In developing the proposal, view these elements as gates, not steps. That is, they are not items that must be rigidly included; rather, they are functions that you move through. You can move through some gates in conjunction with other gates.

A longer proposal will typically contain most of the following elements. (Keep in mind that this is only a general framework. Adapt it to your actual situation. Don't feel compelled to cover each of these categories, particularly if the dollar value of the item you're selling doesn't warrant that much detail. Conversely, add other categories as needed, particularly to address technical points.)

1. Cover, or title page.

Key data to be included on the first page include the title of the proposal, the date (at least to the month and year), and your name, address, and phone number.

It adds a nice touch if you can customize the cover by including the prospect's logo, perhaps copied and reduced from their letterhead.

In government proposals, the RFP (Request for Proposal) number or similar information may be required on the cover page. If you are responding to a government RFP, *read it closely*. You can't fight the bureaucracy and win; you must play by the bureaucracy's rules (as they are at this moment, since they may have changed since your last proposal to the same agency). Trivial oversights can destroy the value of an otherwise fine proposal.

2. Executive summary.

As a general rule of thumb, include an Executive Summary if your proposal runs more than about ten pages. Sum up your key findings and recommendations in a single page.

3. Table of contents.

Include a table of contents if the proposal runs more than about ten pages.

4. Situation background.

Here you briefly summarize why you have prepared the proposal. For example, "This proposal follows discussions with Dr. Arnold Porter, president of Megasystems, Inc." or, "This proposal responds to Department of Agriculture RFP No. 94–46578."

5. Methodology used.

This is an optional section that you may need to include, particularly if the proposal is based on research, such as a survey of the prospect's organization.

For example, you might elect to provide details of the survey approach you used as a way of adding credibility to your conclusions.

6. Statement of objectives.

Here summarize the objectives you and the Decision Maker agreed upon when you obtained the precommitment before writing the proposal. Make it very clear that these are the objectives you jointly agreed upon earlier, and not ones you developed on your own.

The next four elements address the three fundamental "proof logic" concerns: The customer's *Problem,* your proposed *Solution,* and the *Value* of your solution to the customer in filling the need.

7. Customer's present method.

Normally you will not need to go into a great deal of detail here, unless the DM is sufficiently far removed from the actual operation to be basically out of touch with how it is presently being done.

Even if the DM is familiar with the present method, it may make sense to describe the present method in detail in order to make the specific contrast with what you propose more clear.

Note: It is often practical to blend this gate and the one that follows into a single section of the proposal.

8. Problems/needs observed with present method.

Here outline the problems with the present way of attempting to solve the problem that you observed. However, since you are not an all-purpose management consultant, focus on your area of expertise—that is, the area of your product or service. Your objective, after all, is to sell your product or service, not to "fix" the entire client organization.

The present method that you describe may include the use of a competitor's product. Or, the present method may indeed be that there is *no* method at all for dealing with a need.

If your analysis of the need came from your discussions with the DM, make this clear, as a way of refreshing his recollection of that event.

If appropriate and relevant, you might briefly mention how you learned about the present problem or need. This may be your discussions with the DM, interviews with other staff members, or surveys or your analysis of the work flow.

9. Your proposed method.

Describe the solution you propose. Explain clearly and in an objective way how your product will solve the problems described above. This statement should be direct and objective. Leave out the gushing adjectives. If your product or service is solid, and your proposal sound, it will sell. If not, all the adjectives in the world can't help.

Above all, be specific in matching your proposed solution to the customer needs. Of course *you* know just how your solution will solve the client's problem, but what is self-evident to you may not be all that clear to the DM. Therefore, in the proposal, take special care to ensure that the linkage between each aspect of the need and the corresponding aspect of your solution is clearly made.

If appropriate, set up that linkage visually, as in a chart like the one discussed in Chapter 13:

Need	Solution	Value
1. Reduce workload in filling in patient billing data on repetitive insurance forms.	Computer holds "boilerplate" information and format, and so only new bits need to be typed in.	Saves 15 min per patient. At $15/hour, means nearly $4 saving for each visit.
2. Reduce time spent in transcribing doctor's dictated notes.	Computer's spell corrector allows typist to work at 30 percent faster rate without concern for errors.	Saves 90 min/day, or $22.50 per day.
3. Allow doctor to edit and correct these notes without imposing heavy extra typing load.	Computer makes it easy to type in changes, as the original is stored in computer memory.	Saves 30 min/day, or $7.50/day.

10. Cost *plus* statement of value.

In Chapters 14 and 15, we examined the method of stating price or cost, then immediately restating it in terms of value received, so that the buyer doesn't look at cost alone. It's important to do the same on paper in the proposal. If you review the techniques discussed in those chapters, you'll see how they can be readily adapted to use in proposals.

Remember: In showing value, go beyond out-of-pocket costs. Show how your proposed solution will reduce indirect costs, as well. For example, if your solution means that the customer's staff overhead will be reduced, be sure to say so; don't take it for granted that the customer will see that on his own.

Compare the overall costs of implementing your proposed solution with the overall costs of the present system—or the costs of having no system at all.

It may be helpful to express the comparison in a chart like the following. Adapt it to reflect the items that you want to compare. For example, instead of "Present Cost" and "Proposed Cost," you could substitute the cost of your product and the cost of the main competitor the DM is considering.

Item	Present Cost (Annually)	Proposed Cost (Annually)	Difference (Annually)
Labor cost (Annual)			
Equipment cost on annual basis			
Total processing cost on annual basis			Annual Savings

11. Implementation plan and schedule.

Project your confidence that the DM will naturally say yes today by setting up a specific schedule with actual calendar dates for installing your product, or for beginning your service to the organization. (For a model of using an implementation plan in closing, see item 3 in Chapter 18.)

To personalize the proposal, so that the DM realizes that you have paid attention to her actual situation, use calendar dates like "March 15," not generic schedules such as "21 days after signing the order." (Caution: Before setting these dates, check the calendar to make sure they don't fall on weekends or holidays.)

Appendices to the Proposal

Keep the proposal lean and to the point. Put any backup material in the appendices. These appendices may include matters such as the following:

A. Capabilities/staffing/qualifications.

Here you demonstrate that your firm has the staff with the education and experience to deliver what you are proposing. In some situations you would include resumes of the key people who will be working on the project.

B. References/other users.

If appropriate, you could include here the names of other organizations using your products or services. If you do this, also include the name, title, and phone number of the person to contact in that organization.

However, be sure to get clearance from these references before using their names. When you phone to get this okay, be sure to check that they are still satisfied with your work.

C. Additional technical details.

This is the place for the detailed charts, specifications, and other supporting data, so that they don't clutter up the main flow of your argument in the body of the proposal.

Transmittal or Cover Letter

You normally should *not* just drop your proposal in the mail. As a rule, dropping it in the mail will have about as much sales impact as dropping it in your own wastebasket. (Instead, set up an appointment so you can make a presentation of the findings to the DM. That presentation will conclude with your closing for the order. For guidance, see Chapter 26.)

But if you must mail it, then, as a matter of business courtesy, include a transmittal or cover letter with the proposal. This is a separate document, written on your letterhead, that is included in the mailing envelope, but outside the proposal binder.

The transmittal letter should normally be only two or three paragraphs, to the following effect: "Here's the proposal we discussed. Thank you for your cooperation in helping me obtain the background information. I'll be following up with you soon. In the meantime, please call if you have questions."

Chapter 29

Sending and Receiving Nonverbal Messages

In your sales calls, and in the follow-up demonstrations and proposals that serve as proof sources, your overall purpose is, of course, to communicate. But keep in mind that this communication is a two-way process: You communicate your ideas *to* the Decision Maker, Decision Influencers, and others, but you also need to comprehend the meaning of the feedback that they are, consciously or not, communicating to *you*.

This feedback communication can occur on multiple levels. According to one study, **only 7 percent of the messages transmitted during face-to-face communications are carried by the words spoken. By implication, therefore, 93 percent of the communication between you and the prospect is taking place beneath and around the words—via movements, gestures, voice tone and phrasing, and other almost subliminal means.**

In this chapter, we will be focusing on the nonverbal aspects of your communication with the customer. More than enough books examining nonverbal communication in general are already on the market, and so here we will narrow in on some aspects in the selling situation, particularly in stand-up demonstrations and presentations.

Projecting Your Confidence

Presentations and demonstrations are stressful, and that kind of stress can elicit some unprofessional mannerisms. Initial nervousness may cause you to avoid eye contact, to fidget and move your hands with the desperate movements of someone drowning on dry land, and to speak too fast, and with a coercive urgency—all actions

---

The illustrations in this chapter are from one of a series of training guidebooks I developed for the Xerox Corporation a few years ago: *Demonstrations: Sales Representatives' Lesson Guide* (610P8814), part of the *Marketing Skills Reference Library*. Used with permission.

Though the focus in this chapter is on nonverbal communication in the context of product demonstrations or presentations, the basic concepts apply all through the selling situation. Be attuned to the nuances of the customer's nonverbal signals at every point in the sales cycle.

that a prospect could misread, and as a result see you as a shifty-eyed, fast-talking, high-pressure sales type, not to be trusted.

"An experienced salesman makes a conscious attempt to impress with slow, wide gestures; a relatively smooth brow; occasional head-on glances; slow, regular and complete respiratory cycles; a resonant, inflective voice with optimistic timbre; a slightly up-tilted chin, and composed hands."*

Aim to project a sense of total confidence through the nonverbal messages you send. Videotape yourself working through a sample presentation or demonstration, and watch for how others see you. Here are some particular points to watch for.

- *Voice.* The deeper and more resonant, the better, so long as it is natural. This is true for women as well as men. Resonance projects confidence and control.
- *Speech patterns.* Especially at the start, make a point of speaking slowly, as this also projects confidence. Obviously, you don't want to speak too slowly, or you'll lose your audience.
  On the other hand, it is acceptable—even desirable—if your tempo picks up as you get into the heart of the demo, where your natural enthusiasm for the product causes you to get excited.
- *Voice "energy."* Listen to yourself on the tape. Does your voice sound upbeat, energetic, positive? Or bored, tired, tentative, depressed?
- *Posture and gestures.* Stand up straight (just as Mom and your drill sergeant told you). Control your hand gestures; move your hands slowly, confidently, gracefully in broad, sweeping movements, rather than in short, choppy, nervous fidgets.
- *Movements.* No matter what goes wrong, don't let it show. If you project confusion, the customer will read this as an indication that your product is difficult to operate. He may also infer from this that you are inexperienced, easily rattled, or lacking confidence in your product or capabilities. When you walk around the room, walk calmly and deliberately. The half second you may save by rushing isn't going to make any difference, but the sense of insecurity your hurried movements project will make a difference.

Positioning Yourself

How you position yourself and the prospect will vary with what you are selling: Is it big or small? Is the demo in your office or the prospect's? Are you demonstrating a machine or your work output? Regardless, here are some basic considerations.

* From an article, "Sign Language Spoken Here," *The Marketing Magazine,* Dec. 15, 1969.

First, get on the prospect's "right side." If you're working in the DM's office, the desk can be can be a barrier, both physically and psychologically. It helps on multiple levels if you can transcend that barrier so that the prospect and yourself are working "on the same side" of it.

One way of getting past that desk/barrier is to carry brochures and small samples, so that you can reasonably ask if it's okay to bring your chair around so that you and the DM can sit side by side and view them together. Some DMs will suggest that you move to the conference table; if you do, don't let it become a barrier. Or, if the DM has a larger office suite, he may move over to the sofa and chair arrangement. Try to take the chair closest to the DM—though without crowding onto the sofa.

These ideas of staying on the same side with the prospect also apply in stand-up situations like demos and presentations. If you spend most of your time facing the customer head-on, in effect lecturing *at* him, an invisible psychological barrier comes into being.

Therefore, when you are both standing, try to stand *beside* the customer rather than in front of him. That way, you project the subliminal message that you and the customer are working together—which you are.

If you are demonstrating to a group, make a point of becoming part of the group rather than the "teacher" at the front. To accomplish this, you might walk down into the group as you talk, or even casually take a place in an empty chair with them from time to time as the presentation proceeds.

Focusing the Prospect's Attention

The center of attention for the DM and his team should be the product or work samples or other proof that you are showing. If the demonstration or presentation is to be effective, you should unclutter your message so that the prospect team's attention focuses where it should. With the extraneous static cleared away, the demo can be more effective, and the attendees more at ease.

These comments from a memo I wrote while I was developing a series of sales training packages for the Xerox Corporation make the point:

> "The other day I attended a demonstration given by a sales representative, and tried to view it from the customer's point of view. The thing that stands out most clearly is the fact that he sat me in a chair and then stood in front and lectured like he was a professor and I a

student. But he had set up his A-frame on one side of the (unit), and he stood on the other side of (it).

"As I result, I didn't know whether to look at him or at the machine, or at the A-frame. My eyes kept looking for a spot to focus, and I missed a lot of what he was saying.

"Later I attended another demonstration, this one given by a Sales Representative who had been with Xerox only 20 months and was already number two in the branch. The difference was amazing. This time I found my attention focused where it should be all the time, and this made me much more comfortable. In fact, he was so good at his job that he was able to move me around the machine—to operate the controls or to walk down and take things out of the sorter—without my realizing what he was doing."

Positioning and Moving the Decision Maker

Continuing the lessons learned from the good Xerox rep in the section above, it's usually best if the customer is standing during the demo. Even if your product is small enough to fit on top of a table, you can still ask the customer decision team to stand so that they can "get a chance to try it out."

A customer who is standing is a lot less likely to be "sleeping in place." Besides, one who is standing beside you will find it easier to join in with you in using the unit, thereby becoming more comfortable with it.

In moving the Decision Maker (or the group) from point to point, you can ask them in words: "Would you move over here, please?" But you may not want to break the flow of your demonstration with stage directions. Nonverbal signals can usually tell the customer what to do or where to move, without the need for spoken instructions.

If you step backwards in the direction you want the Decision Maker to move, and accompany your movement with broad arm movements, he will tend to be drawn forward to fill the psychological vacuum you have left.

It works best if you keep talking as you move.

To continue the silent guidance, you can gesture toward your product—perhaps even point to a button to be pushed, and the DM will follow your unspoken instructions.

In some cases, you can acceptably guide the Decision Maker by a gentle pressure on the arm above the elbow.

But caution: Be sensitive to the reaction. Some people don't like to be touched by strangers.

LISTENING WITH YOUR EYES

Successful demos and presentations involve more than just your saying and doing the right things. At least as important is picking up and reacting to the feedback you get from the DM and others on the purchasing team.

For example, glazed eyes and an unchanging facial expression signal that you have either bored the person or in other ways lost her attention—perhaps because you are talking in too great detail, or because you are focusing on an aspect that she finds of no interest, or on a use for which she perceives no need. Here are some ways of turning this around:

Any gesture or mannerism is only one part of a communication. View the signal in context to get the total meaning. Here are a few examples to help you begin breaking the code.

A prospect who takes his glasses off may be signaling either interest or disbelief. It may also indicate that he likes or is impressed by what you are saying. Generally, the key to reading the signal is in the person's facial expression.

When you see someone rubbing his eyes at the bridge of the nose, it may be a clue that he is bored and is tuning you out.

It's usually a good sign if you see the Decision Maker cupping his chin in his hand, or rubbing his chin. It probably means that he is thinking of uses for your product. Slow down then to give more thinking time.

A seated DM who is resting his head on his hand is probably bored. You are moving too slowly, or you are talking about areas that hold no interest.

- *Speeding up your tempo* to reawaken interest.
- *Resetting the context*, so that the person understands the relevance of the points you are making—especially their relevance for filling the needs that she earlier agreed were significant.
- *Asking questions* to get the person or group more involved. Partly this is to get the blood flowing again. But you also want to probe the customer's interest in and level of understanding of what you are saying. Perhaps you have unconsciously slipped into the "techno-babble" of your specialty and left the customer behind.

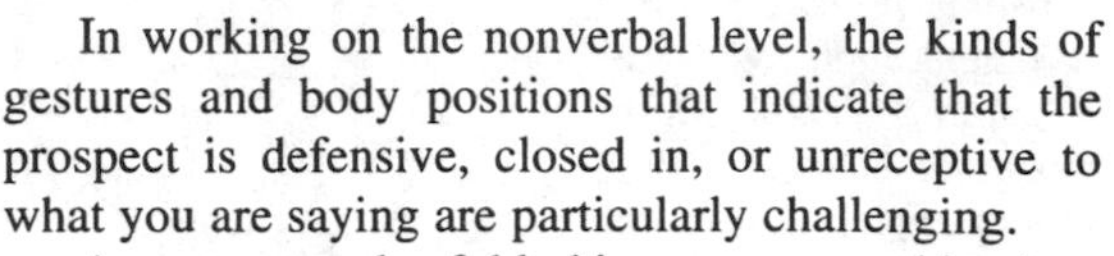

In working on the nonverbal level, the kinds of gestures and body positions that indicate that the prospect is defensive, closed in, or unreceptive to what you are saying are particularly challenging.

A customer who folds his arms across his chest *may* be telling you nonverbally that he is closed in, locked up, unreceptive to what you are saying.

True, folded arms may also mean that his hands are cold, or that he doesn't know what to do with them. But if you can get the arms to open, the mind will usually open as well. Ask him to hold something, even a sheet of paper, or perhaps some samples. It is awkward to hold something with folded arms. Thus he may open up despite himself.

Or ask him to operate your product. His arms will naturally unlock as he handles the controls.

If nothing you say or do seems to spark the customer's interest, try the direct approach: "I sense that I don't seem to be covering the things that are of special interest to you. Can you help me? What should we be focusing on now?"

MAGNETIZING THE PROSPECT

You can often gauge a prospect's degree of interest by how much he comes toward you or your product.

When the Decision Maker leans forward or steps forward toward you, he is typically expressing a high level of interest. He may be ready to buy at that point.

If the customer comes toward you, *do not withdraw.* Keep your heads together.

Similarly, during a demonstration, when you are both standing, the more the Decision Maker leans toward you or your product, the more interested she probably is. Capitalize on this interest—you might even skip ahead of your outline and ask for the order at that time.

The reverse is also true: If a prospect draws back physically from you or your product, he may in fact be drawing back mentally. Thus you need to "remagnetize" him. Shift your focus onto something that does interest him, or even move toward him to "show some details" on a sample.

Or, to respark interest, you might simply ask a question to get him involved again. For example, "Which of these applications do you think would be most helpful at the start?"

But caution: Don't get too close. It's one thing to get your heads together with the DM—that's positive. But it's quite different if the DM feels crowded. There are no hard-and-fast rules. Just be sensitive. If the client backs away, then you should back off a little. If you do, he may come forward again.

Part Eight
Odds and Ends

In this part, we examine some topics that don't quite fit anywhere else. One of these is how you can use indirect marketing approaches to generate sales leads, or to build up your credibility or brand recognition in your area.

Another is how to work with your clients *after* they have bought, so that they remain happy and become repeat customers and generators of positive referrals.

We also consider some ways of winning back those who have slipped away as customers.

Finally, we offer some guidance on practical issues, including organizing for efficiency in selling.

Chapter 30

Follow-up Letters and Other Customer Care

On one level, customers are buying your product or professional service. But on another level, equally important, they also expect to buy your consistent personal follow-up to ensure that all is going well.

If you fail to provide this follow-up care, you convert what could have been profitable ongoing relationships with repeat business and lucrative referrals into single dead-end sales.

Follow-up Letters

By granting time for a meeting, the DM is doing you a favor. (At least, that's how the DM typically perceives it.) You should make a practice of sending a short follow-up letter after the sales call as a way of repaying that courtesy. (Another thank-you note is in order after the contract has been signed, to say thanks for the business.)

That courtesy note is *not* just a courtesy. It's also an excellent way of reiterating the points you made earlier, or of reopening closed doors.

With today's sales-tracking and word-processing technology, it shouldn't be much of a burden to do this. You can merge the prospect's name and address from a database with a basic letter. Most of the letter will be standard, although you can customize it to reflect the special points touched on in your face-to-face meeting.

In your follow-up letter, begin by thanking the DM for taking time out from a busy schedule to meet with you. Then briefly summarize your discussions about the client's needs and how your product can fill those needs, cost-effectively. If appropriate, summarize the follow-up actions that were agreed upon (such as that you would do some research and then get back to the DM with the answers). Respond to any questions that were raised.

It's essential to take notes during, or just following, each sales call. Otherwise, by the end of the day, all the calls will have blurred, and you'll have little idea of what you agreed upon with each.

As with any other correspondence you send, be sure to paper-clip your business card to the letter; even if you have already handed out a couple of cards, they may have been lost. Business cards are cheap, so use them freely.

Tip: When you come to write your follow-up letter, you'll need to have the DM's precise address and the correct spelling of her name, so be sure to get *her* business card while you're on the premises.

Here's a model letter for you to adapt.

YOUR LETTERHEAD

Date

Ms. I. Decision Maker
President
DM Products
1 Pleasant St.
Pleasantville

Dear Ms. Decision Maker:
I appreciate your investing the time to meet with me yesterday to discuss some of the needs you foresee upcoming with your organization this year. These included

- Desire to increase output in the production unit by 20%.
- Intention to hold staffing level during this time.
- Corporate objective of holding capital investments to a minimum.

As I explained, the GEM 2000 will assist in meeting these needs:

- Our customer surveys show that installation of the GEM 2000 has assisted in increasing production output by an average of 15%. Further, its low maintenance requirements allow it to be operated with 11% less downtime, meaning that it could be operated longer hours, achieving the goal of 20% increase.
- The GEM 2000 can be operated by one person, instead of the three staff members needed by most competing machines. This alone would allow you to reduce staffing by two persons.
- We do have a lease program available, which would mean that the GEM 2000 could be in place with no capital investment necessary on the part of DM Products.

Overall, installation of the GEM 2000 would mean high output with significantly lowered cost. As we agreed, I will prepare a cost proposal for the GEM 2000 and present it to you on Thursday, August 12, at 11 A.M. at your office.

Again, thank you for the time and interest, and I look forward to the prospect of DM Products joining our client list.

Sincerely,

J. Seller

Follow-up "Customer-Care" Calls

Once a customer has bought from you, it's good business courtesy to keep in touch through occasional "customer-care" calls in which you check to make sure things are working as promised, with no problems. By showing this kind of interest, you demonstrate your resolve to make sure that the buyer is satisfied. That puts you in an excellent position to gain repeat business from this customer and from other prospects he refers on the basis of your superior performance.

Follow-up customer care calls usually tend to be short, and you'll have a good chance of getting in, even without an appointment. Even if the secretary is unable to fit you in with the Decision Maker, leave your business card, so that the DM knows that you cared enough to drop by to check on things. Phone back the next day, and you'll probably get put through at once.

Although "cold calling"—that is, just dropping in on offices—is usually not a productive use of your time in making *initial* calls, it *is* appropriate for follow-up customer-care calls. Even if the DM is unable to see you, you can at least accomplish your customer-care purpose by appearing and showing interest. The secretary or receptionist will inform the DM that you have been there.

Chapter 31

Winning Back Lost and Wavering Customers

Near the start of this book, we encountered the 80/20 rule: Generally 80 percent of your revenue and profits will come from just 20 percent of your customers. The point is, it pays to give that lucrative 20 percent the attention they deserve, so that they can make your enterprise really profitable.

The trouble is, at the start of a new venture, you can't really do that. At the start, while you're still learning where the important sales are, you have no choice but to spread your time evenly, and then wait to see where the real profits are.

But now, we'll assume, you've been in business for a while, and have gained a list of customers—and lost a few customers, as well.

One thing is clear: Your present customers probably will be those who offer the greatest potential for profitable repeat business. Even your past (or lost) customers offer a greater chance of profitability than most new prospects. Thus it is a very good use of your time to try to salvage the relationship with customers who seem to be slipping away or wavering. Here's why:

- It costs five times as much to find and sell to a totally new customer as to sell to an existing customer. So for every dollar of advertising, travel, salaries, and other selling costs you spend to get a reorder from a present customer, you can expect to spend five dollars to get an equivalent sale from a totally new customer.
- One study found that the odds of selling more product to a new customer were 1 in 16, whereas the odds of selling more product to an existing customer were 1 in 2. (If you keep score of your own success rates, the numbers may vary somewhat, but the basic results will probably be roughly the same: It's a lot easier to sell again to an existing customer than to go through the process of developing and selling new prospects from scratch.)
- Even past customers—including those who have left because of dissatisfaction—can be very cost-effective sales, if approached properly.

From these figures flow some key implications for your marketing policies and practices.

First Implication

The Customer Is Always Right

There's nothing revolutionary about that. It's always been a good policy for companies that intended to survive in the longer term. But I'm suggesting a different slant: It makes sense, even short-term, to give way to the customer in case of a dispute, because it'll probably cost you more to find a new customer to replace this one than to yield on the present point.

It's a good idea to set up a policy that allows the sales rep in the field to resolve a dispute in the customer's favor on the spot, up to some preset limit. (The amount of that limit would depend on the cost of the product.) For disputes beyond that limit, the sales rep is to assure the customer that you (or a sales manager) will be in touch within twenty-four hours.

The Best Way to Resolve Customer Disputes

Begin by setting the context. Say to the customer something on the order of, "You are a valued customer to us, and I want to be fair and I want to end up with you satisfied, so that you continue to do business with us."

Then pass it to the customer: "So that I can be fair, I'd like your input. If you were in my shoes, exactly how would you resolve it?"

A few customers may take advantage, but most will come up with a fair solution—often one that gives them less than you would have on your own. They'll almost inevitably feel a bond to your company because of the way you appealed to their sense of fairness. And they can't very well complain about not having been treated well, since they chose the remedy. Chances are, not only will you win them as permanent customers, but they'll probably begin generating a steady stream of new referrals.

Of course, if what the customer proposes is too costly, you can negotiate. But before doing that, ask yourself whether it wouldn't be better to invest that money in this customer, rather than to spend it prospecting for a new client.

Second Implication

Invest in Caring for Your Present Customers

When orders are canceled, the real reason often is not that the product is faulty, but that the buyer is unhappy with the customer service that came after the sale. Here's a brief checklist of some key steps you can build into the after-sale process. (Add other items to reflect your own situation.)

- Check with the customer after the product has arrived. Is it working well? Are there any problems or questions to talk about? Again, thank the customer for the order, and assure him or her that you intend to stand behind it, and that he or she shouldn't hesitate to call.
- Check back periodically, partly to make sure that all is well, but also to remind customers that you are still in business, and would appreciate repeat business or referrals. (One young lawyer at a legal marketing seminar in Washington said that he found that most of his business came through people he had networked with in the previous forty-eight hours.)

- Check especially with customers that you have not heard from for a while. Even if yours is a once-per-year or once-per-lifetime product, check in a couple of times each year and see how things are going.

Third Implication

Don't Write Off "Lost" Customers

Selling is a game of percentages. You can't hope to win every customer for life. But, at the same time, there's no reason to give up too easily if a customer leaves you.

If you're checking in with present customers, as suggested above, then you should sense if any customers are slipping away to the competition, and take steps to win them back. The key is to treat this as you would an objection: *Probe* to find the reason, *Restate* to confirm mutual understanding, *Respond Positively*, and *Move On* by asking for new business.

In Responding Positively, consider sweetening the pot by investing some of the marketing expense you would otherwise incur in looking for a replacement customer to further strengthen the bond with your present customers. Ways of doing this might include

- Discounts, such as for a longer-term renewal or larger-quantity orders
- Free samples, such as of new or improved products
- Free or reduced cost on upgrades and the like (depending on what your product or service is)

But what if the customer didn't just drift away, but slammed the door on the way out? Again, after a cooling-off period, check back. Treat this like other objections: Probe, Restate, Respond Positively, Move On.

There's no point in trying to ignore the fact that something happened. When you see (or phone) the customer, open by saying, "I realize that something caused us to lose your business. I'd appreciate the chance to talk about that with you. If possible, I'd like to win you back, but even if that's out of the question, I'd like to learn from you, so that my firm doesn't make that mistake again. I'd like to talk to you about it. Can we do that?"

If she says yes, then it's almost certainly worth the investment of your time to go and sit down, face to face, rather than to try to patch things up over the phone. So if she says yes, she will talk, offer a couple of alternatives: "Would tomorrow morning be good, or would early next week be better?"

(If she says she is not willing to talk, ask why: "Is the problem that this isn't a good time for you? I can check back later.")

Once the past customer (who we'll refer to as the DM) agrees to talk, ask an open-ended question, so that she has full latitude to air the grievance. (What you assumed caused the split may not have been it, at all.) "From your perspective, what happened? Why did you decide to stop working with us?"

Probe for more information if you need to. Then Restate, summarizing your understanding. Just summarize first, and check understanding. Only then should you apologize, or explain your side of it. But don't get bogged down in a complicated explanation; that comes across as an alibi, and can reopen old angers. Just state it once, then apologize. (Your apology can be along the lines, "I'm sorry we had this misunderstanding (or disagreement)." That smoothes hurt feelings without necessarily admitting that you were wrong. (Though if you *were* wrong, then *do* admit that.)

After explaining and apologizing, Respond Positively. Here you go beyond explaining or apologizing, and suggest a positive remedy. This can be an attempt to put right what went wrong before, or an offer of a discount or something else to induce them to come back. Some examples:

> "We're sorry this happened, and we'd like to win you back as a satisfied customer. Let me ask you this: Suppose our roles were reversed, and you were in my shoes. What would you propose so that we could make you a satisfied customer once again?"

Or,

> "You've told me that you didn't feel we followed through on installing the product as diligently as you hoped we would. I appreciate the feedback; perhaps we haven't been doing that as well as we should. I'd like to make this offer to you: If you'd like to purchase a new GEM 2000-B, the revised model, we'll credit you 70 percent of the original purchase price as a trade-in. In addition, I will personally coordinate the installation and postsale follow-up, as a pilot program for improving our efforts. You'll gain a brand-new product, perfectly installed, and we'll gain the benefit of your feedback this time so that we can upgrade our process. Does that sound interesting to you?"

Fourth Implication

Recognize that lost and wavering customers can be ideal consultants on your product, your service, market conditions, and the competition.

When you troubleshoot with lost customers, don't just try to salvage the situation. Listen through to any other clues they may be giving you. A customer who says that he feels your product "is no longer cost-effective for us" may be telling you that you have an overengineered product, so that you are selling something like a Mercedes when a bicycle will do the job. Or the same feedback may really mean that the industry is running into a belt-tightening phase, or that there are rumors that one of your competitors is about to drop prices.

Listening through is going beyond probing to put clues together from here and there so that you can make sense of broader patterns and undercurrents.

Fifth Implication

Recognize that oftentimes the core of the problem with a dissatisfied customer is unhappiness with your service and customer relations, and not really with the product.

The customer who complains of your product's not working well, or of its being too complicated or too expensive to operate, is often voicing only symptoms of a deeper, perhaps subconscious, complaint: that you took his money, dropped the prod-

Awakening "Sleeping" Customers

If you're offering a product that requires a refill every week or two, it's easy enough to know when a customer is slipping away. But what if your product or service is something that a customer might need only once per year, or maybe once every five years? In the interval, are your customer's needs dormant, or has the customer forgotten about you?

That's a problem that realtors commonly face. You've just sold a house to a very happy customer (or helped one buy a new home), so *of course* they'll remember you when it's time to sell this one and move to a new one. Or *will* they? How can you remind them you're still around without seeming too pushy?

My candidate for the title of World's Best Realtor—Carol Hawley of ERA/Five Star in Reston, Virginia—sold a house for me about six years ago when I moved out of Reston. This year, I got a packet of seeds (imprinted with her name, address, and photo) and an invitation to participate in a contest using the seeds. Scribbled at the bottom of the contest letter was a bit of gossip about prices in my old neighborhood.

It wasn't just the seeds, not just the contest, not even the gossip, but the whole package of good service plus staying in touch that kept me as an active though distant customer. The result: Not only did she get a plug in a book she didn't know I was writing, but she has gotten from me—recently—a couple of new referrals.

A contest for the best garden photo might not fit your product or service, but maybe there *is* a contest possibility if you look for it. In any case, keep this idea for awakening dormant customers in mind as you move into the next chapter, which addresses the related issue of using indirect

uct on him, and then disappeared ("disappeared," at least, in comparison to what he had expected from you).

On a deeper level, the customer is saying, "You didn't train me well enough in how to use the product," or "You didn't hold my hand enough to get me over the rough spots in the learning curve," or "You didn't warn me about the static I'd be getting for buying this, and you didn't give me anything I could use to defend myself."

Sixth Implication

Every contact with a happy or unhappy customer is a selling opportunity.

Even when you're going in to handle the complaints of a clearly angry customer, approach it from the positive perspective. That is, don't just view this defensively (to minimize your losses), but look at it as a chance to win the customer back and expand the sale and maybe even get some referrals to new prospects. Use the Four-Step process for handling objections as your framework: Probe, Restate, Respond Positively, then Move On by asking for some type of buying action. (The buying action you ask for may be for this customer to buy more of your product, or it may at this point merely be to give it another chance before insisting on a refund.)

Summary

Your existing satisfied customers are your best source of additional sales. But customers who have left, or are in the process of slipping away, are also very much worth following up on: It can be far less expensive to win them back than to go out and begin the process of finding new customers. From this flow six key implications:

1. The customer is always right. That is, in case there is a dispute, it may be better to sacrifice a little profit and keep this customer happy than to lose the customer and have to find someone new to replace that revenue.
2. Invest in caring for your present customers.
3. Don't write off "lost" customers.
4. Lost and wavering customers can be ideal consultants on your product, your service, the market conditions, and the competition.
5. Often the core of a dissatisfied customer's problem is disappointment with the service and customer relations you have provided, and not with the product itself.
6. Every contact with a happy or unhappy customer is a selling opportunity.

Chapter 32

Using Indirect Marketing Tools

In this chapter, we examine some alternative ways of opening doors to Decision Makers.

Referrals

Your best source of referrals will be satisfied customers. When you make a sale, always ask who else the purchaser thinks you should talk to. (Be sure to check that this DM doesn't mind your using his or her name as a door-opener when you make that contact.)

- Ask for a referral even if you don't get the sale. Even though today's prospect genuinely doesn't have the money to buy now, she may nonetheless think your product is great, and so be happy to pass you on to friends in other organizations.
- If the rapport is good, the Decision Maker who has just bought may be willing to phone ahead to others to preintroduce you and your product. Sometimes the DM will welcome this as an opportunity not only to introduce you, but also to network with a counterpart in another firm.

Mail as a Marketing Tool

In this book, we are focusing on face-to-face selling. Marketing by mail is a whole subject in itself, and so we won't go into detail. But there are some basic ways in which mail marketing can augment your direct efforts.

For example, give thought to letting the mail do at least the initial work if you sense that the customer is low probability or low priority, so that a full sales call might be a waste of your time. Mail the brochure or other information, then follow up by phone to explore whether there is enough interest and potential to warrant meeting face to face.

Tip: Even with low-priority prospects, include with the sales material a cover letter saying that you will follow up with a phone call at a specified time, such as "early in the week of January 22." By doing that, you greatly increase the likelihood that the Decision Maker will take the trouble to read the brochure now.

Every piece of sales literature that you hand out or mail should have your own company name, address, and phone number on it. This is especially the case if you are a dealer or representative for another company; if your name is not on the brochure, the customer may contact the factory directly, leaving you out of the loop.

Seminars

You can teach seminars or workshops, or offer shorter lectures. The easiest way is to offer them through other institutions, such as your local community college or the local equivalent of the Chamber of Commerce. Alternatively, you can arrange them yourself, advertising in the local newspaper or business news, or mailing invitations directly to likely prospects. You might hold the seminars at your office, or in a conference room at a local motel.

Think also of the possibility of a joint marketing program with other individuals or firms. For example, if you're working in real estate, check with one of the smaller or newer local banks; it may be interested in a joint seminar. The bank might absorb the advertising cost and provide the use of its facility after hours. In return, a bank officer would share the podium with you, and both your logo and address and the bank's would appear on the handouts. This saves you money and lends you credibility, while the bank expands its outreach to new prospects.

Another approach: Teach some credit courses at the local community college, or teach at the continuing education program of the local school district. But be sure you get credit by name and expertise: "Linda Farr is a real estate broker with the firm of Farr and Cudahey in Pleasantville."

You can even take a page from the Tupperware book and run seminars at home—either your own home or the home of a "sponsor," who supplies the space and maybe also helps promote the seminar to potential attendees. (The sponsor could take a share of the profits, if you charge for the seminar, or get some other consideration.) How well home seminars will work for you depends a lot on your product or service. This could be effective in promoting career training or consulting, for example, or if your business relates to home repair. (The only way to know for sure if it works is to experiment.)

If your business involves construction or building repair, you might talk one of the local building supply or paint stores into sponsoring your seminar at the store, and perhaps even featuring it in advertisements. If you're an interior decorator, you could work out an arrangement with the local fabric shop. If you're a computer consultant, check with the local computer shop. In looking for these seminar possibilities, ask yourself, what kind of enterprises do you patronize professionally? They might be interested in a joint venture.

How useful the seminar/workshop/teaching route is will depend on a variety of factors. Key among these, first, is your ability and willingness to teach the seminars. It takes time to set them up and prepare your material, and it takes a certain talent to pull off standing in front of a curious crowd. Running ads and renting meeting spaces may use up capital.

Another key concern is to what extent your product or service will communicate well in a seminar. On the one hand, you want to build interest, and for this you need to demonstrate your expertise. Yet you don't want to end up giving away the core of what you have to sell.

Decide your objective at the start: Is it to *teach* your clients, or simply to *create a sense of need* in them for your services?

For example, you may have seen advertisements for free evening seminars put on by your local stockbroker. If you attend one, you'll see that the objective is ultimately to create a sense of unease about your present investment methods—sufficient to induce you to meet with an account rep for the full sales treatment. Perhaps you can adapt this to your own situation.

One caution: If you are going to do seminars or workshops, you *must* do them well. Anything less than smooth, organized professionalism is by nature a *negative* advertisement, likely to drive away more prospects than it attracts. (You can get away with less than perfection for your "off-Broadway tryouts," provided they are volunteer work, done at no charge for smaller audiences. Depending on your subject, church and civic groups might be interested.)

Seminar Evaluations

Though it's not essential, it's still a very good idea to ask the seminar attendees to complete a short evaluation of the seminar before they leave the room. (If they don't do it on the spot, you can be sure they never will.)

The evaluation serves a couple of purposes. First, it gives you feedback on how well you did. Second, if structured right, it can give you both other prospect leads and even fresh ideas on what you are marketing. See the next page for a model you can adapt:

Displays at Trade Shows

Trade shows specific to your industry, or to your area, can generate leads and visibility. Whether or not it will pay to exhibit depends on your situation and what you're selling. Here are some general suggestions to get you started.

- Attend at least one similar show to get a sense of how firms like yours operate. Normally, they set up a booth—basically a table or two. The more elaborate may have a backdrop on which to array the product.
- Look also at what kinds of brochures, catalogs, and other handouts are customary. What will your customers want to carry away? Would offering a free sample be useful and cost-effective? Would it help lead to future sales? Would it enhance your message?
- Determine your objective beforehand. Generally, except with low-priced merchandise, the object is to collect qualified leads, not to close sales on the spot. Therefore, think of ways of collecting names, along with information about them.
- At the very least, have a sign-up list for those who visit your booth. But it's hard to get people to sign without a reason; for that reason, some bring a fishbowl in which attendees can leave their business cards, with the promise of a drawing for some prize.
- It's best if the drawing offers a sample of your product or service, rather than something extraneous such as a free dinner or a weekend trip away. Since only potential users would be likely to want a sample of your product or service, this provides a built-in prescreening of applicants. That

Seminar Evaluation

Thank you for attending the GEM Applications Seminar. Would you please help us by taking a couple of minutes to give us feedback on what the seminar meant to you. Scoring is on a scale of 0 (not helpful) to 5 (extremely helpful).

1. Were the topics covered in the seminar on target for your needs?
   0 1 2 3 4 5
   Suggestions:____
2. How would you rate the way in which the presenter covered the material?
   0 1 2 3 4 5
   Suggestions: ____
3. Please rate the facilities (room, location, etc.).
   0 1 2 3 4 5
4. [Add other questions as appropriate to your situation.]
5. What topics would you suggest for future seminars?

   A.

   B.

   C.
6. Do you have any general suggestions on how GEM products or marketing could be improved?
7. Can you suggest any other people or firms who might be interested either in meeting with a GEM representative or in being invited to future seminars like this one? (If yes, may we mention your name when we call on them?)

Name Title Firm (phone and address if known)

1.____

2.____

3.____

Again, thank you for attending this seminar. We look forward to meeting with you again. If you have any further questions or comments, please call us at the phone number on the other handouts you received.)

Optional: Your name_________________________________Phone:_______

***Note*: In the interests of space in this book, I have tightened up the spacing in the model evaluation. Be generous in the space between lines; it may cost a few more nickels to copy that extra page, but by leaving plenty of space, you encourage people to write notes. One good idea pays for a bushel of nickels.**

saves you the later problem of sorting out which are viable leads (and the frustration of paying for a fancy dinner for someone who would never, ever be a prospect).

- As an alternative way of generating qualified leads, take a survey at the trade show, with the promise of the results by mail. For example, you could run a survey on "business leaders' expectations for the local economy next year." (This could be as simple in practice as a basic check-sheet filled out on the spot and dropped in a box at your booth.) When you later mail the survey results, enclose your brochure, along with a cover letter mentioning that you'll follow up by phone in the next few days to discuss the results, and to share other ideas that spun off from the work.

One of the most important factors for long-term success from participation in trade shows is the quality of your handouts. Handouts impress prospects on the spot, but can also be the source of unexpected calls over the following year or so. Some suggestions:

- Hand out copies of any articles you've written, or any articles that have been written about you or your product. (If they are copyrighted, you'll need to get the publication's permission to reproduce these.)
- Given the ease of desktop publishing, you may produce other handouts, such as write-ups on your product that take the form of factual articles or case studies of your successes (with the permission of those clients to use names and data, of course).

But one caution: It can feel lonely standing at your booth, as the crowds walk past paying you no attention. That's the way it is. Not everyone will be interested at the time, so just keep smiling and realize that it takes only one interested customer to make it all worthwhile.

Newsletters and Other Publications

Desktop publishing opens a variety of inexpensive ways of keeping in touch with present and potential clients. In some cases, a simple newsletter may do the trick. The content doesn't have to be all yours, either; once you get it started, you'll often find that your customers send you enough material to keep it going.

Or, use the newsletter as a vehicle for phoning your clients and industry leaders, asking for input. That serves as a way of making your name, and the name of your firm, known in the industry.

If you don't want to undertake publishing your own newsletter, volunteer to serve as a contributor, or even editor, of the publication of your business or professional group. That also gives you a chance to meet key leaders in the group, and to phone or interview others who can contribute news or expertise.

Writing a Column

If you're inclined to writing, you may be able to persuade the editor of your local paper, or of the local business journal, to give you a slot weekly or monthly. Don't underestimate the amount of time and effort it will take to fill that space. Still, it may well be worth the investment of time for the way it builds your name recognition and brings you into some of the local power networks.

You'll also find that you become a "power broker" of sorts, as some of the people you previously couldn't get in to see become eager to talk now that they see you as a channel for the publicity they need.

In negotiating the format of your column, be sure that you get a professional byline: "Dana Slater is an attorney with the firm of Kogins and Slater in Pleasantville." Without that free advertising, it may not be worth the investment of time and effort.

Recognize that your personal opinions—interesting as they are—probably aren't going to sell to the editor. But if you have professional expertise and can package that expertise in simplified form, that probably will sell. For example, a local attorney wrote fifty columns covering a variety of areas in business law, family law, landlord and tenant problems, and the like—and parlayed those columns into a successful run for district attorney.

If you're not up to weekly self-help columns, consider using an interview format, where you meet with local leaders and give them a chance to share their ideas and expertise.

Presenting at State and National Conventions

If your clientele is exclusively local, then going to the state convention may not seem to make a lot of sense. But don't be too quick to turn down the opportunity. After all, the appearance gives you credibility—and may be the subject of a press release that finds its way into your local newspaper or business magazine.

If your subject is interesting enough, you may even find your local media interested in interviewing you—which opens other possibilities.

Further, you can turn your presentation into written form and use it as a handout at trade shows and as leave-behinds with the Decision Makers with whom you meet.

Here's a case study in building name recognition through indirect marketing tools:

> My chiropractor, Dr. Joe Clauss (and his wife, Carolyn, also a chiropractor) moved to town a few years ago and quickly built an exceptionally successful practice. I first became aware of them when I saw notices in the local paper informing their patients that the clinic would be closed for a few days while they presented training at professional development seminars.
>
> The notices were a convenience to their existing patients. But they had the secondary effect of building the Clauss's name recognition, and one could infer that if they were invited to teach several times each year, then their expertise must be respected in the profession.
>
> That didn't cause me to go to them, but it created a climate in which they became my first choice to explore when I developed a back problem (people who write books spend too many hours slaving hunched over hot computers.)

SURVEYS

Back in Chapter 6, we examined "hot buttons" to interest the Decision Maker in spending time meeting with you. Another hot-button door-opener, not mentioned there, is the offer to share the results of an industry or area survey that you have conducted.

If you promise information, then you must be able to fill that promise with useful results, but that may not be particularly difficult. You may already have done much of the work: A needs or market survey that you did for your own use could perhaps be adapted to a marketing purpose.

Keep in mind, too, that in the course of your sales calls, you gain an unusually broad perspective on what is happening, broader than that of any of the individual executives with whom you meet. With a little ingenuity, you may well be able to develop survey results from your present work. (Earlier in this chapter, we looked at a quick survey that you could run at trade shows.)

Indeed, some consulting firms send out a written survey each year across the industries in which they work. The survey serves several purposes. First, it helps the consultants keep in tune with needs. But it also works as a door-opener for later marketing efforts. Summarized into press releases for industry journals, it brings the firm publicity and hence draws inquiries from still more potential clients. Finally, one consulting firm specializing in the legal profession packages both the analysis and the raw data and sells the complete study to major law firms at several hundred dollars per copy. (It's not just butchers who use every part of the pig but the oink!)

The overall point is that, with minimal investment of time and effort, you may be able to package your expertise in a way that may, first, be a salable product in itself, and second, serve as a door-opener for your marketing efforts. If the findings prove useful, then you can become established as a recognized authority—and you will find new clients searching you out.

Crucial: In developing and speaking of this survey and its results, make it clear that your interest is in *broad trends*, so that no potential client thinks you are collecting secrets from one firm to pass to others.

Chapter 33

Prospecting Resources

To provide a complete listing of sources of marketing leads and other data would require several books in itself, and then still would not cover everything in specialized areas. What I can reasonably do is point you in useful directions for beginning the search in your unique market. These are basic sources that will give you a starting point and a foundation on which you can build in focusing on your specific niche.

Marketing Directories

A great deal of American effort has been invested over the years in developing directories that are helpful in the marketing process.

Many of these basic directories are available in public libraries. Some you may already be familiar with; others, probably not. Here's a beginning list to get you started; your librarian can guide you further in finding the directories that are relevant to the specific type of market and geographical area on which you will be focusing.

Some of the more innovative research suggestions in this chapter (as well as in earlier sections on getting through the executive's Screen) were suggested by my wife, Susan, from her experience as an executive search consultant. "Headhunters" need to be at least as resourceful as salespeople in finding and getting through to prospects.

General Business Directories

- *Dun and Bradstreet.* D&B publishes several sets of directories that are useful for marketers. Typical is the *Million Dollar Directory*, for organizations with a net worth of $500,000 or more. But there are a variety of others, one or more of which may be right on target for your needs.
- *Moody's.* This firm publishes a variety of manuals focusing on specific industries, primarily providing financial data. Other manuals provide information on municipalities and government organizations.
- *Standard & Poor's Register.* There are registers of corporations, of corporate directors, and of corporate executives.
- Annual directories published by *Fortune* and *Forbes*. (Work from these listings to find any divisions or work locations in your area.)
- Membership lists of professional organizations relevant to your field. Check for both local and national lists.

- A helpful directory of business directories is *Business Information Sources* (third revised edition, 1993), by Lorna M. Daniels, University of California Press.

Another reference of special value is *Leadsource*. This is a special "reverse" directory that enables you to trace from the type of business an existing client is in back through the Standard Industrial Code (SIC) categories to find other similar businesses. For example, if you find that optical supply houses tend to be good prospects, you can use *Leadsource* to locate other supply houses that you might not have been aware of, or even to locate operations similar to optical supply houses, such as wholesalers selling to them. *Leadsource* can also be used to trace by postal Zip code as well as by SIC code.

Local Business Directories

- *Chamber of Commerce directories.* These may also be found under another name, such as county or city "Board of Trade."

  Similarly, if there is an Economic Development Corporation (or a group serving a similar function under another name), call and ask if it has a directory, newsletter, or other publication. Explain why you are calling, as such a group can usually give you leads on new companies or agencies that are moving to the region.
- *State directories*, typically grouped according to type of industry or profession.
- *Telephone directories*, including the specialized directories for certain industries that are privately published in some cities.
- *R. L. Polk's Street Directory*. This lists all residents and businesses in a metropolitan area.
- *Haines Criss-Cross Directory*. This is a reverse telephone directory, enabling you to look up a street address and find who (or what organization) is listed at that address, and their phone number. (This is helpful when you're "smokestacking.")

  Businesses are listed in bold print. (If there's no Haines for your area, ask the librarian; a similar directory may be available under a different name.)
- *Lists of key local industries* published in an annual special issue in some local newspapers.

Your local library will be the best guide to special directories available in your area or industry of particular interest.

Marketing Lists

Because marketing is itself a major American industry, you will find that in virtually any area in which you may want to market, others have been there before you, compiling lists of potential prospects.

Most of these lists are primarily intended for use in direct mail marketing, but they can be useful as leads for structuring your calls.

For example, if you're selling to doctors, you can rent a list of doctors on which the prospects are sorted according to any of a number of factors: by geographic location, by specialty, by whether they practice alone or with a group, by income, by age, by what magazines they subscribe to, by whether or not they have ever been sued for malpractice, by whether they own or lease their cars, or by whether they have purchased anything by mail recently, and if so whether it was for personal or professional use and how much they paid for it.

This is just one example, but the point is that, relatively inexpensively, you can rent the names of prospects, already presorted according to the characteristics and location you require.

You can rent names for one-time use for about a dime or less each. You will pay a little extra to have the sorting done to your specifications, thereby saving your time.

You may have to pay extra if you use the name for a purpose other than direct mail; thus, if you will be making phone or personal calls, the list house may add an extra fee.

Generally, too, the minimum order from a list house is 1,000 names and so you may be paying for more names than you can use, or for names outside your geographic area. However, the money you spend saves you hours compiling names from directories.

You can find these list houses by checking the telephone yellow pages of the largest city near you, under the heading "Mailing Lists." Or the largest printer in your area may be able to put you in touch.

Who Your Competition Sells To

To research the most significant potential markets for your product or service, take the time to find out who your competitors are, and where their significant sales come from.

For example, suppose you have developed a new billing program that is useful in doctors' offices. It is similar to one that has been on the market a couple of years, although yours is significantly more advanced; we'll call this competitor product COMPET, and your new product NEWBILL.

You know that the doctors' offices that are already using COMPET are the best prospects for your more efficient product. Therefore, to generate leads, you could ethically phone doctors' offices and ask if they now use COMPET, then follow up with those that do and show how NEWBILL is a better product, and more cost-effective, besides.

Similarly, you could check the catalogs or showrooms of dealers who supply the medical profession to see which presently carry COMPET, and make a sales call on them to convince them to carry NEWBILL as well.

What you *cannot* ethically or legally do, of course, is pay someone in the COMPET organization to sell you client lists, or to alert you to the introduction date of Improved COMPET. That's industrial espionage, not marketing research.

But suppose you search, and find no competition at all for your proposed new product. Indeed, there seems to be nothing even remotely similar. That may be wonderful news, for you have unlimited potential to tap. But it may also be terrible news.

First, if your new product is unique, the result may be that you have to *educate* the market. There are few things more difficult to market than ideas—or products—whose time has not yet come.

In order to accelerate the point at which your product's time *does* come, you may have to invest dollars and energy in educating the world about the fact that your offering exists and is needed. That may not be cost-effective. Moreover, you may not have the capital—and hence the time—to do this.

Second, the fact that no competition exists may be an indicator that the world seems to have no need for your product. The idea itself, or one similar, may have been tried earlier, without success.

Third, it may be that the need is being met in a way that you have overlooked. An economist who had spent his career developing business forecasts for a *Fortune* top 50 company was convinced there was enormous potential in bringing a certain kind of data to growing firms in the Sunbelt. He took early retirement and set up a consulting firm to provide the service. After he had burned his bridges and made the investment, he realized that a state agency already supplied the same information at no cost, although it was buried in an obscure newsletter.

Newspapers, Magazines, and Other Publications

Here again, the best source will be your local librarian, or the librarian in a specialized business library. (Some metropolitan areas have business divisions within the public library system; if not, try your nearest university.) In any case, start with these:

Business Publications

Fortune, Forbes, Inc., and other magazines publish lists each year of the most significant businesses within various categories, such as overall largest companies, largest industrial manufacturing companies, or fastest-growing young companies.

These listings can get you started even if you don't happen to be located in these companies' headquarters city. Suppose you've invented a new type of industrial-strength window-washing fluid. On the *Fortune* list you spot General Motors. GM is likely to have a lot of windows, but you don't want to make the trip to Detroit to show your product.

First, look up General Motors in your local phone book—perhaps there is a regional headquarters, a training center, or a subsidiary nearby. If not, send for GM's annual report; it may mention a local center. Then call on the local users, try to sell them, and later use the local user as a wedge into the larger company.

Local Papers and Magazines

Read the business news. Take notes on what firms are expanding or have just received new contracts: Chances are they will soon be in the market to buy.

Take notes also of the names of those who have been promoted to head up new divisions. If you know them personally, don't be bashful about writing a congratulatory note, enclosing your own brochure. If you don't know them, make a note and call for an appointment to explore how you can help them in their new position.

If you are in or near a major metropolitan area, chances are that the local newspaper or business publication publishes a listing of the region's 50 or 100 largest business firms or largest employers (which might include government agencies).

Also, you will find that a special business newspaper or newsletter is published in most major metropolitan areas. The articles, charts, and advertisements will bring you up to date on the significant firms and agencies, including information on their size, number of employees, address, and major projects under way, often with the names of the project managers.

When you see a news article of particular interest, you can phone the reporter credited in the byline. Most will give you a couple of minutes to discuss major problems, trends, players, and the like. Depending on how specialized their beat is, they may be uniquely well suited to bring you up to date in an area or industry. They are likely to know which are the key companies, and who within those companies is in charge of dealing with the areas of interest to your firm.

You can later repay the favor by phoning the reporter with nonconfidential information that might be of interest. Even if you don't know the whole story, your tip could alert her to something newsworthy. If you're lucky, and you develop the ability to "net it out" in brief, quotable messages, she may remember you and call you for comments on developments within your field. The publicity from one of these can do as much for you as a week of knocking on doors.

Even the help-wanted ads can generate sales possibilities. First, they will give you the names of prospect companies that you might not turn up in your other research, especially new firms or those that have moved into the area too recently to be in any directories. Second, the focus of the ads will tell you which companies are expanding, and in what product areas.

Other Sources of Leads

Here's where your creativity and ingenuity come into play. To spark that creative thinking, here are some ideas.

Associations

If it's available in your library, examine the multivolume *Encyclopedia of American Associations*, published by Gale Research Co., Book Tower, Detroit, Michigan. First develop an overview of the range of associations in existence, then target those that might be relevant to your marketing effort. There is an association for almost any kind of working or professional group. (A companion encyclopedia focusing on regional, state, and local organizations is available from the same publisher. This enables you to look up your city and see the range of clubs and other civic and professional groups organized there.) Another source is the American Society of Association Executives, 1575 I Street NW, Washington, DC.

It might be productive to phone the national office of relevant groups to find out if there is a local chapter and, if so, to learn the president's name, address, and phone number. Ask also for a copy of the group's newsletter or magazine; from that you can get names that you can use to network through a series of phone calls.

The local chapter may permit you to join, or may let you use its membership lists. Or you might propose a talk or presentation; most groups are constantly on the lookout for something to feature in their meetings.

"Smokestacking"

Drive around in free time between appointments. Look for factory smokestacks or, more likely these days, office buildings and industrial parks that may contain the offices of likely prospects.

When you find a possibility, park your car and take a look at the building directory. The names of the organizations listed may tell you whether or not they are prospects for what you offer. If in doubt, drop by the office and chat briefly with the receptionist. You won't be the first to do this; salespeople probably drop by exploring like this every week, or perhaps even every day.

Simply say something like, "I was in the area and noticed your company on the directory. Can you tell me what line of business Amalgamated Resources is in?" Unless it's a CIA front company (which happened to me when I was marketing consulting services in the suburbs of Washington, DC) or unless you get an exceptionally timid receptionist or a temporary, you'll learn enough to know whether it's worth exploring further.

However, sometimes the receptionist will pass you on to another person. This is not the time to give a sales talk; try to get the basic information and get out. Almost certainly this person is a "Screen," and has authority to say, "No, we aren't buying any of those, whatever they are," but lacks any authority to say, "Yes, we'll buy." If you get bogged down in the details of what you offer, you will close the door for a later organized sales call on the person who has real buying authority.

At this point, what you want is information, including

- *What the organization does*, and from that, whether it is likely to be a user of what you offer. But it's usually better to infer that on your own; if you ask, the Screen may say, "No, we sure don't need any of those," just to get rid of you and get back to his desk.
- *How large this operation is*. Again, your eyes and inferences are usually a better source than a direct question. But do ask whether this office is part of a larger organization.
- If the organization seems to have enough potential to be worth coming back to, *the name of the person who is likely to have the authority to buy what you are offering*. In a small operation, the person with buying authority will typically be the company president, or the senior partner in a law or accounting firm. It gets more complicated in larger organizations. (For the reasons examined in Chapter 3, the purchasing manager is usually the *wrong* person.)

Information Swapping

As you make your rounds, you'll cross paths with others who are selling related but not competing products. Get acquainted with them, because you can help one another. If the other person sells only paint and you sell only brushes, you can trade industry data and even specific leads without hurting your own prospects.

Referrals

When you make a sale, don't leave without getting the names of other prospects from the person who has just bought. If she believes in what she bought, she'll believe in it enough to expect that her friends and coworkers will want it, too. First ask the general question: "Who else do you think I should go see?"

Get the first names that come to mind, then give the customer a little more help by prompting in specific categories: "Is there anyone else in the company I should see? Maybe your counterparts in other divisions of this company?" (Write the information.) "What about in other companies? Anyone in this industrial park?" (Write the information.) "How about your counterparts in other companies?" (This implies competitor companies, which is fine, so long as your offering doesn't give a competitive edge.)

After you get the leads, check on how you can use them: "Is it okay if I mention to Ms. Perkins that you suggested I call?" If the answer is yes, then that will be your strongest opening when you make those calls: "Mr. Treadwell at Amalgamated suggested that I contact Ms. Perkins."

If some of the people you sell to seem particularly enthusiastic about your product, they may be willing to phone others before you call, in effect introducing you. This is excellent, if they are willing, but don't press your luck. Realize that they are busy with other duties. Realize, too, that an introduction like this may be seen as an endorsement; unless they have already used your product or service for some time, they may not feel prepared to take this step.

Ask for referrals even if you *don't* get the sale. Although this company may not need your product at the moment, or may not have the budget now, the decision maker you've met with may nonetheless have been sufficiently impressed that he or she will want to pass you on to others.

Talks, Workshops, Free Seminars, Appearances at Trade Shows

These acquaint the world with who you are and what your product or service can do. Although you may not make any sales on the spot, these efforts usually help you build a network of contacts. The exposure can open doors later when you make follow-up calls.

One consultant friend of mine presented a single workshop when he first set up his business. When he analyzed his clientele ten years later, he discovered that 90 percent of his business could be traced directly or indirectly to the attendees at that first session.

A Survey Spin-off

In Chapter 32, we examined ways in which you can develop survey results and use them as door-openers for sales calls.

But be creative in mixing and matching approaches. For example, with some ingenuity, you may be able to use the survey results as an even broader kind of business development tool if the findings can be adapted as the basis of a talk for appropriate groups.

For example, if your survey focuses on local business trends, the area Chamber of Commerce or Rotary Club would be a good prospect for sponsoring your talk. If the subject is specialized, propose a talk to appropriate professional organizations.

Your talk should be genuinely informative, and definitely not a "hard-sell" marketing presentation. The objective is to establish yourself as an authority on the subject and to pass on some of your knowledge. Any mentions of the product or service you offer should come only in passing, such as incidentally by way of illustrating your points.

That's not to say that you need to keep your product a secret. Find out who will be introducing you, and provide that person with a brief biographical sketch detailing your background, and mentioning your firm name and what it does.

A tip: When you prepare this bio sheet, keep it short and emphasize what you want emphasized. If you don't focus this introduction on what *you* think is relevant to your business purpose, you may well find that vital data such as your credentials and company name and address are glossed over in favor of some obscure, irrelevant point in your bio sheet.

Another tip: When the announcements of your talk are being sent out, make sure that the organization's publicity director includes both your name and your firm's name, along with the city in which your office is located. The city is particularly important if you're located in one of the suburbs of a metropolitan area. In the Washington, DC, area, you could be listed in any of three different phone books—Washington, northern Virginia, or Maryland. There is no point in making it difficult for prospects to find you. (Even better, arrange to get your street address and telephone number included in this handout, as well.)

Those who are real prospects will search you out after the meeting or in the weeks to come with questions. With these people you can be more specific in how your product or service can help them.

Give handouts to make it easier for the attendees to follow what you say—and to make it easier for them to find you later. The handouts may contain copies of key visuals so that the attendees don't have to take notes from what you are showing on the overhead projector. Or the handouts may consist of an outline of your talk—but *never* the full talk, or the attendees will wonder why you bothered to waste their time reading it to them when they could have read it faster on their own.

Each handout should carry your name (and company name), address, and phone number. A classy but subtle way of accomplishing this is to use your letterhead as a cover sheet for the handouts. Add the title of your talk, the name of the group, and the date.

If you prefer not to use your letterhead as a cover sheet, tape your business card to the lower corner of the title page so that it will be duplicated on the first page of the handout. To avoid shadows around the card, completely cover the edges with clear tape.

When you have found a technique that works for you, look for ways to creatively springboard from it. For example, if you find a hot button that catches the interest of dentists, explore how you can adapt it to work with physicians, psychologists, physical therapists, and any other group on your prospect list.

Chapter 34

Organizing for Sales Efficiency

Prospects will flow on and off your priority list, and it will take skill to keep your weeks organized so that you can manage your time and travels efficiently. In this chapter, I'll be introducing you to a basic model that you can adapt to your special situation.

Here we'll focus mainly on scheduling your sales calls on new prospects. However, it's important to keep a balance of other necessary activities as well. Sales calls will normally take up most of your working week, but don't neglect other tasks that also need to be carried on. These include

- "Customer-care" calls—stopping by to check on how those who have bought your product are faring.
- Preparing proposals and dealing with correspondence, phone calls, and the like.
- Administrative activities, such as reordering from your suppliers.
- Keeping up your professional proficiency.

Some of these tasks can be performed between your scheduled appointments. For example, you can keep up with your professional reading while in customer waiting rooms, and you can drop in on existing customers as you pass by on your way from one scheduled call to another.

In the first part of the chapter, we'll give a basic overview of the tasks involved. You can accomplish these tasks using paper (notebooks and index cards), or you can use a computer-based system to accomplish most of them.

We'll look at the role of computer-based sales management systems at the end of this chapter. But whether you use paper or computer, these tasks need to be accomplished if your efforts are to be organized and systematic.

The Model System

1. Map your territory.

Get a map of the territory in which you will be working, and divide it into quadrants. To illustrate the approach here, we'll assume that the territory that you're covering consists of a single city, and that the time frame is one week. (On the other hand, if your territory is an entire state, it may be more appropriate to plan on a monthly basis, with a week, or even two, spent in each quadrant.)

The quadrants will not necessarily be equal in size. A busy downtown area that consists of only a few square blocks might be one quadrant, and the entire southern and eastern suburbs might be another quadrant.

Here we're using the term "quadrant" loosely—it's not necessarily one of four areas or a pie-shaped wedge. It can be any reasonable grouping that makes sense in minimizing time lost to unnecessary travel. If you are working in a very large area, such as a part of a state, you may have a dozen "quadrants," or working areas. These might be centered around the major cities or a natural barrier, such as where two interstates intersect.

You might also divide by industry, so that all the doctors are in one "quadrant" (using the term even more loosely), all the lawyers in another, and all the Indian chiefs and factory managers in a third.

2. Assign prospects to quadrants.

Assign each prospect to a quadrant or sector, and mark that quadrant on the prospect data card. (We'll cover the details of the prospect data card below.) Code the quadrants by number, location, or grouping: "1," "West," or "northern suburbs."

3. Set up your calendar.

In setting up your calendar for the week, allocate one day to each quadrant (Monday in quadrant 1, Tuesday in 2, and so forth). As the weeks go by, shift the days, so that you are not always in quadrant 2 on Tuesday.

Remember, this is the *model* approach; you can adapt it to fit your needs. For example, if you are working in a larger geographic area, your cycle may be longer than one week.

4. Phone for appointments by quadrant.

Before you begin phoning for appointments, group the prospect cards by quadrant, and focus on one quadrant at a time. Decide on which days of the following two or even three weeks you are going to work in each quadrant, and then push for appointments to match.

If you schedule your time two weeks ahead, you will have backup dates ready, just in case the Decision Maker is interested but unavailable.

The quadrant system is a tool for making the most of your working day, and helps prevent your racing back and forth across the city. But be flexible; don't automatically pass up the chance for a promising meeting if it means crossing into "tomorrow's" quadrant.

5. Prepare a prospect data card after obtaining an appointment.

When you get an appointment, note it both on your daily working calendar and on the prospect data card.

After you make the call, note the outcome and any action steps that need to be completed on the prospect data card.

6. Balance other sales-related activities.

It's important to be out making sales calls, but it's a mistake to neglect other necessary activities.

Build in some office time at least every other week for catching up on these tasks, including paperwork, professional reading, correspondence, and the like.

Plan ahead, in both the short and the long term. Phone for next week's appointments. Deal with any supply problems. Develop any proposals or survey reports you have promised. Read up on the industries you are working in, as well as on what your competition is doing.

Organizing Your Key Data on Prospects

Here's a basic system for keeping your information on existing customers and future prospects organized with a minimum of effort. You can adapt it to a computer-based system if you prefer. But if you do, keep in mind that your objective is to make sales calls, not to develop the world's most perfect database.

The basic system consists of two key elements: prospect data cards and customer information files. (If you are computer-inclined, you can find software packages to organize this for you. But if you're just starting out, it's probably a good idea to operate with a simple paper-based system, so that you get the chance to know what to look for when you do go high-tech.)

Prospect Data Cards

Prepare a *prospect data card* for each potential client. (As you begin, this can be as simple as a blank 4-by-6 index card. You can customize it to your specific needs as they become clear.) This should contain the prospect company's name and address, and the name, phone number, and address (if different) of the key Decision Maker.

If the lead came from a referral from another client, note that source here.

After the prospect has been converted to a customer, relabel the card as a customer data card, or put on a colored tag as a code.

Jot down any brief essential notes. If these amount to more than a few words, set up a prospect file, which we'll examine below.

On the prospect data card, keep a record of the results that transpire from each contact. Note on what day you started phoning for an appointment, and how many calls it took to get the meeting.

Record also the progress made at each meeting, along with any tasks you need to do in following up, or any special objections you need to be prepared for.

For instance, if the Decision Maker indicates that she is interested, but needs to get the results of quarterly earnings before deciding, write that callback date on the prospect data card. Flag it with colored ink. (You may also want to write a brief note to yourself of what was said during that conversation.) In addition, supplement that by marking the callback date in a tickler file to remind you. The tickler file may be your appointment book or a more elaborate accordion file system.

File these data cards in the way that is most comfortable for you. One option is to file them alphabetically. Another is to organize them by their priority status, with high potentials in a hot file, lows in a back-burner file, and so forth.

A third, and the method that I found worked best for me, is to file the data cards by the quadrants into which you have organized your territory.

Put a red stick-on dot on the top corner of the card to flag the high potentials. Remember that generally 80 percent of your sales will come from just 20 percent of your prospects, and so it makes sense to focus on the high potentials, rather than trying to give all equal coverage.

CUSTOMER INFORMATION FILES

As you research prospects, or work with those that you convert to customers, you'll collect a pile of information: company brochures, handouts, notes from meetings and phone conversations.

To get these data under control, set up a separate file folder for each of your present or prospective customers. Add any newspaper clippings you come upon that are relevant to either the prospect company or its industry. Note on the prospect data card that you have opened a file, so that you remember to check the file before taking the next step.

YOUR MONTHLY REPORT—TO YOURSELF

One of the benefits of being an entrepreneur is the freedom from having to report to a boss on how you have been spending your time. Still, it can be helpful to keep a record nonetheless, as it can help you see where your time is going. It is also a motivational tool: By keeping a monthly record, you can compete with yourself to improve your productivity.

Here's a simple worksheet that you can adapt as a model for your own situation.

Monthly Record of Calls and Selling Activities

MONTH: ________________

Activities	Week 1	Week 2	Week 3	Week 4
Orders				
Sales calls				
Demos				
Presentations				
Proposals				
Customer-care calls				
Talks given/other indirect efforts				

COMPUTERS AND YOUR SELLING EFFORTS

The range of software products available to help manage the selling process is changing and growing so quickly that it's impossible to list specific products in a book—by the time the book gets to you, half the products will be off the market, replaced by others, and the other half will have been updated beyond recognition. (By one estimate in the magazine *Mobile Office*, sales of sales management software will balloon from $413 million in 1991 to an estimated $2.5 billion by 1997. You may be thinking that *that's* the industry you should be targeting as an entrepreneur!)

In any case, here's a checklist of some of the key factors to watch for when and if you do shop for software to automate your selling efforts. (In the new jargon, that's called "sales force automation," or SFA.)

In shopping for a sales management product, the key question is, Precisely what do you want this package to do for you? (There's no sense paying for the super bells-and-whistles version if all those options are just going to get in the way, and quadruple your learning time.) Among the things you may want the software to do are these:

- Help the Sales Rep (you or your staff) keep track of prospect data. (This is generally referred to as "sales contact management.")
- The above, plus automating the sending of sales letters.
- The above, plus keeping a calendar of appointments, plus providing a tickler system to remind the sales reps when to get back to certain prospects.
- The above, plus passing on information on the sales and prospects to other departments, such as production, shipping, and billing, without anyone else having to reenter the information.

Other considerations:

- Will the software also supply sales reports—such as on prospects sold and pending and on the sales reps' activities—in a format that meets your needs? (On this, decide what data you really do need to do your job; don't get drawn into processing data just because they are available.)
- How easy to use is the software? (You want yourself and your sales reps selling, not fighting against the software.)
- Is it flexible? Can it be adapted to any special needs you might have? Can it be expanded as your sales force grows? Can it be used on a network, so that all reps and departments can easily share data?
- Is it compatible with other software you use, such as word processing systems?

Given the right combination of laptop computer and software, the sales rep can carry an electronic catalog with her, updated every day to show current inventory. With other software, the laptop can serve as a presentation device, letting the prospect see short video clips of the product in action.

To get a sense of what software is available to meet your needs, start by scanning relevant magazines at a good newsstand, as the computer and sales publications will be most up to date.

Magazines, like software, tend to come and go, so it's difficult to predict what will be helpful when you go looking. However, *Success* magazine has been publishing for close to 90 years, so the odds are that it'll still be around when you're ready to shop for SFA software. Particularly helpful is the May issue of *Success* each year, which focuses on sales. In addition to a lot of good information on what other marketers are doing, you'll find reviews of the latest sales software. *Success* even runs a mail-order operation, so you can order software and sales books directly, if your local dealer can't help you.

However, before investing in new software, check to see what may have come already bundled on your computer. My Microsoft Works has templates for a variety of business tasks, including customer database management, key contacts, and even templates for developing employee profiles. These models, maybe with some minor customizing, may be all you need until you get to that first $1 million in annual profits.

Chapter 35

Selling Tools: Office Space, Computers, Sales Kits, Etc.

Here are some final practical details, first on equipment and the like, then on what to carry with you on your sales calls.

Essential and Not-so-Essential Equipment

1. *Business cards, letterheads, envelopes.* You can't do business without them. This is an area in which to splurge a little, upgrading your image through better paper and perhaps even investing in a graphic designer to ensure an attractive layout.

   Attach a business card to everything you send out. Stick a business card on every letter, every brochure, every newspaper clipping you mail. Every time you visit a prospect, give a business card to the receptionist, the secretary, and the Decision Maker. Pass out business cards to everyone you meet with whom there is any reasonable potential business connection. Granted, maybe only one in a hundred or one in a thousand will pay off with a lead or a sale, but since even the fanciest card costs only pennies, it's still a good investment.

2. *Brochures and other sales literature.* Don't invest a lot of money in developing glossy sales literature at the start. What you and the pricy graphic designer think are great may not make the selling point with actual prospects. Perhaps for the first month or so you can make do with just typed sales literature to test out the ideas with customers. (Your marketing approach, and even your prices, may change.)

   For most selling situations, testimonials from actual customers will carry far more weight with prospects than all the best efforts of copywriters and

High-Tech Business Cards

Putting one's fax number on business cards is common now, and more and more people are putting on their E-mail addresses as well. Some even list several E-mail addresses, including those for CompuServe, the Internet, and GEnie or other systems. If you've got it, flaunt it. More avenues by which clients can reach you can only help.

photographers. Granted, you may not have testimonials at the start, but stay on the lookout for them. If you know that a client is pleased with what you have done, ask for a short letter. Even a single strong sentence can be a powerful addition to your literature.

3. *Office space.* An office, especially in a good location, used to be an important factor to clients, as it supposedly demonstrated stability. But now, with the growth of sole entrepreneurs and the boom in home offices, an office is generally much less important, unless you need a place to meet with clients, or unless you have others working with you.
   If you need a business address, look into using "mailbox" services. These will, depending on the firm, supply you with mail service, telephone paging, and perhaps conference rooms, fax, and secretarial service as needed.

4. *Computers.* It's hard for me now to imagine surviving without my computer. Even if I were spending more time selling consulting services, instead of writing books, I would still find a computer, and appropriate software, essential for writing follow-up letters, preparing proposals, designing handouts and presentation materials, and the like. (Plus, as discussed in the previous chapter, a computer and the right software can be a great help in organizing and tracking prospect data.)
   If you already own a computer, look for ways of integrating it into your selling efforts. If you don't own a computer, should you buy one just for the sake of your marketing efforts? That depends on your budget. You may need to go three months, six months, or maybe even longer before any cash flows in. If in doubt, better hold onto the cash to keep the operation running that many weeks longer.

5. *Voice mail.* You must have some way of being reached by phone. If prospects can't reach you, then you can be sure they'll never convert from prospects to customers. Whether your "voice mail" is a simple answering machine or something more elaborate is up to you and your needs (and your pocketbook). Just have something.

Your Briefcase or Selling Kit

Inevitably, the Decision Maker is going to judge your company and your product by what he sees in you. If you are organized and professional, the DM is likely to assume that your firm will provide reliable deliveries and service.

The reverse is even more the case: Your product is going to be judged harshly if you appear disorganized, or if your sales kit is a mess.

Every day, in every city, sales are lost because a salesperson forgets to replenish his stock of brochures or order blanks. Other sales are lost because the salesperson arrives late to a sales call because she didn't have the right change for the parking meter.

To help you avoid these unnecessary handicaps, here's a beginning checklist for reviewing your briefcase or sales kit. Add to the checklist to fit your special needs, or as other items occur to you.

- Prospect data cards (and optionally customer information files) for everyone on whom a call is scheduled today.
- Prospect data cards or files on all others you may see, such as for customer-care or cold calls.
- Your brochures, samples, etc.
- Supply of
  - * Business cards
  - * Order forms (or equivalent)
- Clipboard, paper, extra pens, paper clips, stick-on notes
- Calculator
- Change for parking meters, subway, phone
- Reading material for waiting time
- Map (or in your car)
- Appointment book with phone numbers for other calls you may make today

Two suggestions from my wife, Susan:

- For women, an extra pair of stockings, in case of a run.
- For men, an extra necktie in case of food stains. (If you're a messy eater, carry either an extra tie or a bib, though we don't recommend bibs for crucial business lunches with potential clients!)

I haven't included in this checklist any high-tech gadgetry that you may use, such as a laptop computer (which may contain your prospect information, replacing the data cards, etc.), cellular phone, pager, and the like.

Part Nine
Expanding Your Sales Organization

Up to this point, we have focused on the how-to of selling, particularly on how you, as a new or sole entrepreneur, can get started in selling one-to-one with customers.

But with hard work and good fortune, organizations grow, and so now we look at how to expand your sales operation from one person—you—to more than one, whether that's just you plus a single new hire or many new hires.

Moving on is a big, even intimidating, step. On one of the morning programs a few years ago, Mary Kay Ash, founder of Mary Kay Cosmetics, said that one of the hardest decisions she ever had to make was to determine whether to stay small, so that she could keep full control, or to expand, which meant giving up some control and relying on others.

First Basic Decision: To Expand Marketing In-House, or to Use Outsiders

In deciding how to expand your marketing capability, you have two basic choices: Either hire your own selling staff or contract with outside organizations or individuals to handle the marketing for you. A variety of selling organizations and networks are in place across the United States for you to tap into, including

- Dealers
- Wholesalers
- Sales reps who handle a variety of lines, and who work solely on commission
- Catalog operations

Whether outsiders are appropriate for you, and, if so, which type is best, depends on a number of factors, including what your product is and its price range, and also whether you have a single product or a range of items.

Suppose you are producing one or a few types of innovative kitchen implements that retail for, let's say, $10 each. At this price, there is no reasonable way that it could be profitable for you—or for the members of an internal sales force—to travel across the country visiting individual store owners.

In this situation, the most appropriate marketing approach would probably be to sell your utensils through one or more national direct mail catalogs directed to people who are known to buy cooking-related products.

Alternatively, a good marketing channel might be the wholesale operations across the country that supply regional networks of dealers and shops. You might even interest one of the TV shopping channels in featuring your line.

If you do decide to market through outside channels, which is the best approach—catalogs? dealers? wholesalers? No one can say for certain. Particularly at the start, testing provides the best answer. Talk to, or write, a few of each, tell them about your product, and ask their input: Is the product something that would be of interest to them? Can they sell it at a price that will enable both you and them to make a profit? If not, what do they suggest?

Developing Your In-House Selling Capability

Enough about outside marketing channels. Our focus here is on the other option: Choosing to expand your own selling staff, rather than relying on dealers, reps, and the like. (In practice, even if you do sell through other large marketing forces, you may still need to have your own in-house selling staff to sell to these larger firms.)

In expanding your internal selling staff, you face several decision points, which we will be addressing in the pages following.

- Who to hire? How to hire the best for you? (These will be covered in Part 9.)
- How to develop a pay and compensation plan for your salespeople that makes them *want* to *work* for you (with deliberate emphasis on both "work" and "want"). If the good people don't want to join you, then you're not going to make progress. Also, a pay plan that makes your salespeople so comfortable with their base salary that they lack motivation is not in anyone's best interest. (We look at compensation in Part 10.)
- How to manage your sales staff (be it one person or a network spread nationwide). Once you take on a single person, you become a manager. You can manage by default and hope that everything works out, or you can do it right and help your people and your organization work up to full potential. (We address these issues in Part 11.)

Chapter 36

Defining the Job You Need Filled

One of the key messages of the earlier parts of this book is that to sell effectively, you begin by helping the prospect define what needs exist, and only after that do you speak of your solution.

Now the approach remains much the same, but with a twist: In hiring, you begin by defining very clearly just what need exists, and only after that do you think about the actual mechanics of hiring.

It's an obvious point, but one that is often overlooked—which is how new entrepreneurs can find themselves saddled with the wrong people. You meet someone who has the aura of "super-salesperson," and who just happens to be between engagements. Or you have a brother-in-law who is reported to be a great salesman. You're overworked handling all roles, and your impulse is to say "Hired!" just to take some of the pressure off yourself.

It's only later that you realize that you didn't really need a salesperson, at all; what you should have hired was someone with very different skills.

Or, still overworked (as all new entrepreneurs are), you meet a person who's a clone of yourself, someone with exactly your blend of expertise and skills. It seems a dream come true, and again you say, "Hired!" But as the weeks and months pass, you realize that you've made the common blunder of hiring in your own image. Now both you and your clone want to stay back in the lab dreaming up great new products, and there's nobody out selling them. Or maybe you're both out selling, and there's nobody back doing the administrative stuff like shipping orders, billing, and so forth.

Defining Your Need

In determining what kind of person you really need to hire, focus on the needs, not the person.

We'll be referring to "hiring" here, but that doesn't necessarily mean adding people to the payroll. Although you may find you need to "hire" someone, be open to taking that person on as an outside contractor or consultant, rather than as a full-time employee. (One caution on using "contract" employees: There are certain tests used by the Internal Revenue Service to determine whether or not someone is independent for tax purposes, so check this with your tax person.)

To keep the discussion simple, we'll assume that you are a one-person operation, now thinking of adding one more body. The principles will be the same if you multiply the numbers by two, by ten, or probably by twenty. (If you're already the size of General Motors, I don't expect you're looking here for advice.)

1. What is the actual need? What is the precise job that needs filling?

Maybe you do need to add a sales type. But, on the other hand, maybe *you* are the best possible salesperson at this stage, and what you really need is someone back in the office, or at the production line, to take over the little tasks that are keeping you from selling as much as you would like. Or maybe you know that your real strength is as a creative developer, or as an administrator or financial person. You don't want to spend your time selling (or don't do it well).

Perhaps your need is for a salesperson to go out and make calls. But, then again, perhaps what you *really* need is a strategic marketer. Instead of adding one or an army of people to go out and sell, perhaps this is the time to take on—as employee or consultant—someone who can put together a "big picture" strategic plan, pointing out that this is the time to move away from selling directly to end users, and instead roll the product out nationally, working through the kinds of dealers, wholesalers, or catalog houses we discussed in the introduction to this part.

In short, even more important than finding the person for the job is determining what job actually needs doing. Just what do you ultimately need now: Someone to do what you don't have time for? What you don't do well? What you lack training in, and don't have the time to learn? Or do you need someone to contribute at a different level, adding a level of vision or expertise that you as a new entrepreneur can't hope to have?

Example: A new entrepreneur, the inventor of a $50 consumer product, went to an executive search firm looking for help in finding a good national sales manager. But some probing by a senior search consultant revealed that the entrepreneur's ultimate need was for a marketing strategist, because the selling effort to that point had been erratic, responding to opportunities without any overall plan. Although sales were good, they were below what they could have been for the effort and dollars invested.

2. If you are going to add one or more sales types, what does the job—or jobs—call for?

Let's assume that you have given it plenty of thought, and you have concluded that yes, you really do need to beef up the sales function. Other considerations flow. Just what will the new salespeople be doing? Will they be

- Selling "inside," that is, staying back in your place of business and selling to the prospects that come through the shop door
- Selling "in the field," that is, going out to find prospects and selling them at their homes or places of business
- "Telemarketing," selling over the phone, either by initiating calls or by converting those who phone in for information into customers

Clearly, very different types of people would be appropriate for each approach. And a still different type would be appropriate if the job encompassed all three approaches—which could easily happen as a business grows, or as it moves into different markets.

Example: Jeff started selling computers in college, then expanded into a retail store after graduation. As the business changed, most of his customers bought at the retail shop. He hired various people to staff the store.

But, because he was losing out on the larger, more lucrative group sales to businesses, he began adding "field" sales reps. He found that they needed different skills from those needed by the people who stayed back in the shop. This was partly because the job involved locating prospects, but also because these business prospects had more interest in systems and networking applications than most of the retail customers.

Now he is adding a telemarketing specialist to scout for leads farther afield, and to handle sales of low-ticket items such as supplies. This telemarketer will have a package of skills different from those of both the shop and the field salespeople.

3. What skills, knowledge, personal characteristics, and the like does the specific job require?

Ideally, you look for a person who has not only selling skills and experience but also technical knowledge of the field and the industry, plus other nice-to-haves such as appearance, manner, "style," and the like.

That's the ideal. Depending on your luck, and the state of the job market, you may find that perfect person. More often, it becomes a matter of settling on the person with the best balance of several factors. Three of these factors are appropriate to every field; add other factors that are particularly appropriate to your industry or other needs.

- *Selling skills and experience.* But caution: While a background in selling is definitely an asset, there are pros and cons attached to hiring a salesperson with significant experience. We'll discuss them below.
- *Personal characteristics and capabilities.* Among these are factors such as the ability to ask good questions and listen well, to learn quickly, to adapt ("think on one's feet"), to present well, and definitely to project energy and enthusiasm, as well as to instill confidence and trust.
- *Product- and industry-specific knowledge.* This can take a variety of forms:
    - *Technical knowledge of your product or service.* For instance, the programmer who helped you design the software package or the data service that you are now marketing has technical knowledge of this sort. Even a programmer who didn't work on the product would probably have enough technical expertise to understand it. But keep in mind that knowing how a product was built, or how it works, does not automatically translate into an ability to talk clearly, to help potential customers recognize their need, or to help them see how your product can do the job for them.
    - *Technical knowledge of the industry or general field,* whether it is the area of electronics, printing, transportation, or whatever. One might know virtually everything there is to know about a field, yet still not

have a real sense of how to match your product with a prospect's real-world needs.

* *Knowledge of the marketplace, the competition, and competing products.* This is useful, as that kind of knowledge can put your product into perspective—how it can help customers and how it compares with what's already available.
* *Contacts in the field or industry.* Knowing who's who can be a real marketing asset. But not all contacts are equal. Determine whether these contacts are at the Decision Maker level, or further down the hierarchy.

Developing a Job Description Letter

If you've worked in a large, bureaucratic organization, the words "job description" may be off-putting. The job descriptions churned out in big organizations tend to take a lot of words to say very little that's really useful. But, then, what can you expect? Most of them are lawyers' documents, intended not so much to define the work to be done as to protect the organization in case of disputes.

As a new entrepreneur, you need to develop a different kind of job description: job descriptions that are real-world and useful, because they reflect what needs to be done in real-world jobs that relate, in a measurable way, to the bottom line of profitability. Here's how:

Sum up the conclusions you reach about what you need in your new selling job. First, develop a list or outline of your findings on the skills and abilities needed. Then flesh out the list in the form of a letter. That letter serves as your job description, and it is helpful in a variety of ways. (I suggest using the form of a letter, as most people find that easier to write and read than a formal job description. Alternatively, you can stay with the outline form, provided it can be understood by others.)

For one thing, you'll find that the act of forcing words onto paper will itself help focus and clarify your thinking about the kind of person (and skills) you need for the job.

The letter also serves as your base point as you search for candidates. After you have met someone who seems good, go back and reread your letter describing the job you need to fill. Does this candidate really meet all those criteria?

If not, two possibilities arise: Either this is not the right person, despite the charisma, or the job description letter needs to be revised. It's not written in stone; it's only a working tool that you can and should continually fine-tune.

The job description letter also serves as a helpful tool in communicating to the leading candidates just what you expect from them. A sales job is not just about selling. It will generally also include other duties, such as maintaining good relations with customers, keeping up-to-date records, even dressing in a way that reflects well on the company's image.

The job description letter can be the basis of your final negotiation with the top candidate, so that you and she or he agree on precisely what the job entails. You may, even at that late point, revise the job description letter to reflect ideas suggested by this candidate, or to adapt the job to capitalize on this individual's unique strengths.

Finally, the job description letter that you settle on at hiring can be the basis of your ongoing performance reviews. You can, as appropriate, negotiate changes in it as the work relationship proceeds, to reflect the realities of the person's strengths or weaknesses, or to reflect changes in the organization. (For example, as the company grows, you may add other specialized staffers to take over certain duties, such as the telephone side of marketing, and that would be reflected in your expectations of other staff members' duties.)

Checklist of Possible Elements in the Job Description Letter

To get you started, here are a few key points of the kind that you may want to include in the job description letter. These are only starting points, so be sure to add your own particular requirements. In addition to selling, which is the core of the job, are there other aspects, such as these?

1. *Installation.* That is, the salesperson responsible for setting up the product or service and getting it under way?
2. *Training customers* in the use of the products sold?
3. If the unit breaks down, is it the salesperson's responsibility to repair it, or to arrange for repair?
4. Is the salesperson expected to actively sell small peripheral products related to the main product? (For example, if you sell copiers or printers, does the Sales Rep also have the responsibility for selling toner cartridges? What if the customer runs out of toner, and puts in an emergency call—is the salesperson expected to deliver the toner as a priority task?)
5. *Assisting with other general selling functions*, such as helping to staff booths at trade shows, giving talks and presentations, and the like.
6. What responsibility does the salesperson have for *other customer relations activities*, such as the following?

    - Periodic *customer-care callbacks* to make sure that all is well, keep in contact, and remind them that your firm is there for any further orders.
    - *Socializing with clients*, such as playing golf, etc. If so, is time spent on this considered company time? A company expense? Is there a limit on entertainment expenses that will be reimbursed? If this is done on company time, how much time is appropriate?
    - Keeping up *attendance at or membership in professional and civic groups*. Is this done on company time? Who pays for the dues and dinners?

Summary

Don't hire a person because he or she looks like a potential selling whiz. Instead, invest real time and effort in thinking through just what the job is that needs to be filled. Instead of a salesperson, you may need someone to fill your other roles, so that you can do more selling (or vice versa). Consider these questions:

1. What is the actual need? What is the precise job that needs filling?

2. If you are going to add one or more sales types, what does the job—or jobs—call for?
3. What skills, knowledge, personal characteristics, and the like does the specific job require? It will generally involve some combination of factors like these:
   - Selling skills and experience
   - Personal characteristics and capabilities
   - Product- and industry-specific knowledge, including
     * Technical knowledge of the product or service you sell
     * Technical knowledge of the general field or industry
     * Knowledge of the competition and the marketplace
     * Contacts in the field or industry

A job description letter helps you boil your thinking down, and also serves other purposes, including defining your expectations to potential new hires, forming the basis of the final negotiations before hiring, and serving as a continuing reference for future performance reviews.

Chapter 37

Finding Appropriate Candidates for the Sales Job

With the job description letter drafted, you should have a good sense of what kind of package of skills and abilities you are looking for. Now it's time to begin developing a "menu" of candidates from which to choose.

In this chapter, we'll examine some practical ways of developing that menu of candidates at reasonable cost, and some of the key factors to watch for as you begin to narrow in on the top few contenders.

However, keep in mind that your selection criteria, as reflected in the job description letter, are subject to revision. They may well change as you see what kinds of skills are actually available in the hiring market in the compensation range you can afford.

Ways of Finding Candidates

1. Networking.

As you probably know from your own job searches in the past, the most productive approach to finding a good job is to network among friends and people you know in the industry or geographic area, subtly (or not so subtly) spreading the word that you are open to a move.

Networking is equally useful now that you are on the hiring side of the table. Sending out feelers among the people you know in your field greatly increases your chances of finding compatible, knowledgeable people who come with known references and records of accomplishment. (It may even happen that the people whom you ask for leads are themselves open to the possibility of joining you.)

In networking for candidates, don't stop with the people you know. Those first calls are only the first step. In your initial networking calls, ask two kinds of questions:

- Who do they know with a selling background (or other relevant marketing skills) who might be looking for a new opportunity? *Also*, whether or not they are able to give you names of potential candidates, go on to ask,
- Is there anyone else they suggest who might also be able to give some leads? (If they do, clarify whether or not you may mention their name when you make the contact.)

As you see, networking for potential new hires is actually a lot like networking to develop your prospect list for selling, as described in this book's Part 1, "Locating Priority Prospects." Many of the techniques (and information sources) discussed there are equally useful in networking to find good salespeople.

Incidentally, some of the people with whom you network may be willing to serve as "reality checkers," giving feedback on how appropriate, relevant, and real-world your job description letter really is. Not everyone will be able to spend time discussing it in detail, but most will be pleased to be asked.

Who and where to network depend on the specifics of your field or industry, but there are some common starting points:

- *People with whom you used to work* before going off on your own.
- *People you know from professional associations*, either in your region or nationally.
- *People from other civic organizations or church groups* (provided, of course, that you're not working in too specialized an area).
- *Suppliers to your new business*. For example, if you're manufacturing a product, then you deal with various kinds of suppliers, ranging perhaps from specialized parts manufacturers to retailers of office equipment and supplies. Any of them may know of salespeople who are looking for a change, or may put you in touch with others who know more about your field.
- *Your banker* may be able to help, although bankers can't always speak freely because of concerns for the confidentiality of clients.
- *Professors and instructors* who work in your field. Begin with your old school, but don't overlook the institutions near where you are now located.
- *Your best competitors*. Find out who the sales and marketing people in competing companies are, because these folks might just be open to moving to a smaller company where they see more opportunity and a brighter future. Consider also any salespeople who may have been let go from these companies: Given the way corporate downsizing occurs, this may be no reflection at all on their abilities. It may even mean that they were so competent that someone above them on the organization chart found them a threat.
- *Other successful small companies with a similar product* may also be a source of trained, eager salespeople who want to get in on the ground floor of a new venture.
- *Even the superstars of your profession*—people you don't know personally, and have only read about or heard about—will often be willing to network. For one thing, they may be flattered that you searched them out for advice. For another, they may appreciate the opportunity to pass on names as a way of repaying favors to others.

2. Letting candidates find you.

Once you start the networking process, you'll find it working both ways. You'll begin networking your way to good candidates, but they will also begin finding their way to you through those same networks.

As soon as you start the process of networking, word will begin getting out, and job seekers may begin calling you. Have a netted-out description of what you are looking for, along with some qualifying questions in mind to help you sort out those who are high-potential from those who don't quite fit. While you don't want to reject anyone too soon, it's most efficient for both sides if you can screen out noncontenders before they and you waste unnecessary time or effort.

The analysis you put into preparing your job description letter should give you the material for these qualifying questions and statements.

But be open-minded, because the candidates may educate you on what you should really be looking for. Be particularly open to candidates who have both the strength to phone you and the presence of mind to ask useful, persuasive questions. Those are two of the key abilities of an effective salesperson. Although these candidates may not initially seem to fit the profile you are looking for, listen: They may open your mind to other kinds of skills or areas of expertise that mesh with your needs.

Other potential candidates may find their way to you on the basis of their own research, or in response to some publicity you or your product or service has received. Although the calls may come from unexpected angles, be open to the fresh possibilities they may raise. Again, the fact that these people have the initiative and creativity to find their way to you, and the courage to make the call, is a good indicator that they may have the energy, enthusiasm, and drive to succeed with you.

3. Placing job advertisements.

Job ads are certainly worth trying, but an ad opens you up to the world, and the world may inundate you with responses, few of them on target with your needs.

In what publications to advertise and whether to use display or classified ads depend on your unique circumstances. For example, if you are looking for a salesperson to help expand your garden supply shop to serve the commercial building market, it probably would not pay to advertise in a national gardening journal. On the other hand, if you have bought a struggling small-town AM or FM radio operation, you probably would do better advertising for a sales director in a national trade journal.

Suppose you live in a medium-sized city, say 200,000 to 500,000 people, and you want to advertise for your first salesperson. The product is not so specialized that you need to use a trade journal. You decide to put an ad in the local paper. Should it be a classified ad (which is relatively cheap to run) or a display ad in the main body of the paper (costing probably a few hundred dollars for an insertion)?

Another question to consider: Which day is best for running your ad, Sunday or a weekday? The answers depend largely on local custom. Watch what others do. As a general rule, the Sunday paper will be best, as it reaches the largest readership, and as people have more time to read ads—and to respond.

Running a classified ad is taking a shotgun approach: You're shooting in the dark, as you generally won't go into much detail, and the respondents will be shooting back in the dark, and a lot of them will be off-target.

A good display ad can catch the eye of people who are not necessarily looking to change jobs—and they often turn out to be the best candidates. A display ad also gives you a better opportunity to describe in some detail what you are looking for. For models, check any big-city Sunday paper or the *Wall Street Journal*. Notice that some name the company advertising the opening, whereas others are "blind" ads, with replies going to a box at the paper. In either case, most of these ads are placed in the employment or classified section (even though they are larger display-type ads, with larger type) because that's where job seekers look.

To stand out from the crowd of other job ads, consider writing yours in plain language (not the standard phrases that are generally used in job ads). Describe exactly the kind of person you're looking for, and what your company is about.

In listing your requirements, think again about what you actually need. For example, is a degree really necessary, or is it just a shorthand (and not necessarily accurate) way of describing certain skills and qualities? If so, then list those skills, which might include "quick learner," "able to absorb technical information in the area of health sciences," "able to interact comfortably with senior management," "able to use databases in both technical and business areas to conduct marketing approaches."

For this kind of ad, or any other, you have several choices in how to receive the replies. You can include a mail reply address—either that of your office or post office box, or (for an additional fee) the newspaper's reply box, from which ads they are forwarded to you.

If you are adventurous, and you want to get a sense of the candidates quickly, put your business phone number in the ad, and say that you'll be by the phone during certain hours that Sunday and one or two evenings during the week from, say, 6 to 9. Invite qualified people to call and talk about the job and why they think they may be right for it. If there is a fit, you can ask them to send a resume or to bring the resume with them to an initial meeting.

Here's a model job ad to work from. It was suggested by my wife, Susan, a former executive search consultant. It seems simple enough, but contains a number of "code words" used by head-hunters.

A small, fast-growing, aggressive computer services company seeks a sales representative with skills including ____, _____, and _____. We offer a dynamic team environment with growth potential, and look for someone with a proven track record of success in this or a related field. Compensation salary plus commission. Reply to Post Office Box ——.

It seems basic, but there are some key words that should elicit the interest of the right people: "small but fast-growing" (there is opportunity for upward mobility if you join us); "aggressive" (be prepared to work very hard to keep up with the rest of us); "dynamic" (there are no rigid hierarchies and bureaucratic procedures; if you need a rule book to work by, don't bother applying here, because you'll hate it—we want someone to help us invent the company as we go along); "team environment" (no lone-wolf or prima-donna types, please); "growth potential" (if you're stuck in a rut where you are, we can offer you the chance to expand your skills; may also mean that the money at the start isn't going to be dazzling, but if you're good at your job and we prosper, so will you); "proven track record of success" (we're looking for a winner; may also mean that if you don't quite have a great record yet, we'll still listen if you can convince us you have the potential).

4. Letting headhunting firms search for you.

The main disadvantage for start-up firms in using headhunters is cost. Count on paying in the area of 30 percent of the first year's compensation to the firm, plus expenses. That 30 percent usually comes out of your pocket, up front: it's not something you can charge back to the candidate you ultimately hire.

But the advantages are many. For one thing, reputable search firms generally offer a guarantee: If the person you hire at their recommendation leaves (or is fired) in the first six months or so, they will either refund the fee or, more often, find you a replacement at no additional charge.

Headhunting firms tend to break into two major categories: "retainer" firms and "contingency" firms.

As the name implies, retainer firms ask for a retainer up front before beginning work. They generally tend to be oriented to executive or managerial types earning upwards of $50–75,000 or so (though that can vary with the area and industry). Retainer firms favor calling themselves "search consultants."

Contingency firms are paid *when* and *if* they find someone.

As a ballpark figure, figure that both retainer and contingency firms will expect to be paid around 30% of the person's estimated annual income, though there is usually room for negotiation.

Though a headhunter's fee may seem expensive, balance it against factors such as these:

- *You save your time.* When you retain a search firm, you are free to spend your time doing what you do best, not skimming resumes and interviewing.
- *You increase the odds of getting the right person, and on the first attempt.* Search firms are experts in matching people to jobs, whereas your expertise is in other areas. If you choose wrong, you may waste several months waiting to see if the person will work out. Then, if you do terminate the individual, you may face liabilities ranging from commissions on pending sales to, even, a lawsuit for any reason a hungry, creative lawyer can come up with.
- *You better the odds of filling the right job.* Part of the service a good headhunting firm offers is a thorough preliminary analysis, working with you to define precisely what needs you have to fill. (Your job description letter starts this process, but as experts the search firm can carry it further.)
- *You better the odds of getting the right personality "fit."* Search consultants have seen thousands of faces on both sides, and have well-honed senses for what personality matches will and will not work. For example, if they sense that you are an adventurous, free-spirit entrepreneur with a seat-of-the-pants management style, they would save you from hiring—despite the resume—an overly security-oriented person.
- *Many search firms specialize in one or a few industries,* such as electronics, construction, transportation, law, marketing, and the like. That means you don't have to educate them on the key players in your field. They are already tuned in, probably more than you, to who's who, and who's looking for a change. They may also have stacks of resumes on file (or computer), shortening the time required. And, if yours is a unique need, they know where to begin networking. If you are working in a specialized field (for

example, software design), a head-hunter who targets that specialty may be better for your needs. For help, try the Association of Executive Search Consultants, 230 Park Avenue, Suite 1549, New York, NY 10169.

Look Not for the "Best," but Instead for the Best for Your Situation

If you are basically a start-up company looking for a sales manager or senior salesperson, you will probably be looking for someone with credentials like the following, as a minimum:

- Proven track record of taking a start-up company and expanding it. You want someone who has done it successfully at least once already. You can't afford to take on a person who is learning as *you* learn.
- Ideally, this person's track record will include taking some similar product and growing it from close to ground zero up to some respectable figure, over a span of at least a couple of years. It doesn't necessarily need to be a product even remotely like yours, but it should be a start-up product, and it should be in the same basic area: consumer products, electronics, etc. An individual's breathtaking success record as sales manager for a start-up cosmetics firm might not be a predictor of the ability to do the same for a new consulting firm or a medical equipment manufacturer—and vice versa.

Someone who has spent his or her career up to this point in a big, stable company may not be up to making the transition to a fragile new operation, where he or she lacks not just a sense of job stability, but also the perks and logistical support he or she is used to.

Summary

Once you have a sense of what job you need to fill and what skills and capabilities you're looking for, look for candidates through channels such as these:

1. Networking
2. Letting candidates find you (reverse networking)
3. Placing job ads
4. Leaving the searching to headhunter firms

If you are a small, start-up firm, recognize that "ideal" candidates coming from large, established firms may have serious adjustment problems in adapting to small, fast-moving firms where the job is being constantly re-created, and where they are trading perks for challenge and opportunity. Don't write those people off, but make sure they understand what they are getting into, and what they are sacrificing.

Chapter 38

Selecting Among the Candidates

Now you've done your networking, or run some job ads. The replies have come in, and it's time to begin narrowing the list. Preliminary screening is usually based on four main factors:

1. *The written documentation* the various candidates provide you, including resume, cover letter, and perhaps backup materials including samples of their past marketing successes.
2. *Your initial telephone contact.*
3. *Your face-to-face meetings.* We think of these as "interviews," but it's better to view them as the candidates' sales calls on you. Some may be interviews, others may be demonstrations of their selling skills, or presentations of their work results.
4. *References provided,* including those from past employers and perhaps even previous customers. Take the time to check those references. When you call, always ask, "If you had it to do again, would you still hire this person? Would you rehire them now? Why? Why not?"

Interviewing Candidates

There are shelves of books on the subject of interviewing job candidates, so there's no point in duplicating that advice here.

The important thing to keep in mind is that hiring a salesperson isn't really like hiring people for other kinds of jobs, such as secretaries, supervisors, and technicians. People are hired to *do* those jobs, whereas salespeople are hired to *sell.* For salespeople, the key assessment factor should be just how well they sell you on themselves.

Put differently, with a salesperson you are not just hiring a staff member. Instead, think of yourself as a purchaser, since you are considering purchasing this person's selling services. Project yourself forward, and look at her as if she had been hired and now was trying to sell you the product or service that is the core of your enterprise. How would your customers look on her?

- Does this person come across well on the telephone—is she to the point, enthusiastic, confident? Does she interest you in meeting with her? If you play hard-to-get, and perhaps throw out some objections, is she flexible and appropriately persistent?

- If the person sends written documentation, such as a resume, is it an effective "selling instrument"? That is, does it reflect a flair for eliciting your interest, or is it just another ho-hum resume?
- When you first meet this person, do you get the sense that he presents the image you want to associate with your product or service? Trust first impressions (but don't be locked in on them). Does the person seem likable, or arrogant? Is he dressed well—and dressed for business, not for an ad in *Vanity Fair*? What does his body language project?
- Whether or not he is familiar with the techniques in this book, does he have the ability to listen well, and probe to find out what you are looking for so that he has a clear target to match with his capabilities?
- If you give the person a short selling test, does she have the ability to adapt on her feet to an unexpected product or unexpected circumstances? (It's an old sales manager's test to hand the candidate a pencil or stapler, and say, "Sell it to me." That's a good idea, in concept. But try to come up with something new that candidates aren't likely to have rehearsed.) Also, if you do run this kind of test, watch particularly for the ability to use even a rudimentary version of the Selling Wedge: Does she ask good questions first, or does she just start talking?
- Overall, does she make the best possible case for herself? After all, this is the single most important "sale" she will make in her career with your enterprise, since if she doesn't make this sale and get the job, she will never get the chance to sell anything else for your firm.
- Finally, does the person have a track record of success in past jobs, whether they involved selling or not? Success breeds success. Success as a chemist, for example, does not necessarily predict success in selling chemical supplies, but failure as a chemist is generally a more accurate predictor of probable failure in sales.

Cautions

1. Check references, then check some more. It's a lot easier to get married than to get divorced, and it's a lot easier to buy something than to sell it. It's easy to hire, but it can be hellishly difficult to live with the consequences—and then even more difficult to terminate.
2. Just how hard it will be to terminate depends on factors such as the size of your company, in what jurisdictions you're located (and hence what the laws say), and what assurances you gave at the start. If there are sales in progress (with commissions pending), that can further complicate the process.
3. Even if you're a one-person operation, it may pay to consult a professional before hiring, to make sure you're in compliance with laws and regulations. Alternatively, look for a workshop at your local community college, and invest half a day there.

Chapter 39

Hiring/Orientation Meeting

Now we're at the point where you have narrowed your search to the leading candidate—the person who's your Number One choice on the "menu" you developed. You could phone that person and tell him he's got the job, but it's usually a better idea to get together for one final meeting to confirm your mutual understanding, particularly regarding three main factors.

1. A shared understanding of precisely what thc job entails.

You will have had some discussion of this earlier, but probably only in general terms. You may have worked from your job description letter, and you may even have shared a draft of it with this candidate. But by now your perception of what the job should involve—and the priorities—may have changed. This candidate or others may have given you some new ideas that you have decided to incorporate. It makes sense, before extending your offer, to review the job description and ensure that you are in total accord.

2. A clear understanding of the compensation plan under which the person will be working.

You will have discussed at least the general outline of the compensation package earlier, but now is the time to pin down the specifics. Your earlier discussions may have been in the nature of negotiations, with various offers and counteroffers moving back and forth; as a result, each of you may have slightly different ideas. Or, again, you may have been educated by meetings with other candidates since your first meeting with this person.

3. A clear understanding of other matters you consider relevant.

In addition to these two key factors, there may be other matters that you consider equally important to settle at this point. Here are a few to start with; add to them from your own experience. Clarifying these factors would be particularly important with younger salespeople, particularly if this is one of their first jobs after leaving school.

- *Your expectations on dress.* Is the person to wear a business suit when calling on prospects? While you can't really dictate styles (without imposing, and paying for, a uniform), you can clarify whether your expectations tend, for example, toward conservative business dress, rather than trendy designer styles that might grate on potential customers who are used to more conventional business dress. (Your salespeople might argue that it's really none of the customers' business how they choose to dress. But they need to face the reality that those customers also have the freedom not to take them seriously if their dress doesn't match expectations of how business people should look.)

- *Your expectations on automobiles*, if relevant. For the sake of your firm's and your product's image, you will expect that, at the least, the person will keep his or her car clean. If prospects are going to be riding in the car (as would real estate prospects), then a sporty two-door would not be appropriate. If you will be supplying the car, then clarify expectations on its use outside of work, and use by other drivers.
- *Your expectations on work hours*. Though you're hiring sales types to produce sales, not to punch a clock, with new people it's not unreasonable to set certain parameters, such as what time you expect them to be in the field, and the like. You would also want to set expectations regarding such things as attendance at team meetings.

Be Prepared to Walk Away, if Necessary

Depending on the circumstances, and the relative bargaining and persuasive power of both you and the candidate, the discussion of these factors may be only a formality, or it may involve serious bargaining and negotiating.

Before you go into the meeting, decide just how important it is to hire this particular candidate. Unless this person is head and shoulders above the others, be prepared to walk away from the table if necessary. It may be a nuisance to come this close and still not have a salesperson on board. But it would be far more of a nuisance to find yourself saddled with a person who doesn't share your perception of what the job is about, or what its priorities are.

Orienting a New-Hire Salesperson

If you and the new person come to terms, then you will need to orient that person to the job, and to what you expect from him or her. This could take place as soon as you hire the person, or during the first day or two on the job. Among the topics you will want to cover in this orientation are these:

1. *Ethics policy*. If you don't have a policy yet, at least confirm your expectations on basic principles. Here are some suggestions, as starters:
   - The firm does not condone any illegal activities.
   - We give no gifts to prospective customers, although it is permissible to buy a prospect lunch, the cost of which will (or will not) be reimbursed.
   - We are working with our customers for the long term, and we do nothing to jeopardize that relationship.
   - If a customer disputes a charge, you are authorized to decide on the spot in the customer's favor if not more than $50 (for example) is involved. Above that, tell the customer that I will be in touch with him to discuss it within twenty-four hours, and notify me immediately.

2. *Company benefits*, including health plan, policy on time off, vacation time, etc.
3. *The policy on absences*, excused and unexcused.
4. *Special customer care*: how often follow-up calls should be made, and what should be covered.
5. *Administrative procedures* and other paperwork, including how to get supplies.
6. *How the product is installed*, if appropriate, including
   - Timing
   - Who must be present, who must be scheduled
   - User training
   - The customer's responsibilities, such as to supply working space, staff, and other assistance, and to meet deadlines so that your work can proceed on time
7. *How the product is serviced:* repair procedures, warranty, policy on returns.
8. *Car-related issues,* if relevant: how parking and tolls are accounted for, and if they are reimbursed.
9. *Other travel expense policies*, if relevant.
10. *General expenses*: which are reimbursable, and how they are accounted for. What receipts and documentation are needed. What authorizations are needed, such as for expenses above a set limit.
11. *Internal communications*: use of answering service, phone calls, etc.
12. *Definition of the sales territory:* by geography or other method.
13. *Overview of the paper flow* from the sales order to delivery of the product and customer billing.
14. *Your expectations regarding the salesperson's recordkeeping* and other areas of self-management.

Part Ten
Developing a Productive Compensation Plan

In developing a successful sales team, the design of your compensation plan is at least as important as the people you select. Compensation is one of the keys to motivation, and motivation is the key to selling.

Compensation, to trace it further back, is also one of the keys to attracting good salespeople. The best salespeople tend to have an entrepreneurial streak, and tend to be less motivated by steady paychecks than are other people. Good salespeople like to have a stake in their own success: If they sell well, they want their compensation to directly reflect their success.

Good salespeople also tend to be competitive by nature, and, as billionaire H. L. Hunt put it, "Money is just a way of keeping score."

Looking at it from the other direction, a poorly designed sales compensation plan can sabotage you in several ways, by

- Failing to attract people who can really sell
- Failing to challenge and motivate
- Antagonizing your best people, if they find that the compensation plan works against them

There is no single best compensation plan, as the plan must reflect factors such as how much cash you have available up front for salaries, the length of the product's buying cycle, and precisely what kind of selling behaviors you want to emphasize, such as the ratio between selling new products and selling existing products.

In this part, we give an overview of some of the key characteristics that should be part of your compensation plan. We also look at the options you can mix and match to achieve what you want the plan to accomplish. The end result is a framework that you can adapt in designing a compensation plan to fit your specific needs—and your bankroll.

Chapter 40

Characteristics of a Well-Designed Compensation Plan

Productive compensation plans share four main characteristics.

1. A good compensation plan elicits the kinds of behaviors and results that are appropriate for your overall marketing strategy.

Not all sales are equal. For example, if you want the sales rep to invest the extra time and effort it may take to develop new prospects, then the comp plan should reflect that by paying more for new customers. Similarly, if you want the sales team to make the effort to emphasize new products—which may not be as easy to sell as established lines—then the comp plan should make that extra effort worthwhile for the salespeople.

2. A good compensation plan is clear enough that a salesperson can see a direct payback for investing time and effort right now.

Suppose it's the end of a long day. There's one more call the sales rep could make. If he can see a clear link between making this call successfully and increasing his compensation check this Friday by $____, he'll probably be motivated to make the call. But if he feels there's no clear link between this call and the money he takes home, he'll be less likely to invest the effort. Or if just how much a successful sale nets him won't be determined until the compensation formula is worked out by the accountants next December, he again will be less likely to make the call.

3. A good compensation plan "feeds the eagles and starves the turkeys."

A productive comp plan motivates your best sales performers to stay with the company. It also motivates the least productive people to realize that their best opportunities lie elsewhere.

4. A good compensation plan is simple enough that it can be administered without requiring inordinate time and effort.

You're in the business of creating and selling better mousetraps (or whatever), not of working out complicated formulas to determine sales commissions. Unfortunately, good comp plans can't always be worked out on the back of an envelope.

Fortunately, computer software rides to the rescue. Software packages exist (and new ones are coming onto the market constantly) that assist in developing and then administering sales compensation programs.

As this is written, the top of the line is VI Comp, developed by VI Comp Management, Inc. (21 Worthen Road, Lexington, MA 02173, 800-INCENTIVES (800-462-3684), or 617-674-2624). The disadvantage: The cost ranges from $25,000 up. Depending on your business, it may be right for you.

Alternatively, talk to your local software dealer. By the time you read this, there will probably be many more packages on the market. Alternatively, the dealer, or a computer-literate friend, may be able to provide what you need by adapting an existing spreadsheet program.

Also, keep up with the magazine *Sales and Marketing Management,* where you will find the latest sales software and other tools advertised, along with helpful practical articles on—not surprisingly—selling and managing salespeople. Even if you're a sales and/or marketing manager with a staff of one, this is an essential read, for reasons even beyond keeping up with new products. (*Sales and Marketing Management Magazine,* Subscription Service Department, P.O. Box 7719, Riverton, NJ 08077. One year, 12 issues, $48.)

Factors to Consider in Designing the Compensation Plan

We'll outline each of the main compensation options, along with its key advantages and disadvantages, so that you can begin to mix and match these options in designing your plan. In comparing the options, watch the effects on these areas:

1. *Incentive or motivational effect.* How well does this compensation approach motivate the sales rep to perform the tasks you need, when and how they need to be done?
2. *Your ability to control the salesperson's behavior, priorities, and the like.* If you pay strictly on commission, then you have virtually no ability to step in and tell the sales rep how to do the job, or which customers to focus on. A sales rep working on pure commission is in effect an entrepreneur herself. If she chooses to hit only the most promising prospects, "skimming the cream," then you must either live with that or terminate her.

   On the other hand, if you pay straight salary, then you have almost complete control, because you are in effect buying the salesperson's time, and so you can dictate priorities and approach. The trouble is, if you pay straight salary, with no bonus or commissions, you pay the same for good work or bad, and you don't have much of a motivational "carrot" to induce harder work.
3. *Ease of application.* A practical comp plan shouldn't be so complex that it takes many hours to work out. Similarly, it should be fairly easy for your salesperson to work out so that he knows the clear payoff for investing the extra effort to get this order.
4. *Sales Reps' predictability of income.* Good salespeople tend to have an entrepreneurial streak, and enjoy having a stake in their own success. But they also have fixed expenses like mortgages, car payments, and dental bills. If a portion of their income is predictable, they can budget that and focus their energies on selling, not on wondering if they will be able to pay their basic bills next month.

5. *How much cash out of your own or your company's pocket it will take.* This is particularly important if you are a start-up. Do you have the cash to pay salaries, etc., without first having sales? Can you take the risk of committing to a fixed salary for someone who may produce nothing?
6. *The degree to which the salesperson is motivated to look out for the company's interests,* especially its longer-range interests.
7. *Loyalty to company, and reduced turnover.* It's expensive in time, dollars, and lost revenue to hire new people and get them up to speed, and so you don't want to devise a comp plan that inadvertently encourages unnecessary turnover.
8. *The likely effect on customers' satisfaction with your product and company.* The worst situation would be to set up a comp program that pushes the sales force to think short-term, as that can result in actions that alienate prospects for years to come.

Bottom line: For a productive compensation plan, the optimal mix is probably going to be a combination of one part fixed income (salary, base, or "draw") and one part variable, based on success. (That variable or "contingent" part may take more than one form, such as commission plus end-of-year bonus for overall performance. It may be further supplemented by special awards or contests.)

The Most Powerful Motivator

Although we have focused here on financial motivators, don't overlook the single most powerful motivational tool: your personal recognition for a job well done. For some people, that can be hard. It's easier to sign a check, and even easier to say what has not been done well, than to say, with sincerity, "Great job." Yet it's the recognition that will fire up many, if not most, salespeople and create a sense of loyalty and esprit de corps. The good ones may know that they can go elsewhere and earn just as much money, but they may not be so confident that they can move and still feel appreciated.

Summary

Productive compensation plans share four characteristics:

1. They elicit the kinds of behaviors and results that mesh with your overall marketing strategy.
2. They are clear, so that the salesperson can see a direct payback for investing time and effort now.
3. They "feed the eagles and starve the turkeys."
4. They are simple enough to be administered relatively easily.

In the next chapter, we'll look at some of the main compensation options, such as salary, commissions, and the like. But in mixing and matching these, watch the effect on these areas:

1. Incentive or motivational effect
2. How much ability to control the salesperson's behavior and priorities you retain

3. Ease of application
4. The sales rep's predictability of income
5. How much cash it takes out of your pocket at the front end, before sales come in to cover the outlay
6. The degree to which the salesperson is motivated to watch out for the company's interests, and not just his own
7. Loyalty to company and reduced turnover
8. The likely effect on the customers' satisfaction with your product and company

The greatest motivator will usually be your recognition and spoken appreciation of a job well done.

Chapter 41

Comparing the Main Compensation Options

There are seven main options from which to choose in putting together a compensation plan that accomplishes the kind of positive results you want. We'll compare them in this chapter, contrasting the pros and cons of each. (You can combine the approaches to target your needs. For example, you might offer a straight salary with the prospect of a bonus or commission for sales beyond a certain threshold.)

1. Salary

A salary is a flat hourly, weekly, or monthly paycheck. It may vary with the number of hours worked, but it goes neither up nor down with the number of sales that the person makes.

Advantages of Paying by Straight Salary

- The system is easy to administer.
- It builds company loyalty.
- It is predictable for both employee and employer.

Disadvantages

- As employer, you are locked into meeting that payroll each week, whether or not sales—and payments—come in.
- By agreeing to pay by salary, you gamble on the productivity of new hires. Whether or not they earn their keep, you are still obligated to pay them.
- An assured salary may create too high a comfort level, leading to complacency. If the salesperson can neither win nor lose by making extra sales (or failing to bring in extra sales), why should he invest the effort?

Best Use

- A salary may be appropriate in a store operation where customers come to buy, so that there is no real need for extra initiative: The manager can easily supervise hours, attitudes, and selling approach.
- A salary is also good in a situation where the cost of the goods is so low (and the volume so high) as to make it impossible or impractical to bother calculating commissions.

2. Draw

A "draw" is an advance against expected commissions. It's like a loan, with the salesperson drawing a weekly check. The "loan" is, in theory, to be paid back from commissions when earned.

Advantages

- A draw levels out the salesperson's income, so that she can plan on at least a predictable base.
- A draw gives new hires some cash flow at the start to tide them over the period until the real sales begin.

Disadvantages

- As with salary, committing to paying a draw means that you have to come up with the money—which could be a problem if you are also just starting out and there is little inward cash flow.
- Also, as with paying by salary, if the new hire doesn't work out, or if she gets too far behind, she may move on without ever earning enough to repay the draw. While in theory you could sue her to recover the unearned amount, it would probably not be practical: The amount at issue would probably not be enough to interest a lawyer in taking the case, and so you'd have to do the work yourself. Even if you win, it's questionable whether the person will have the money to repay you. Will she have other creditors waiting in line ahead of you? Finally, if her finances are really bad, she may move to another jurisdiction, out of state, making it a logistical nightmare to track her down and get her to court.

3. Commission

Commission compensation is paying the salesperson a percentage of the selling price. (In some cases, the commission is based on the wholesale price.) Just what that percentage will be depends on the custom of the industry and the area, and on the deal that you negotiate with the individual salesperson.

The commission may not be constant. For example, you might pay 5 percent on sales up to a certain level, then 6 percent on sales from that level to another level, then 7 percent, and so on. Or you might not begin paying commission until a certain level of sales has been reached. (If you are paying commission in conjunction with a salary or draw, the system could be set up so that commission earnings don't begin accruing until the salesperson has pulled in enough to cover the salary or draw.)

Some companies make a practice of "capping" commissions so that the sales rep can't earn above a certain figure. This is a penny-wise, pound foolish approach: Ross Perot left IBM when he found that by February of one year he had already sold as much as his commission cap would allow him to be compensated for over the entire year. You don't want to turn off your most effective salespeople by a short-sighted comp plan. As one put it, "Tell me what day my earnings top out, and I'll tell you the day I stop working hard."

Advantages of Compensating by Commission

- It is highly motivating to the beginner: Sink or swim. Sell or don't eat.
- It is also motivating to the confident, experienced salesperson who finds the possibility of open-ended compensation exhilarating.
- Because you pay only after the product has been sold, you, as a cash-poor start-up entrepreneur, don't have to come up with pay in advance.
- Because the link between effort, success, and payoff is clear and short-term, the salesperson will be motivated to put in the extra effort now.

Disadvantages

- If you are compensating solely by commissions, then the sales rep is in effect an independent entrepreneur, and may have a different agenda, and a different time frame, than you do. Presumably, you want to build a business for the long term. But the pure commission rep's long term tends to be the next payday.
- Since a sales rep working strictly on commissions is in effect an independent entrepreneur, he will not be likely to develop the kind of company loyalty and esprit de corps that you might hope for.
- If the commission is based on gross sales (rather than profits), then it is in the salesperson's interest to generate sales at all costs. If you are paying selling expenses (such as parking, travel, etc.), then the salesperson will be tempted to spare no expense to bring in that extra sale. Similarly, it won't really matter to the sales rep that your product A yields twice as much profit to the company as product B. Also, if the commission remains the same regardless of the payment terms or discounts the sales rep negotiates with the buyer, you'll probably find that almost every purchaser gets a discount, as that speeds sales, and hence commissions.
- Also, when you compensate only by commissions, you generally lose all real control over how and when the person works. You can't expect to dictate selling priorities. You can't insist on all of the recordkeeping and other paperwork that you might like. Similarly, you can't really count on the individual's coming in to staff a booth at trade shows and the like unless it is clearly in his best interests.
- Working on straight commissions tends to shorten the individual's horizons, so that he may be less likely to invest time and effort now in developing business that will ripen only in the future. Similarly, the person will be less likely to take a risk on working with customers who are small now but may grow in time.
- In some cases, people who accept a sales job paying only commissions may have poor work records. Check their references, even though it seems that you have nothing to lose. While it's true that you pay only if they sell, they can do long-term harm. Incompetent people can squander leads that others could sell, and may even permanently alienate your client base.

- Another risk: Others who may be drawn to pure commission jobs are those who make a practice of spending a short time with a firm, "skimming" the easiest sales. This may be an advantage for you at the start, as that can get cash flowing and build a base of "installs." But it can work against you in the longer term, as the wider customer base doesn't get built up. Besides, a commission skimmer sees customers as one-shot opportunities, and so may not be sensitive to developing good relations.
- A pure commission plan probably won't work well if the selling involves team selling, such as sharing leads, or in situations where one person locates prospects and another does the closing.

Best Uses

- Despite the disadvantages, a pure commission plan is often the ideal arrangement for newer businesses, as it offers a way of attracting experienced salespeople whom you could not afford on a salaried (or partly salaried) basis.
- A pure commission plan is also productive when the sales team is made up of confident high performers who are content to work without the safety net of a salary and who have demonstrated, through their past professionalism, that they will not just "cherry-pick" prime prospects, but will instead look long-term for both their own and the firm's interests.

Incidentally, many professional firms, in law, accounting, and consulting, in effect compensate on what is in fact a pure commission schedule (although perhaps supplemented with a draw). Thus even people who are not nominally salespeople (consultants, accountants, and lawyers) are expected to bring in their own business. Their annual compensation is based on a percentage of the business they bring in and then handle (less a cut for the firm's overhead and other expenses).

4. Bonus

A bonus is a special payment tied to some specified performance, such as selling a certain number or dollar value of products or selling certain products. The time frame can be short or year-long.

Bonuses can be set up to reward individual or team effort. (If you can't figure out an equitable way to allocate the bonus among the team, let the members work out the split among themselves; there may be friction, but it will provide good feedback to any who are not used to doing their fair share.)

Advantages

- Bonuses are good for stimulating short-term effort, or effort toward achieving special objectives, such as developing new accounts.
- They are also good as a tool to speed the introduction of a new product or to encourage the development of new accounts, as the special bonus may overcome the reluctance of salespeople to take on the extra effort.
- If targeted to that end, bonus programs can boost team spirit, and can encourage team members to teach and help one another.

Disadvantages

- Bonuses are unpredictable; the salesperson may invest extra effort, yet not win the bonus. Or, a poor-performing rep may drop his regular work and focus exclusively on the bonus program.
- Bonuses can cause inappropriate internal competition, depending on how they are designed.

5. Special Awards and Contests

Awards and contests are a lot like bonuses, but tend to be more focused on a short time frame, such as a month or a quarter. While a bonus program usually rewards in money, awards and contests may pay off in merchandise or travel, and the like.

The award can be given to an absolute winner (such as the one who sells the most this month) or to those who achieve relative success (such as all who exceed their sales quota this month, or who exceed it by a certain percentage).

Advantages

- These programs can be helpful in boosting short-term effort, or in focusing efforts in defined ways, such as new product introductions or the development of new customers.
- They can also be useful in spurring the sales force during otherwise slack periods.

Disadvantages

- Unless you set up a handicap system, the rich will get richer, and the lower-performing reps won't have a chance—and so may choose not to play the game. But tailoring handicaps to each person's past sales record is difficult.
- The rewards may not be equally valued by all. The sales rep who logs 200,000 frequent flyer miles each year may not be particularly motivated by the idea of another trip.
- The competition may (or may not) cause internal friction and morale loss.

6. Profit Sharing

This is a good idea in theory, but it is hard to compute, and it is even harder to determine in advance just how an individual's performance will actually affect profits. Besides, do you really want to open your books to everyone? You might have to do that if any disputes arose.

7. Equity or Ownership Share

In practice, this means taking the other person on as a partner or giving some shares of stock. It's a great idea in theory, but a potential disaster in practice, particularly for small or start-up firms.

For most entrepreneurs, a partnership is the worst possible business arrangement. First, you lose a degree of control. Instead of making the decisions yourself, as a sole entrepreneur can, you'll probably need to get agreement from your partners. (There may be ways around that by setting up a distinction between limited and general partners, but that only creates more work for the lawyers.)

Second, in a partnership, you can be held responsible for any expenses or debts the partner runs up. This is true even if you put up 99 percent, or even 100 percent, of the capital and the partner doesn't contribute even a penny.

Example: You reward your best salesperson by making him your partner. Though you have put up all the capital, you bank on him to produce the sales. But your partner runs up some debts in the partnership name, does something to provoke a lawsuit, then cleans out the bank account and takes off overseas. The law says that even though you had already put in all the capital, you're still liable for 100 percent of the losses and 100 percent of the bills, including those stemming from the lawsuit. (Sure, the partner is also liable, and you can in theory collect from him. But if he's in bankruptcy, or in Brazil, then you're stuck.)

If you operate in a corporate form, you can grant shares with less risk than giving a partnership interest. But once you get into corporate form, life can get more complicated than it is worth for most small entrepreneurs. While good lawyers and accountants can minimize some of the difficulties of sharing equity, do you really want to be spending money on lawyer's fees that should be going to developing your customer base? (There *are* good reasons for using the corporate form, such as to limit your liability. Do talk to a lawyer about that.)

Summary

There are seven main options that you can mix and match in designing your compensation plan. Each has advantages and disadvantages, and so the best solution is usually some combination.

1. Salary
2. Draw
3. Commission
4. Bonus programs
5. Special awards and contests
6. Profit sharing
7. Equity or ownership share

Part Eleven
Managing the Sales Effort

Parts 1 to 8 of this book focused on the how-to of selling your personal "better mousetrap." By Part 9, "Expanding Your Sales Organization," it was time to begin looking to add extra salespeople (or, alternatively, outside dealers, independent sales reps, or stores). Part 10 focused on setting up a productive compensation plan.

Now, in Part 11, we move on to the new role you undertake: that of managing the sales team. Once you add even that first extra salesperson, your role changes: You take on a new role as *sales manager.*

As a sales manager, your focus is quite different from your focus as a salesperson. As a sales rep, your job is to *do*. As a sales manager, your job is to *accomplish through others*.

As a manager (whether of sales or of any other function), your function is to accomplish tasks through others. Therefore, your role as sales manager is to increase sales *through others.* You multiply yourself by coordinating other people to handle the majority of the tasks.

Note: Here we're speaking of the sales management part of your work. When you hire your first sales rep or two, you may both manage them and continue selling in your own territory. Just keep the different roles in mind, so that you accomplish *through* the reps you manage and don't attempt to *do* it for them.

Two Fundamental Rules of Successful People Management

Rule 1: Don't Do the Work for Them

Keep in mind that in the territories for which the sales reps are responsible, you are the manager, not the doer. Several implications follow:

- You can't be everywhere at once. To expand, and to keep on top of your various responsibilities, you have to let go of some things. If you had enough confidence in your salespeople to hire them, be ready to let them do the work. (This is not to say that you turn them completely loose and forget about them; you may still have to train, give feedback, coach and counsel, and monitor performance.)

- If you overcontrol people, then you sap confidence and initiative, and create dependency on you. There's a fine line to draw. You need to set up the conditions so that they can be successful, but at the same time you need to give them freedom to experiment, and even to fail in the short term.

  Yes, do keep watch over what your people are doing, and yes, set clear expectations regarding their work, then monitor them to be sure they are working hard and working effectively. But don't feel the need to hold their hand at every step. Turn them loose, and let them produce: sink or swim. (If they are sinking, then do intervene, and help as needed. Just don't set up the pattern of stepping in too soon to start helping those who don't really need help.)

Rule 2: Keep Out of the Way of the Work Being Done

As the manager, you need to be available to give guidance as needed and to solve any problems that can be solved only at your level. But a lot of problems are best solved down there at the field level, by the people closest to the situation. Let that happen.

Some of these problems will relate to selling, while others will involve interpersonal relations with other members of your team or with customers. Most of the time it's best to give the people involved the freedom to work it out for themselves.

However, that is not to suggest that you ignore these situations. Rather, be aware of what is happening, but generally don't intervene unless you must. When *would* you intervene? Intervene if there is a significant risk of permanent damage to relationships with customers or within the team. Intervene also if the situation is taking too long to resolve, and hence is draining energy that could be used more productively.

Your Two Principal Roles as a Manager

A manager wears many hats, but they tend to reduce to two main roles: administrator and coach/problem solver.

First Role: Sales Manager as Administrator

In your "administrator" role, your function is—figuratively speaking—to keep the trains running on time. That is, your function is to make sure the necessary paper flows, and to deal with the internal matters necessary to keep the sales team functioning. Typically, that means coping with any personnel matters; keeping supplies of necessary forms, brochures, and the like up to date; and dealing with any other similar "overhead" problems, such as those involving office space, telephones, and expenses.

That's all I'm going to say about the administrator function in this book, as just what tasks it entails depends on your specific business.

The key point to bear in mind is this: *Do* perform whatever administrative functions are necessary so that your sales team can function efficiently. But don't get bogged down in the administrative aspects to the detriment of the rest of your sales management responsibilities.

SECOND ROLE: SALES MANAGER AS PART COACH, PART PROBLEM SOLVER

The problems we're referring to here are "people" problems, that is, problems of subpar performance by the members of your sales team, such as people who

- Work below potential
- Demonstrate by their actions or manner that they are clearly demoralized and discouraged
- Seem to create an unusual number of misunderstandings and hard feelings with customers
- Keep sloppy records or send in incomplete paperwork for orders and other communications

These are only a few of the possible problems of deficient human performance, but they show some of the range of people issues that you need to be equipped to deal with.

In the chapters in this part, we work through some tools that are helpful in dealing with human performance issues. In Chapter 42, you'll learn to use three fundamental questions to diagnose the core reason for the difficulty, and you'll learn to select the remedy that is most appropriate for the specific situation.

Then in Chapters 43, 44, and 45, we examine the implications behind each of these three core questions, along with the appropriate remedies that flow from each type of performance difficulty. Finally, in Chapter 46, we move on to the practical how-to of coaching and counseling the sales team.

Chapter 42

Diagnosing the Cause of Below-Par Selling Performance

Think of something you're good at. It may be playing tennis or golf or the piano. Or doing magical things on your computer. Or gardening or making money on the stock market.

Whatever it is, think of it, and try to figure out exactly *why* you are good at it. Chances are, you'll find three common elements at work:

1. You know what to do, and how to do it.
2. You want to do it.
3. Nothing blocks you or prevents you from excelling (other, perhaps, than lack of time to do it as much as you might like).

Why are we talking of golf or gardening or computers? Because, if we turn those three elements around and look from the other direction, they tell us what to watch for if sales reps (or any other people with whom you work, or even family members, for that matter) are having difficulty performing a task as well as they might.

That is, if one of your salespeople is failing to do the job as well as you think he or she is able, it's almost certainly because one (or more) of these three reasons is operating:

1. He or she doesn't know
   - What to do
   - How to do it
   - How to do it the precise way you want it done

2. He or she is not properly motivated to do it, often because
   - He or she lacks confidence in his or her ability to do it.
   - Doing the task, or doing it right, doesn't pay off sufficiently well to make it worthwhile.

3. Something in the system or the work environment prevents him or her from doing it, or from doing it well.

These three main concerns, as a quick diagnostic checklist, boil down to

1. Does the person *know* what to do?
2. Does the person *want* to do it?
3. Is the person *allowed to* do it by the system or environment?

Once you have diagnosed the cause of the subpar performance, then the remedy follows.

1. If the person doesn't know what to do or how to do it, then give some kind of *guidance, feedback, training, or even a simple job aid as a help.*
2. If the person isn't properly motivated, then *change the motivational approach or get rid of the factors that undercut motivation.*
3. If the system or work environment is hindering performance, then *revise that system.*

These are the three core reasons for poor human performance on the job, and the corresponding core remedies. We will be looking at each of these in more detail in the following chapters.

Chapter 43

If They Don't Know What to Do, or How to Do It

Quick review: If one of your salespeople is failing to sell as well as he or she should, it's almost certainly because of one of these three reasons. Run through this three-question checklist:

1. Does the person know what to do, and how to do it?
2. Does the person want to do it? That is, are the actual consequences of doing the job positive, or positive enough to motivate the kind of work you need?
3. Is something in the system or environment preventing or hampering good work?

In this chapter, we'll focus on the first of these, examining the background of this cause in more detail, and exploring the practical remedies you can apply.

Thus if one of your salespeople (or anyone you manage, for that matter, whether in sales or in another function) is not performing up to par, focus on the specific tasks that person is not doing well, and ask,

> Does this person know what to do?
> How to do it?
> And how to do it the precise way I want it done?

Your first inclination may be along the lines of, "Well, *of course* she must know what to do! After all, this is an experienced salesperson, who has been working in this field for the past five years."

Well, not necessarily.

- Despite all that sales experience, the individual may be having trouble making the shift to a new industry or new product.
- He may be lost without the guidance provided by the sales manager in his previous job.
- He may be finding it difficult to shift from selling products to selling intangible services (or vice versa).
- He may be stumped by finding that the selling approach that made him a star in his previous job just isn't working now, for a reason he doesn't understand.

- A technically skilled person who has shifted to selling may not know how to boil down his expertise in a way that comes across well to prospective customers.
- He knows how to do the job his way, but he doesn't know what *you* want, or doesn't know how to make the shift to the style you encourage.

These are only some of the ways in which even knowledgeable and skilled salespeople can, in practice, not "know" how to do the job you want done.

The list can be far longer if you are working with people who are new or relatively new to selling, or to your product or the industry in which they are working. They may know *most* of what is needed to succeed in the job, but lack one or two crucial skills.

Tests for Determining if the Cause Is a "Don't Know" Problem

Obviously, if people have had no training or experience in selling, or none in the technical area of your product, then it's very likely that they have wide-ranging deficiencies in the necessary skills and knowledge. (Are you sure they have read this present book thoroughly, and worked through all of the exercises? Have you talked them through the key elements? Have you role-played with them so that they have a sense of working through the steps with a customer?)

More often, people know *most* of what they need to know, but have certain limited skill or knowledge gaps. Begin by trying to narrow in on the specific area or areas in which someone is having particular difficulty. Generally, even the most unproductive people can do some or even most tasks at least reasonably well. (In this, they're like the person who knows how to hold a golf club properly, how to swing, and how to get distance, but just can't quite get the ball to go straight. A little targeted instruction and practice can help them.)

Concentrate on one specific skill deficiency (something as defined as "ability to close for a sale" or, even more defined, "ability to use an action plan close effectively"). With that in mind, ask these eight questions:

1. Could this person do the task properly or successfully if $10,000 in cash were riding on it?

If the person couldn't do it right even for an instant $10,000, then she definitely does not know what to do or how to do it. If she *could* do it right for cash on the line, then the cause is definitely *not* any lack of skill or knowledge. In other words, she knows what to do and how to do it, but she either doesn't want to do it or is prevented from doing it by something in the system.

2: Has this individual had specific feedback on what he or she is doing wrong and right?

"Specific feedback" is not something on the order of, "You're not asking the right questions." Useful specific feedback is something like, "You asked the customer _____. Did you notice how she responded? Was that favorable to you? What if, instead, you had asked _____?"

Also, useful "specific feedback" is given to the *individual*. General feedback given to the whole group is not always particularly helpful, as each person may assume that the errors were being made by the others, and not by him or her.

3. Are you sure that the individual knows precisely what you are looking for, or precisely how you want the job done?

It's easy to take it for granted that your expectations are clear, and clearly communicated. Are you certain that you gave clear instructions at the start? Do you continue to give clear, specific feedback along the way? Does that feedback point out the contrast between what you want and what you are seeing? Are you giving that feedback to the individual and not just to the group, assuming that the right individual will get the point?

4. Can *anyone* do the task well? Does anyone do it *consistently* well?

If the task is something that certain people can do and others can't, then it is a skill that the others can learn. But if no one can do it (or do it consistently well), then the problem is not one of training or feedback. It may well be that the job is impossible.

For example, if you can sell your better mousetrap, then others can learn to do the same from you. But if even you—or the best salesperson—can't make a go of selling it, then the problem is *not* one of learning how to sell it. Instead, the problem may lie in pricing, in the strength of the competition, or in a lack of customer need, or it may just be that it's not a good product. That is, if no one can do it, then perhaps the task is not doable, and something deeper needs to be changed.

5. Are individuals on the sales team telling you that they don't know what to do, how to do it, or when to do it?

"Don't know how" can be a blanket alibi, but it can also be right on target, so don't rule it out.

6. Has there been adequate training and feedback in this *specific* task?

Even the best people can't necessarily automatically transfer skills from one task to another. Even though selling stocks and selling your product both involve most of the same tasks, an individual may need some customized "bridging" training to help him or her make the shift.

7. Was there opportunity to practice or apply the skill or knowledge as part of the training?

To listen to someone talk about a subject is not necessarily to be trained in that topic. Implication: If you conduct training for the team, or if you have an expert in to discuss a subject, don't take it for granted that the salespeople have mastered the subject just by listening, or even by watching someone else do it.

Build in some practice exercises, such as role plays or case studies, and make sure that each individual is personally actively involved in the application practice.

8. Was the training (or practice session) so long ago that the ability may have deteriorated?

You'll often find this to be the case when you train people in special techniques used only for certain situations or types of customers. The difficulty stems from the fact that they don't get a chance to apply the new learning for weeks or months.

Remedies if the Difficulty Stems from Lack of Skills or Knowledge

If people don't know what to do or how to do something, the solution is obvious enough: Help them learn. But precisely *how* to help them learn is not always clear-cut.

- Your *telling* them is not necessarily the same as their *learning*.
- They may already "know" what to do, but just need practice in *translating that "knowledge" into actual behavior.* (For example, one might "know" ten ways of closing for the sale, in the sense of being able to list all ten from memory. But that's far different from being able to use them smoothly and confidently when in front of a prospect.)
- Sending them off to a formal training program may not have much benefit; they may already "know" 99 percent of the task, but just can't put the parts together successfully.
- They may not know that they are doing something wrong, or may not know precisely what is wrong within an overall job that they are doing basically successfully.
- They may be doing the job or task adequately by some standards, yet not be meeting your expectations of what should be done or how they should do it.

Basic Tools for Solving Skill or Knowledge Difficulties

Suppose the new Sales Rep you've taken on just can't seem to get the hang of using the Selling Wedge productively in getting customers to recognize and discuss needs. You've ridden on sales calls with her, and there's no doubt about it: She just can't get the question sequence right.

You have an array of options open to you to help that SR fill that skill or knowledge gap. (These same approaches are equally useful as tools in helping to solve any other kinds of skill or knowledge difficulties.)

A. Training, formal or informal.

Training could involve sending this SR off to a course in selling skills (perhaps at the local community college, or perhaps a short course put on by a sales training organization).

The trouble with most formal training courses, though, is that the content is fixed, and your salesperson could leave the course without having remedied the precise difficulty. (It would be a different thing if you were fortunate enough to come upon a course that specifically addressed "selling by asking questions." But those are rare, at least unless you tap in on expensive corporate training programs.)

In this case, informal training might be a better approach. You could cover the topic at a meeting of the sales team (if your organization is large enough to have meetings). Or you could simply refer the person to this book, pointing out appropriate chapters to study. Even better, you could then get together and talk through the topic, and work through some short practice role-plays in applying techniques from this book, from your personal experience, or both.

B. Demonstrations.

Better still, while sitting with that individual, you can bring the techniques from this book to life by demonstrating how you use the Selling Wedge when you're with prospects. You could do that in practice role-plays with just the two of you, then take her along to observe it again in your actual sales calls on prospects.

But even the best demonstrations are not always miracle cures. It may be that the individual doesn't know what to look for. She may be feeling stressed, wondering if

TO MAKE ROLE MODELING AND DEMONSTRATIONS MORE EFFECTIVE:

- Provide structure and perspective so that the trainee is able to put the parts of the demonstration in perspective.
- Whenever possible, show, not tell.
- Highlight the essential elements to watch for: Develop the trainee's "looking skills."
- "Self-edit" your demonstration. Avoid drowning the trainee in a flood of words. Avoid information overload.
- Be alert to the feedback the trainee is giving you—concerning overload, points not understood, or points that *are* understood and don't need any more coverage—and respond accordingly.
- Provide the opportunity for immediate, supervised practice, with immediate feedback on what is done both incorrectly and correctly. Don't be reluctant to praise.

her job is riding on the outcome of this meeting with you. Besides, a demonstration happens quickly, and the key questions may come and go before she has a chance to recognize and absorb what is happening.

That's why demonstrations should usually be coupled with other approaches, such as practice with immediate feedback and the use of job aids. We explore these below. (Another possibility: Repeat the demo, this time doing it in slow motion, or repeat it, "stepping aside" from time to time to point out what you are about to do, and why.)

C. Practice with immediate feedback.

Given the pressure of other things that need to be done, it's tempting to say, "There. I've shown you how to do it. Now you can go and do it with your customers tomorrow."

But it doesn't work that way. Even if the individual absorbed your demonstration perfectly (which isn't likely, for reasons we'll discuss), the odds of her being able to remember everything and apply it perfectly later are in the range of zero to none.

First, even if you repeat your demonstration several times, you still can't be sure that the salesperson is seeing the key points the way you intend them. People sometimes focus on the wrong details, and overlook the main points. Or they are unable to sort out from the whole demonstration those precise areas in which they are failing to do things the way you do them. (It's a rule of thumb in baseball that retired superstars don't make good coaches because things always came naturally to them, and so they can't break down what they do into how-to steps.)

That's why it's essential to follow up your demonstration by allowing the trainee to copy your approach, with immediate feedback. That gives him the chance to pull together what he has just seen and to get the "feel" of doing it and putting the actions and words together.

But don't let him go off on his own to do this. Give him a chance to try it while he's still with you, so that you can give him immediate feedback—and any additional coaching necessary. That way, the trainee gets immediate feedback so that he is assured that he is doing it right this time. If the trainee is going to develop new habit patterns, you'd better make sure early on that these are the *right* habit patterns.

But be aware that by what he does (and fails to do), the trainee is giving *you* feedback, unintentionally, on how clear and effective your demonstrations and explanations really are. (Keep this in mind: *If the student hasn't learned, the teacher hasn't taught.*)

TO GIVE USEFUL FEEDBACK:

- Make the feedback specific; focus on particular points.

  Useful feedback: "You did X well, but you had difficulty with Y."

  Not useful: "You always mess up your closes."

- Make the feedback objective, nonpunishing, nonthreatening.

  Useful: "I felt your first close was weak, because it ____. Suppose instead you had ____."

  Not useful: "That was the worst close I've ever seen in my life!"

- Link the feedback to precise behavior: "In closing, you said, ________. Did you notice how the prospect drew back in the chair? Why do you suppose that was? What could you have done to compensate?"
- Put the feedback in context. If the behavior was 90 percent correct, make this clear first, before focusing on details.
- Give feedback for both correct and incorrect performance. No news is usually taken as bad news.
- Be patient. How to do it right may be obvious to you, but then you're not the person learning something new.

It can be frustrating to give what you feel is a perfect demonstration of a skill, and then see the other person botch it as she tries to repeat it. Granted, it *could* be that she wasn't paying attention. Or it could be that she's just not very bright (but, if not, then why did you hire her?).

More likely, she is simply mirroring what she saw, or didn't see.

If you have the time and budget, you can take the demonstration and feedback/practice sessions to another level of usefulness by videotaping both parts, then sitting down with the trainee to critique what went well and what needs more work. (Don't be surprised if you learn as much from watching yourself as the trainee does.)

D. Job aids.

Useful job aids come in many forms. Airline pilots use job aids in the form of checklists religiously (at least I hope they do!) Service technicians rely on manuals and flow diagrams. Lecturers have outlines or index cards to keep them on track. Lawyers and doctors use job aids in the form of question checklists—sometimes on paper, sometimes presented on computer screens—to help them ensure that they collect all the necessary information and consider all the possibilities within a case.

The worksheets you developed in the earlier chapters of this book are aids in doing the sales job. For example, back in Chapter 11, a worksheet provided you a list of model questions appropriate to each phase of the Selling Wedge, and you had a chance to translate these model questions into questions appropriate to your product or situation. The result was a job aid, in the form of a reminder checklist.

Now, if you need to help the salespeople on your team develop skill in using the wedge, you can refer them back to the book to review these worksheet job aids that they customized for themselves. They can then refer to these job aids as they work through a couple of practice role-plays with you.

If you want to carry the job aid a step further, you might type up, in a similar format, a checklist of actual questions that you have found productive in your own sales calls with your specific product. That can serve as a tool to help new people get a sense of how to ask the right questions.

What if they still need a little help from the checklist of questions for the next few days? Help them integrate the job aid into their approach so that they can use it in an inconspicuous way. They should be taking notes while with prospects. If they use a portfolio kind of clipboard that opens up like a book, they can clip the job aid onto the left side and have it available for reference; they can subtly refer to it while jotting notes onto the pad on the right side of the portfolio. As they become more familiar, their need for the checklist will drop off.

If your field is technical, you can build the job aid (such as a checklist of probing questions) into a worksheet for the salesperson to use with customers. This kind of job aid is not uncommon; you'll see bankers using something like this to guide them in collecting loan application information. Some law firms have similar job aids to guide lawyers and paralegals in collecting information from new clients.

SUMMARY

In Chapters 43, 44, and 45, we are building toward a job aid for you as sales manager that ties together the three key diagnostic questions and the appropriate remedies. Here is the first "slice" of that chart.

Key Question: Does this person know what to do, how to do it, and how to do it the way I want it done?

If you see these indicators:

1. Could the person do the task properly if $10,000 were riding on it?
2. Has this individual had specific feedback on what he or she is doing right and wrong?
3. Are you sure that the person knows precisely what you are looking for, or precisely how you want the job done?
4. Can *anyone* do the task well? Does anyone do it *consistently* well?
5. Are individuals telling you that they don't know what to do, how to do it, or when to do it?
6. Has there been adequate training and feedback in this *specific* task?
7. Was there opportunity to practice or apply the skill or knowledge as part of the training?
8. Was the training (or practice) so long ago that the ability may have deteriorated?

Try these remedies:

A. Training, formal or informal
B. Demonstrations
C. Practice with immediate feedback
D. Job aids

Chapter 44

If Motivational or Attitudinal Factors Hamper Sales Performance

Reminder: If some of your salespeople are failing to sell as well as they should, or if they are failing to do what they should as well as they should in a particular area, define the core difficulty by asking these three questions:

1. Do they know what to do, and how to do it?
2. Do they want to do it? That is, are the actual consequences of doing the job truly positive, or positive enough to motivate the kind of work you need?
3. Is something in the system or environment preventing or hampering good work?

In this chapter, we focus on the second of these factors: The person does not "want" to do the job, or do it well, most commonly because of motivational deficiencies, attitude factors (including low morale and low confidence), or inappropriate incentives.

It's easy to take these motivational factors for granted. After all, we might think, "Of *course* they're motivated: they have a job! What more motivation should they need? The paycheck should make them want to do it. And as for morale and attitude, they're adults, and professional salespeople, reason enough to focus and get on with it."

That makes sense in theory, but if the people aren't working up to par, we have to probe through to the realities of the problem.

It could be that the compensation isn't enough to motivate quality work. Or perhaps they're disappointed to find that they're not taking home as much money as they had expected when they joined your enterprise.

Or it could be that they've become discouraged and demoralized by the daily grind of knocking on doors without achieving the level of success they had hoped for. Despite all the people one meets, selling is a lonely profession. They may feel isolated, and not understand that selling is a matter of working through the nos to find the few yes responses that make it all worthwhile. Or they may not grasp that your product involves a longer selling cycle than they had anticipated, and so the rewards will come, but later than expected.

Then again, your compensation plan may be generous enough, but not be targeted correctly. You may be rewarding the wrong behaviors and failing to reward, or even inadvertently punishing, the ones you actually do want. Your salespeople may be selling well enough, but not selling the products you want (the ones with the higher profit margins), or not opening up the new customers that will mean longer-term strength.

Tests for Determining if the Cause Is Related to Motivation, Attitude, or Inappropriate Incentives

1. Are the actual consequences of doing a good job (or of doing this particular task) positive?

Sometimes, if you look through to what's really happening, you'll find that there is no special reward for good performance. Good work may even be inadvertently punished.

For example, in some organizations, if the salespeople exceed their quotas this year, then this year's results become the baseline for next year, so that they have to produce that much again just to fulfill the minimum requirement (which may not be easy if, for instance, market conditions were especially good this year). This becomes unintended punishment, and is a disincentive to excel.

Or take the sales organizations where compensation is "capped," so that no salesperson can earn more than a manager. In this case the consequences of doing a good job are not positive. The inadvertent result may be not just slowed productivity but anger against the system, which further drains sales output.

Here's another example of an organization unconsciously failing to provide positive results for doing a good job:

A food company developed a hot new kind of candy. It had gotten a lot of publicity, and kids around the country were eager for it. Even better, it was so cheap to manufacture and so profitable per ounce that it was almost like selling diamonds made out of sugar.

When corporate management investigated further, they found that the candy wasn't always available in the stores, even though everyone across the country under the age of twelve (and in some cases under the age of ninety-two) was eager to buy. When they explored further, they learned that the company's salespeople hadn't been bothering to make much of a selling effort with the network of wholesalers. Why not? Because the company's compensation plan didn't give them any worthwhile incentive to try to sell it.

The marketing team for the candy had overlooked one key reality: In that company, sales commissions were based on tonnage sold, not the dollar value or profitability of the products. Compensating by weight had made sense when most of the products were sold in cans and boxes. It just didn't seem worth trying to compute a commission on one can of tomato soup.

But these intensely profitable little candies only weighed an ounce or so each, so that enough of them to send all the kids in Cleveland or Dallas into sugar shock still wouldn't weigh as much as a few dozen cans of soup. Reasonably enough, from their perspective, the sales reps weren't bothering to push something that had such marginal impact on their own income.

2. Does the compensation for each task match the effort and time required?

The compensation for the job as a whole may be adequate, but the payoff for doing one task or one part of that job may be either inadequate or actually negative.

Here's an example: The manufacturer of a line of early word processors found that the sales force was not bothering to sell some very profitable accessories, such as ribbons. Company management assumed that the reason must be that the sales force needed training, and so they called me in, as a consultant, to develop some special product-knowledge training to fill the need.

As in all of my consulting projects, I began by going out to the field to ride with the people in the real world—the sales reps. (As a consultant, I had learned long before how much more useful knowledge could be picked up in the field than by talking to the people isolated back in corporate headquarters.)

Once I got out to ride with some field salespeople, I found that the last thing they needed was training. They already knew how to sell ribbons and other peripherals. The problem was, they just didn't *want* to sell those things, for two reasons.

First, the people isolated back at headquarters had made the management decision that, since these items were relatively low cost, it wasn't worthwhile to calculate a commission payment on their sale. So the salespeople got nothing for selling them. These sales didn't even count against the salespeople's quota for the month.

Even worse, the sales reps had strong *disincentives* to even try to sell the ribbons. If a sales rep once sold a box of ribbons, then the customer would rely on that sales rep from that point on to keep it supplied with ribbons and things. Thus it often happened that a sales rep would get an emergency call: A customer had run out of ribbons, and needed another dozen delivered right away, drop everything else. The result was that if the reps once started selling ribbons, they would end up wasting productive selling hours servicing unhappy ribbon customers—and get absolutely no compensation for it.

(The solution, by the way, was to set up a separate telephone marketing sales force to concentrate on the ribbons and supplies market—which worked to the benefit of all.)

3. Is this individual having special difficulty in dealing with the ambiguity of sales, or does he or she lack the patience required to wait for a longer selling cycle to work out?

This may be especially with the case with people who have recently come to selling from structured jobs where the hours and pay are set, and the tasks are clearly defined.

4. Is the individual feeling demoralized or discouraged? Is his or her self-image taking a beating from an actual or perceived lack of success in selling?

Selling is not for some people; the daily process of knocking on doors and facing rejection grinds them down. It's best for those people to move on early, and find work that *is* right for their talents, rather than to waste months, years, or a career in the wrong field.

But not everyone who is down should get out of selling. Some cycles of discouragement are normal. Virtually every person who is successful in selling today went through "down" phases along the way. Some of the most successful salespeople I worked with as a consultant admitted that at times they have felt discouraged almost to the point of quitting. But they held on, and worked past that phase.

A significant part of your role as sales manager is to help keep your people motivated and confident. In the remainder of this chapter, we'll be examining techniques for addressing various kinds of motivational, attitudinal, and incentive difficulties that tend to afflict salespeople.

General Remedies

Obviously enough, the remedy should follow the cause. In this section, we'll give an overview of the range of remedies available to you for addressing this group of motivational, attitudinal, or incentive-based difficulties. Now, we examine the remedies appropriate to the four main causes discussed above.

A. Adjust the compensation plan to better target specific kinds of markets or prospects.

For instance, if you find that your salespeople are selling only to existing customers and not developing new areas, look at your comp plan. Chances are, it doesn't provide a special incentive to make it worthwhile for the sales rep to invest the extra effort it takes to locate, contact, and win over new customers.

Sure, the sales reps should "think long-term" for the sake of the company, and should go out and open up new markets on their own without any special incentive. But project yourself into the minds of your salespeople. If you were a new hire with a start-up company (a company that you didn't have an ownership stake in), would you be thinking long-term, or would you be inclined to go for the quick sales that help you make next month's rent check?

B. Adapt the comp plan in other ways, such as to give a larger base or draw to reduce the anxiety level.

This may be particularly helpful with new hires. In theory, there is no better kind of motivation than a comp plan that is based totally or nearly totally on commissions. Then—so the theory goes—the sales rep becomes his own entrepreneur, and can see the direct link between every sale and his paycheck.

That's the theory, and it works well with experienced, confident salespeople. But working with their backs to the wall can be counterproductive for those who haven't yet become "tigers." Instead of thinking how they can persuade a prospect to double the order, they may be looking for ways to minimize the risk of blowing the sale. Instead of going out and finding lucrative new prospects, they will be inclined to go with the safe, sure, comfortable small sale.

Besides, buyers are like dogs: They smell fear. They sense a salesperson's lack of confidence, and they may assume that it is due to a lack of confidence in the product and its ability to do the job. The result is no sale.

Thus, be open to the idea of changing the mix, so that the salesperson has a higher percentage of assured income. Granted, that's money out of your pocket (and that pocket, particularly if you're a start-up entrepreneur, may not be very deep). If you advance it as a draw, it may never be repaid, so you do need to be careful. Still, the bit of security that a draw provides may make all the difference in the individual's confidence and effectiveness.

C. Invest time and effort in coaching and counseling your low-confidence low performers.

It takes time, dollars, and "opportunity cost" to hire salespeople and get them up to speed. Thus it may be far more productive for you to invest a little more time and effort in coaching your existing salespeople than to start the whole cycle over with fresh faces.

We discuss the how-to of coaching and counseling in Chapter 46.

D. Team up old hands with those who are having trouble.

It's usually helpful for a new person to ride with an experienced, successful practitioner, both to absorb how-to skills and to pick up confidence that the product *can* be sold successfully.

The pairing is often equally helpful for the old hand, as well: "I never really knew my subject until I tried to teach it," more than a few have said. The experienced person may well gain nearly as much from this temporary partnership as the person he or she mentors.

SUMMARY

In Chapters 43, 44, and 45, we are building toward a job aid for you as sales manager that ties together the three key diagnostic questions and the appropriate remedies. Here's the second "slice" of that chart. (You will find the complete chart on page 275.)

Key Question: Does this person *want* to do it?

If you see these indicators:

1. Are the actual consequences of doing a good job (or of doing this particular task) positive?
2. Does the compensation match the effort and time required?
3. Is this individual having special difficulty in dealing with the ambiguity of sales, or does he or she lack the patience required to wait for a longer selling cycle to work out?
4. Is the individual feeling demoralized or discouraged? Is his or her self-image taking a beating from an actual or perceived lack of success in selling?

Try these remedies:

A. Adjust the comp plan to better target specific kinds of markets or prospects.
B. Adapt the comp plan in other ways, such as to give a larger base or draw to reduce the anxiety level.
C. Invest time and effort in coaching and counseling your low-confidence low performers.
D. Team up old hands with those who are having trouble.

Chapter 45

If Something in the Work Environment or System Hampers Sales Performance

Again, if some of your salespeople are failing to sell as well as they should (or if they are failing to perform as well as they should at any other kind of task), define the core difficulty by asking these three questions:

1. Do they know what to do, and how to do it?
2. Do they want to do it? That is, are the actual consequences of doing the job truly positive, or positive enough to motivate the kind of work you need?
3. Is something in the system or environment preventing or hampering good work?

In this chapter, we examine the implications if the answer to the third question is yes.

Sometimes it jumps out at you that the cause is a hitch in the system or environment; other times you arrive at this by a process of eliminating questions 1 (Do they know what to do?) and 2 (Do they want to do it?) as causes.

Tests for Determining if the Cause Can Be Traced to Environmental or Systemic Factors

1. Are there competing demands on the Sales Reps' time or attention? Are they distracted by other duties?

2. Have they organized themselves and their sales kit and equipment well? Have they taken the trouble to organize their time and territory? Do they have the necessary supplies, brochures, order forms, and the like?

In your role as Sales Manager, you should be spending an entire day riding with each Sales Rep from time to time. (How often depends on the individual.) When you are with a Sales Rep, look beyond selling skills alone, and be alert to the whole work environment within which the Sales Rep operates.

When you ride with one of your salespeople, try to surprise that person with the pleasure of your company. The Sales Rep may not like that at first, and may say, "Can't we make it, say, next Wednesday, instead? Today is just not a typical day." Well, chances are it *is* a typical day, and he's embarrassed about it. If the day is disorganized, that's something you definitely want to know.

In the next chapter, we'll be discussing some of the how-to's of coaching and counseling Sales Reps. We're a little ahead of ourselves here, but some of the points made there relate to attending to factors such as these:

- *Do they have the brochures, order blanks, and other materials that they need?* If not, why not? Have they failed to pack them? Or are some key items, such as brochures or samples, lost in your own system, so that they don't get out to the people in the field?
- *Where does their time go through the day?* As you ride, try to get in the mindset of an outsider, someone there to look at the situation objectively, like an outside consultant.

Don't rely on impressions, collect data. Record the actual amount of time spent on the telephone, in transit, dealing with paperwork, and the like. (You won't have to do this every time—just often enough for it to serve as a useful reality check on what actually happens in the field.)

Do you find that an inordinate amount of the working day is consumed by travel from one prospect to another? Could this be improved by reorganizing the territories? Or do the sales reps need some guidance on managing the work more efficiently?

Small things can make a big difference. This was brought home to me once when I rode with a pair of Xerox sales reps in the same city on two successive days. The first rep spent a lot of time and energy fighting traffic and looking for parking spaces. "The company only gives us a $90 per month parking and tolls allowance, and that's never enough, so I really have to work at it so I don't go out-of-pocket," he explained.

The person the next day breezed through two extra sales calls, with no sense of stress. He used the expressways more, electing to pay a toll to go just one exit if it cut out several traffic lights. And he didn't hesitate to use pay parking lots and garages, instead of cruising looking for open meters. "Sure, I spend more than my allowance each month, so it does come out of my pocket. But it's worth it, because the couple of dollars I spend to park buys me extra time in front of customers. The way I look at it, I'm in business to earn money, not to try and save nickels."

- *Do they work by plan, or by crisis?* In theory, working by plan is best. But maybe that's unrealistic, given the nature of the business or given the prospects' expectations. *Is* a better way possible? Can you redesign the whole system to minimize crises? Could you hire someone *just* to troubleshoot crises? ("Crisis" here may mean keeping key customers happy.)

3. Are the salespeople distracted by peripheral duties?

A sales rep's main duty is to sell, of course. But in many organizations, peripheral or "overhead" duties begin consuming more and more time, drawing the sales reps away from calling on customers. Some of these peripheral duties are high priority, others are not. It may be that some of the peripheral duties that are important can be handled by someone else, freeing the salesperson to do what she does best.

You may have anticipated some of the peripheral duties and built them into the job description letter you drafted. These might include

- Periodic *customer-care callbacks*, to make sure buyers remain satisfied (and to write any new orders)
- *Attending sales team meetings*
- *Keeping useful sales records*
- *Passing along market intelligence*, such as customer feedback on your product line, information on what the competition is up to, and developing trends in the industry

These are just a few of the useful peripheral duties. For the most part, they are tasks that must be done. But the time they consume may have grown beyond your original expectations. The sales rep may not realize that, or may have become so accustomed to distractions that he thinks they're normal.

For example, what you had envisioned as a few hours a week of customer care calls may have mushroomed because the customers are demanding more and more service. You may have expected to train one person in the customer's organization in the use of your software. But it may be that the customer has grown, or has constant staff turnover so that there's a new person to train every month.

Since there's no one else to do it, your sales rep gets stuck with the job, and it takes half a day or more each month—time that should be spent selling. (If this is the case, then either clarify expectations with the customers or consider hiring a staff member to specialize in conducting this training, in order to free the salespeople to do more selling.)

Or, if you market to retail shops, you may find that the shopkeepers have been calling on your rep to fill in to help stock the shelves, or to staff the area at special times. (The solution is the same: Clarify expectations or add a specialist to free your salespeople.)

Staffing booths at trade shows and preparing for trade shows are important tasks that have the effect of taking the salesperson out of the field, and away from calling on customers. Whether that work is a worthwhile use of time isn't something you can settle in the first months of a new venture, but it is something to consider.

Constant "emergencies" may be one of the costs of getting started and learning one's way around. But they cost an inordinate amount of time.

Even keeping up with the paperwork you request can take an inordinate amount of time. In the past few years, major companies have been issuing computers to their field sales staffs, on the assumption that the equipment necessarily helps save time. (This is part of the "Sales Force Automation," or "SFA" trend—terms you need to be attuned to now that you are involved in marketing.)

However, some companies have found that the real effect was that the sales force got bogged down in the system: There was too much data coming to them, or headquarters wanted too much input back. The effect was that time that should have been spent calling on customers was being spent out in the car pounding the keyboard.

4. Are the Sales Reps caught in a bind between official and unofficial policies?

Recordkeeping and data input are often at the core of the conflicting priorities affecting the sales force. It sometimes happens that if the salesperson were to do everything by the book, he wouldn't have enough time left to make sales calls.

5. Is the selling time cost-effective?

It's possible that if you pay close attention, you may come upon a real eye-opener. In some cases, certain low-cost, low-profit products take more time to sell than bigger, more profitable ones. That could mean that the best strategy is to move responsibility for those low-profit products from field sales reps to an alternative marketing channel. You might try marketing them by phone or by mail, or even hand them over to an outside sales organization.

6. Are the supervisors good role models?

You may be the founder of the Better Mousetrap Company, its chief engineer, and its national (and only) sales manager. Or you may have a couple of echelons working for you. Whatever the situation is, the example the supervisors set on factors such as use of time, attitude, and the like becomes part of the working environment that affects the work and attitudes of the sales force.

One practical implication: When you do ride with your field sales reps, *put in the kind of full day you expect from them.* You convey a certain message, like it or not, if you start your day with them at 10 in the morning, then cut out after lunch because of "important things to do back at the office."

If you don't have supervisors to act as role models, look at what kind of role models the more experienced, or older, sales reps are.

7. Do the salespeople feel limited by their job descriptions? Do they feel that the job description insulates them from having to do any tasks that are not specifically noted?

8. Is there a good, productive team spirit?

9. Do the reps have appropriate control over their schedules and resources?

People who have proven themselves should have maximum freedom to set priorities, and to do the job the way they think best. Less experienced people will need more guidance.

But in looking at this issue of control over schedules, look at the impact of how "emergencies" (both real and those that result from poor planning) can disrupt productive working time.

Remedies

A. Break down any barriers that impede the work.

The systems—including the data systems—are there to facilitate the work, not to get in the way of work being done.

B. If appropriate, rethink and redesign the paper flow and recordkeeping you require.

If you see your salespeople sitting in their cars filling out forms during productive selling hours, be open to the possibility that the entire system might work better with fewer checks and less documentation.

C. Modify the compensation plan.

The compensation plan should target the products and customers that are most profitable for the company. Alternatively, use focused awards or contests to achieve special purposes, especially in the short term.

D. Consider using a telephone sales staff.

Such people can take over some duties if you find that the field salespeople are getting unduly bogged down in customer service or in selling lower-cost, lower-profit items.

If you're a small operation, this "telephone staff" might be as nominal as encouraging the field reps to stay in the office a couple of hours each week to do this telemarketing inexpensively by phone, rather than spending expensive commuting time making face-to-face calls.

E. Clarify territories or areas of responsibility.

If some duties, or some customers, fall through the cracks between your various sales personnel, the situation needs clarification. Perhaps you should write a company policy making these duties clear.

F. Consider revising the job description as well as the comp plan to highlight what you want to happen.

SUMMARY

In Chapters 43, 44, and 45, we have built toward a job aid for you as sales manager that ties together the three key diagnostic questions and the appropriate remedies. Here's the third "slice" of that chart. (The complete chart follows.)

Key Question: Is something in the system or environment preventing or hampering good work?

If you see these indicators:

1. Are there competing demands on the sales reps' time or energies? Are they distracted by other duties?
2. Have they organized themselves and their sales kit equipment well? Have they organized the territory well? Do they have all necessary supplies?
3. Are they caught in a bind between official and unofficial policies?
4. Is their selling time cost-effective?
5. Are the supervisors good role models?
6. Do the sales reps feel limited by the job description? Do they feel that the job description insulates them from having to do any tasks that are not specifically noted there?
7. Is there a good, productive team spirit?

8. Do the sales reps have appropriate control over their schedules and resources?

Try these remedies:

A. Break down any barriers that impede the work.
B. If appropriate, rethink and redesign the paper flow and recordkeeping.
C. Modify the compensation plan.
D. Consider using a telephone sales staff to handle some duties.
E. Clarify territories and areas of responsibility.
F. Consider revising the job description and compensation plan.

Diagnosing and Resolving People Problems

Putting it all together, on the following page you will find a summary chart that ties together the three questions that are useful in diagnosing why people aren't working up to par, the typical indicators that indicate when each cause is involved, and the appropriate remedies.

CHECKLIST: DIAGNOSING AND RESOLVING PEOPLE PROBLEMS

Key Question: **Does this person know what to do, how to do it, and how to do it the way I want it done?**

If you see these indicators:

1. Could the person do the task properly if $10,000 were riding on it?
2. Has this individual had specific feedback on what he or she is doing right and wrong?
3. Are you sure that the person knows precisely what you are looking for, or precisely how you want the job done?
4. Can *anyone* do the task well? Does anyone do it *consistently* well?
5. Are individuals telling you that they don't know what to do, how to do it, or when to do it?
6. Has there been adequate training and feedback in this *specific* task?
7. Was there opportunity to practice or apply the skill or knowledge as part of the training?
8. Was the training (or practice) so long ago that the ability may have deteriorated?

Try these remedies:

A. Training, formal or informal
B. Demonstrations
C. Practice with immediate feedback
D. Job aids

Key Question: **Does this person *want* to do it?**

If you see these indicators:

1. Are these actual consequences of doing a good job (or of doing this particular task) positive?
2. Does the compensation match the effort and time required?
3. Is this individual having special difficulty in dealing with the ambiguity of sales, or does he or she lack the patience required to wait for a longer selling cycle to work out?
4. Is the individual feeling demoralized or discouraged? Is his or her self-image taking a beating from an actual or perceived lack of success in selling?

Try these remedies:

A. Adjust the comp plan to better target specific kinds of markets or prospects.
B. Adapt the comp plan in other ways, such as to give a larger base or draw to reduce the anxiety level.
C. Invest time and effort in coaching and counseling your low-confidence low performers.
D. Team up old hands with those who are having trouble.

Key Question: **Is something in the system or environment preventing or hampering good work?**

If you see these indicators:

1. Are there competing demands on the sales reps' time or energies? Are they distracted by other duties?
2. Have they organized themselves and their sales kit equipment well? Have they organized the territory well? Do they have all necessary supplies?
3. Are they caught in a bind between official and unofficial policies?
4. Is their selling time cost-effective?
5. Are the supervisors good role models?
6. Do the sales reps feel limited by the job description? Do they feel that the job description insulates them from having to do any tasks that are not specifically noted there?
7. Is there a good, productive team spirit?
8. Do the sales reps have appropriate control over their schedules and resources?

Try these remedies:

A. Break down any barriers that impede the work.
B. If appropriate, rethink and redesign the paper flow and recordkeeping.
C. Modify the comp plan.
D. Consider using a telephone sales staff to handle some duties.
E. Clarify territories and areas of responsibility.
F. Consider revising the job description and comp plan.

Chapter 46

Riding with the Salesperson: Coaching and Counseling

A quick review to put this chapter in context: As a sales manager (whether you're managing one person plus yourself or managing a great army of salespeople spreading out in every direction), it's important to abide by two fundamental rules:

Rule 1: **Don't do the work for them.**
Rule 2: **Keep out of the way of the work being done.**

As a manager, you have two principal roles:

First Role: **Sales manager as administrator; that is, keeping "the trains running on time" and the paper flowing, and doing similar "overhead" tasks.** This is important, but don't get bogged down in the role of administrator and neglect the second role.

Second role: **Sales manager as part coach, part problem solver.** It's the coaching part of the job that we focus on in this chapter.

In coaching and solving job performance problems, three questions are helpful:

1. Does this person know what to do, and how to do it?
2. Does the person want to do it? That is, are the actual consequences of doing the job truly positive, or positive enough to motivate the kind of work we need?
3. Is something in the system or environment preventing or hampering good work?

What Good Coaches Do

The coaches I've known fall into three broad types. There are coaches who motivate by fear, and those who try to motivate by "Rah-rah, you-can-do-it" half-time pep talks. But both fear and words may fade before the job gets done.

That's why I suggest that you as sales manager learn from the third coaching style, which focuses on extending the capabilities of the team members. One of the best was John Wooden. Here's how *Psychology Today* described one of his key coaching skills and his ability to provide quick, useful examples or models:

> Perhaps the example of greatest artistry is his use of modeling. His demonstrations are rarely longer than five seconds, but they are of such clarity as to leave an image in memory much like a textbook sketch.

When You Coach and Counsel

Your coaching and counseling as a sales manager can occur in any of a variety of contexts:

- While you are riding on sales calls with a salesperson
- In one-on-one meetings with salespeople (this is best done in an informal setting, such as at a coffee shop, rather than in your office, where roles get in the way)
- In the course of your sales team meetings
- On the fly, as you cope with questions and problems brought by your people

Your Coaching Tools

We have already discussed most of these tools in the previous three chapters as we looked at the performance diagnosis questions and the remedies that flow from them. These are summed up in the chart at the end of the previous chapter. In coaching, you put these questions and remedies together in ways that fit the specific needs of specific people.

Coaching Checklist

In the previous chapter, we looked at some of the issues in the salesperson's *work environment* that you should watch for as your ride with her in the field. These are concerns such as whether she has the appropriate sales materials, whether she uses her time effectively, and the like.

Now we move from background and environment to actual selling skills. The purpose is to help the salesperson overcome any weaknesses or errors in her approach, and also to allow her to tap into the mindset of an experienced person in planning and executing effective sales calls. It's not just the specific selling tasks that make for effectiveness, but also being attuned to the whole sales process, before, during, and after the call.

This checklist gives you an outline of the kinds of concerns to address with your sales reps as you ride on calls. This is just a start; add to it other items from your own experience that you find helpful.

Precall Planning

Before you go into the call, talk through the salesperson's plan with him, addressing questions such as these:

- Why are we calling on this customer? What is the sales potential?
- Are you confident that this person really is the Decision Maker, with Authority, Need, and Dollars?

- Are there any significant Decision Influencers in this organization? Will they be present? Are they favorable to our product?
- What background precedes this call? Have you called on this person before? With what result? When you called for an appointment, what was the tone—interested or just neutral?
- What approach do you plan to take? Why?
- What product will you focus on (assuming that you offer a range of products)? Why that one rather than another?
- What buying action do you plan to close for on this call? What is your primary objective? Your backup?

Before the call, work out with the salesperson how you will be introduced to the Decision Maker. Also, settle on what role you will play in the call.

If you are there to observe the salesperson in action, it will normally be best for you to be introduced by the salesperson as "Ms. X, from my company." If you were introduced as "my manager, Ms. X" or "Ms. X, founder of the company," then the dynamics of the call would probably change. The Decision Maker would shift his attention to you, bypassing the sales rep—which would defeat the purpose of your riding on the call: to watch that person in action.

In this chapter, we are focusing on the situation in which you as sales manager ride with the rep in a coaching role. *This is not the same as "team selling."* In team selling, the normal salesperson on the account brings in another person or several more people as specialists to assist with particular aspects of important transactions.

In a team selling situation, the sales rep *would* introduce you and the others by your full title and reason for being there. In a team selling call, you and the rep, and any others present, would each have a role in the call, which you would work out in advance.

Here we're focusing on a different situation, where you're riding as coach and observer, *not* as co-salesperson. Sports coaches, remember, leave playing the game to the players, and you should normally do the same as a sales coach. That is, barring disaster, you should have no role in the sales call other than to observe.

What that means is that it's important to let the salesperson work in her own style, and even make her own mistakes if need be. If you jump in and take over, then the sales rep will lose both "face" with the customer and confidence. You'll end up carrying the rest of the call, and you will learn nothing more about the sales rep's strengths and weaknesses. (Of course, if you're seeing a crucial sale, on which the future of your company rides, slip away, then do intervene. Short of that, it's better to sacrifice this one sale for the longer benefits.)

During the Call

Observe. If you take notes, don't be too obvious. Jot down your notes at points in the call when the DM will assume that you're taking notes on his input.

After-the-Call Debriefing

Very important: When you debrief, do *not* begin by telling the salesperson what you think he did well or poorly. Instead, ask him what he thinks went well and not so well. Listen to what he tells you. The reason: If you tell him, in most cases he will find that threatening, and much of his energy will go into being defensive. He won't listen, and he may not learn.

But if you give him the chance to critique himself first, from his perspective, you'll find him much more open to your ideas. If the salesperson has had his say, then he can see this as a joint problem-solving session, not an attack on him.

Also, by listening to the salesperson's perceptions of the call, you'll get a chance to tap in on his thinking, and find out more about his actual strengths and needs.

Here are some questions to get you started in debriefing the sales rep after the call.

- What was your overall impression of the call? Did it go well?
- If it didn't result in a sale: Is it your sense that this Decision Maker is favorable to us and our product? Why? If not, how can we change that?
- If you had the chance to make this call again, right now, what would you do the same? Differently?
- Were there any conflicting messages from the DM or others?
- Were there any clear nonverbal messages?
- Did the DM send back any other subtle messages, such as that she was ready to be closed earlier than you did? Or that she was feeling that you pushed too hard?
- What is the next action step from this point with this prospect?
- Did the DM pass on any other useful feedback, such as on our product? pricing? competition? other potential uses or markets for it?

Once the salesperson has given his perspective, then you can amplify, or suggest alternative approaches that might have worked better. Be careful, though, as you don't want your feedback to be a game of "Gotcha!"

- Begin your feedback by pointing out the things this person did well. With a very green salesperson you may have to look hard to find things to compliment, but do it, so that the person can build from strengths, rather than be overwhelmed by criticism.
- When you do give feedback, follow the guidelines in Chapter 43 (which focused on what to do if someone doesn't know what to do or how to do it). That is, be specific, make sure it comes across as objective and non-punishing, and be patient.
- Give the person a chance to respond to your feedback, perhaps to ask questions to clarify your point or to briefly role-play the approach you suggest.
- End by again putting these suggestions in overall perspective, so that the person can see that these are certain skills needing work within an overall job that he does at least reasonably well.

Another point: As coach, you want to build independence and self-sufficiency. One way is to set up the pattern that if your salespeople come to you with a problem to be solved, they are also to bring you at least two or three options for solving that problem, along with reasoning pro and con for each.

One Final Point

Not everyone is cut out for sales. Not every person who can sell is necessarily cut out for your company. So, unless you are very fortunate in your selection of people, there will come a time when you need to let someone go.

There are good ways and bad ways of terminating people. The worst way, both for them and for you, is to send signals and hope they take the hint and move on of their own accord. You may have experienced some of this (which may be why you're now an entrepreneur).

Some of the more common "no-longer-welcome" signals include cutting the person out of meetings and get-togethers, ignoring her, moving her office (if she has one) to Siberia, changing her territory, taking away perks, hassling, nitpicking, slights, and open insults.

The trouble—even apart from the issue of business ethics and whether anyone should be treated like this—is, first, that signaling is often not very effective. For the person on the receiving end, it's hard to be sure at first whether a message is being sent, or whether it's just a coincidence that people forget to tell her things, or that you seem distant when you and she meet.

The second problem with using a signaling approach is that it makes you look weak. A manager who doesn't seem to have the strength to speak up and put voice to concerns will inevitably lose the respect of the others (and probably his own respect, as well).

Third, once an organization slips into the mode of communicating by signal and innuendo, *everything* becomes suspicious. Paranoia develops, along with hostility, backbiting, and all the other petty human traits that get in the way of real work being done.

What *is* the right way to terminate? First, give feedback along the way, so that the person can develop a sense of what she is not doing well, and try to correct it. Second, if the day must come, then say it directly so that both you and the other person can get past it.

A special note: Be aware that, particularly if you're in a midsized or larger company, there may be internal policies or government regulations to be complied with regarding terminating employees.

But you can comply with all those mandates and still terminate in a decent and effective way, as I suggest above.

The Last Word

Editors, by the nature of the job, tend to get in the last word—after all, somebody has to clean things up before they go off to the printer. A reader usually isn't aware of the editor's final input.

But in this case, I'm going to give Dick Staron, my editor on Selling 101, the overt "last word." Through this book, we've been focusing on the *How-to* of selling. But it's important not to take the *Why* of selling for granted, and nothing I know of puts that Why of selling better than what he calls *Staron's First Rule:*

> "There's nothing wrong with any company that more sales and more profits can't cure."

What Else Would You Like To Know? What Selling Secrets Would You Care To Share?

Thank you for buying and reading Selling 101. I hope it proves helpful to you. Now I'd like to ask your help by giving me feedback on a few questions.

1. Whether (and specifically how) Selling 101 has been helpful to you.
2. What else would you like to see covered (or covered in more detail). How could the approach be improved?
3. Are there marketing (or management) tips you would like to pass on to others, including things you learned by trial-and-error?
4. In terms of going into business, or into selling, what do you wish you had known (or done) sooner?

At this point, I'm not sure how I will use this feedback. It could reflect in another book for new entrepreneurs, in a newsletter, or in other forms. To echo what I've been saying in the book, the "solution" (such as it is) will flow from the needs that turn up.

It's up to you whether to include your name, company name, address, and the like. (One thing I will definitely NOT do is sell your name to a mailing list, though I may contact you with later products that I develop.)

Unless you clearly tell me otherwise, I will assume that I am free to use any of your responses to the above questions or other responses in any future books or other projects. So either don't send anything that's "sensitive," or at least flag that it shouldn't be used. For legal reasons, I must advise you that by responding you consent to having your responses published in an upcoming book or other kind of publication, and that you consent to releasing to me any property rights in those words or ideas. (If you don't want to give that consent, make it clear that you do not.)

Also, make it clear if you DO NOT want your name or company name used. (On the other hand, I can't guarantee that your name will be used.) Sorry, I can't promise to respond to individual questions. (Among other reasons, I may not know the answer!)

You can reach me on-line at MTMcGaulle@AOL.com or through the publisher:

Michael McGaulley, Selling 101
c/o Adams Publishing
260 Center Street
Holbrook, MA 02343

Index